Building Reputational Capital

Building Reputational Capital

Strategies for Integrity and Fair Play
That Improve the Bottom Line

Kevin T. Jackson

OXFORD
UNIVERSITY PRESS
2004

OXFORD
UNIVERSITY PRESS

Oxford   New York
Auckland   Bangkok   Buenos Aires   Cape Town   Chennai
Dar es Salaam   Delhi   Hong Kong   Istanbul   Karachi   Kolkata
Kuala Lumpur   Madrid   Melbourne   Mexico City   Mumbai   Nairobi
São Paulo   Shanghai   Taipei   Tokyo   Toronto

Copyright © 2004 by Kevin T. Jackson

Published by Oxford University Press, Inc.
198 Madison Avenue, New York, New York 10016

www.oup.com

Oxford is a registered trademark of Oxford University Press

Library of Congress Cataloging-in-Publication Data
Jackson, Kevin T.
Building reputational capital : strategies for integrity and fair play
that improve the bottom line / Kevin T. Jackson.
p. cm.
Includes bibliographical references and index.
ISBN 0–19–516138–6
1. Business ethics.
2. Leadership—Moral and ethical aspects.
3. Organizational behavior—Moral and ethical aspects.
4. Industrial management—Moral and ethical aspects.
5. Reliability.
6. Honesty.
7. Goodwill (Commerce)
I. Title: Reputational capital.
II. Title.
HF5387 .J297 2004
658.4'08—dc22   2003025581

1 3 5 7 9 8 6 4 2

Printed in the United States of America
on acid-free paper

To my Zhenni

Contents

Acknowledgments

Heartfelt thanks to my wife Zhenni for her inspiration, insight, and steadfast love. My son Brendan and daughter Wenlan, my parents James and Elaine, brothers Jim and Jay, in-laws Shiyu Li and Zhentao Yu, and other family members have been guideposts for my explorations.

I am grateful to the following people at Oxford University Press for their assistance with the book: Tim Bartlett, Catherine Humphries, Peter Harper, Robert Tempio, and Matt Sollars. Special thanks also to Joelle Delbougo. I appreciate the opportunities the following individuals gave me to present, develop, and extend my ideas for this book in the news media and at various forums: Jenny Eisenberg (United States Department of State); John Cirincion, Esq. (LOMA); Paul Gomperz, CLU, ChFC (Society of Financial Services Professionals); Allen Dodds-Frank and Rhonda Shaffler (CNN); Allison Slater (Bloomberg); Michelle Snipe (Fordham University); John Blythe (WFUV); and Edward Wyatt (*New York Times*).

Building Reputational Capital

Introduction: The Economics
of Character and Credibility

The value of a business increasingly lurks not in physical and financial assets that
are on the balance sheet, but in intangibles.

—*The Economist*, June 12, 1999

The most valuable asset, the most powerful force behind your business is right
in front of you every day. Yet for most it lies unnoticed, the most neglected
of all assets. I call this intangible, yet very real asset *reputational capital*. This book
is about increasing your firm's supply of it so it can be leveraged for strategic
advantage and long-term financial performance. When properly harnessed, reputational capital has the potential to unleash extraordinary benefits for your firm's
bottom line.

Perhaps you're thinking: "If reputational capital is such a valuable asset, why
haven't more companies realized this and done a better job of cultivating it? How
can so many people have been so oblivious to the economics of character and
credibility for so long?" I believe the answer is simple: Many people in business
operate under a now defunct premise that "business is business" and that corporations can't afford to be moral.

The Fable of Flatland

Mathematician Edwin Abbott creates an imaginary world, Flatland, as a metaphor
for one-, two-, and three-dimensional space and beyond. Abbott's "Linelanders"
are creatures trapped in a one-dimensional world called Lineland, comprised of
only lines. "Flatlanders" inhabit Flatland, a two-dimensional world. I find this
notion a particularly apt way of grasping the different mindsets with which people
approach the world of business.

Lineland: For people living in this world, business is only about making money: How do we get from point A (running a business) to point B (maximizing profits)? The business of business is business, period. It's one dimensional. All that matters is maximizing your bottom line. If you can make more money for yourself or your firm by breaking the law, and think you can get away with it, go for it. Let's refer to companies whose leaders champion the Lineland mentality as "Alpha" firms. The only reason to obey the law is to avoid the monetary cost of noncompliance.

Flatland: People with a Flatland outlook believe that businesses must stay within the letter of the law while seeking to maximize profits. Theirs is a two-dimensional world: one of law and economics. Moneymaking is constrained only by legal restrictions. We'll call companies operating in this territory "Omega" firms. In Abbott's geometric vision of Flatland, when a three-dimensional figure, say, a sphere, passes through Flatland, everybody sees it merely as a circle, which starts out small, expands, then contracts. The symbolism illustrates my point perfectly. When an ethical problem (a sphere)—a reputation-impacting matter, that is— comes on the scene, an Omega firm always reduces it to a matter of economics and law (a circle).

Realland. This is the "Zeta" firm's world. It's the one we want to inhabit. It is the real world. Business is about economics, law, *and* reputation. Being successful requires finding the right balance among the dimensions of commerce, compliance, and credibility.

The moment you begin to draw your attention to the intangible dimension of your company, to the reputational dimension of business, you achieve a higher level of awareness. You start to realize that there is a vast expanse of wealth beyond physical assets. You see that the things that matter most to your business, that enable it to work, to be productive—trust, integrity, fair dealing—exist beyond conventional measurements of the firm's value.

I define reputational capital as a firm's intangible long-term strategic assets calculated to generate profits. Reputational assets are distinguished from the firm's image in the same way that one distinguishes a person's *character* from their *personality*. A firm's reputation may enhance its image, but image alone will not build a reputation. Indeed, even individual people, professions, industries, and countries possess reputational capital and can lose it just as certainly as a firm can.

As you take the journey with me through these pages, I encourage you to reflect on questions you may not have considered:

- If our firm is motivated to improve its reputation purely by the wish to make profit, can we still grow reputational capital?
- How is our company's reputation affected by the other firms with which we deal? By its culture? By the way it treats employees, customers, suppliers?
- How does our firm's reputation impact its future prospects?
- How can we measure the impact that our reputation has on our firm's bottom line?

Don't worry. We're going to walk through all of this step by step. The time you take to carefully study what I have to say in this book will be worth every minute. The world of business has changed and will continue to do so. I hope that I can help you keep pace—so you get oustanding results now and down the road.

Each moment of each day your business operates is spent either building or eroding its stock of reputational capital. Why? Because today's companies have acquired a new moral status that has changed the essential core of what reputational capital is.

Paradigm Shift in Values

Today a new global business ethic brings rising expectations of corporate social responsibility. Genuinely global corporations, beyond the regulatory purview of any national government in particular, have paved the way for a radical transformation of values for business. A new business paradigm has been born, and Zeta firms move within it. The new paradigm presupposes and expresses timeless principles and values—human rights, responsible citizenship, corporate credibility and character—that are not just passing fads, nor simply the product of parochial legal regulations and local cultural mores. This movement toward values means that now, more than ever, your firm must proactively build reputational capital for strategic advantage or be punished for its failure to do so. In the new paradigm business is fundamentally about integrity and fair play. Intangibles like authenticity, trust, dignity, compassion, and respect are, in reality, much more basic to commercial relationships than any tangible assets. Successful business is about interdependence. It's about relationships that engage the real lives of other people who are essentially just like yourself.

The public's heightened expectations of today's corporations are putting Alpha and Omega firms on the endangered species list. Even the most powerful firms—that is, viewed from a standpoint of physical assets alone—are exceedingly fragile entities. Companies whose financial statements reveal seemingly secure assets will collapse if they lack sufficient reputational capital. Consider Enron. Just before its demise, it was the seventh largest U.S. company.

Alpha and Omega firms not only miss out on the first mover advantage gained from strategies pursued by Zeta firms, but they also hemmorage enormous amounts of reputational capital as crises inevitably flare up.[1]

All of the attention spent on tallying up the staggering financial losses from the collapse of Enron, Global Crossing, WorldCom, Aldelphia, Tyco, Arthur Andersen, and many others over the past few years ignores a much greater—and more significant—loss of wealth from the parade of corporate scandals: a catastrophic exodus of reputational capital from the business profession at large, from regulatory systems, and from corporate leaders. Bottom line: In these days of profound suspicion about business, the firms that can build and sustain reputation will get stronger. Those that ignore reputation or fail to learn how to cultivate it will fail. The choice is yours.

Corporate credibility is the defining business issue of today. My research has determined that the annual loss of reputational capital to corporations from unscrupulous conduct exceeds the combined profits of the top 40 corporations in the United States. All this economic waste cries out for more than a public relations makeover.

I am going to show you how to start realizing your firm's full earning potential. Until you take the right first steps, you won't accumulate reputational capital and will in fact continue to lose it right from under your nose, given that every firm, even the most noble, inevitably gets attacked by somebody for something. Such change takes patience, sincerity, and dedication.

The strategies I give in this book work together. They help you meet these basic goals:

1. To increase your firm's competitive advantage by turning the prevailing climate of cynicism and crisis of confidence about business to your benefit.
2. To enable you to proactively control and manage the reputational risks facing your firm.
3. To enable you to master the art of balancing financial mandates with social imperatives for long-term success.

The strategies will help your business, no matter what it is. The strategies come from my countless consultations with executives and managers, from small advertising companies to multinational investment firms. Many of these corporate leaders, steeped in enormous technical knowledge about financial affairs, came to me clueless about how to deal with the so-called "soft" sides of their business. The strategies are specific and practical, yet they have universal applicability. Whether your firm is a sole proprietorship or a huge conglomerate, whether it is publicly traded or privately held, whether domestic or global, whether it is in the manufacturing or services sector, is not the most important consideration. Why? Because uprightness is the primary attribute of commercial relationships. If there's no trust, there's no deal, period. So the laws that govern the accumulation of reputational capital cut across all secondary or derivative categories in today's business world.

Today's firms move within networks of ongoing relationships. Firms are linked with their customers and suppliers, sometimes even with rivals by strategic alliances. A lot of companies are entering into intricate arrangements with government regulators, the news media, local communities, and special interest groups. Such relationships are, in a profound way, reputational networks. This creates two special problems: First, a crisis affecting one part of the network tends to spread to infect the entire network. The uncovering of accounting irregularities at Enron led to suspicion about the firm's auditor, Arthur Andersen, which in turn led to widespread mistrust of the entire accounting profession. Second, when you add all the expectations up, those of your company's business partners and stakeholders cannot all be met. Responsibilities owed to multiple consituencies often conflict with managers' personal and organizational duties. Such conflicts generate deportment dilemmas for your firm.

I sometimes come across businesspeople who talk about business ethics as if it were something that wasn't possible in the "real world." "The competition is brutal," they say, "nice guys finish last." But the attitude beneath such comments is misguided. Everything in my experience suggests that nothing could be further from the truth. Companies that operate ethically, that safeguard and cultivate their reputations, gain a competitive edge over rivals that don't.

Behaving ethically carries some short-term costs. Walking away from deals tied to demands for illicit payments, refraining from pushing unnecessary services on a customer, or disclosing adverse side effects of a drug may all add up to lost business opportunities. Everyone knows that. But the consequences of ethical failure—loss of credibility and trust—are much greater. They are long term. Credibility and trust are essential, irreplaceable musts for all constituencies of your business.

Ethical people who want to work in a place that fits their own values will leave an unscrupulous company. So sound ethical behavior is a competitive advantage. In business trust is everything.

When it comes to building credibility, everyone wins. Companies win because people make better decisions. And people win because their companies support them. Everybody can step forward with confidence. When companies are steadfast, when they stand up for what's right, they have a positive impact. Such actions simplify decision making by distilling frequently perplexing dilemmas down to the fundamental question: Will my action bring about a favorable reputation for myself and the firm? Because the firm's moral bearing is acknowledged to be a precious long-term asset, your financial responsibilities merge with your social and humanitarian responsibilities. Commerce, compliance, and compassion are fused together to form your core mission. Members of your firm will cultivate an instinct for knowing what they shouldn't even think about doing at work, and even off the job. Gaining the respect of clients, competitors, and your own people is what reputational capital formation is all about. In the long run, nothing is more important than that.

The literature on business ethics, the kind of stuff that deals seriously with principles, values and virtue, and the complexity of moral dilemmas, is highly theoretical and philosophically sophisticated. But it is out of sync with how businesspeople think and act. When I go to conferences about corporate ethics and social responsibility I am amazed at how stuffy and arrogant academics can get about their overwrought theoretical concoctions that are often utterly unusable in the business world. On the other hand, when business ethics tries to mesh with the real world of business—with plain talk and practical suggestions—the result is all too often superficial. It is all about quick fixes, creating brand images linked to corporate citizenship and organizational public relations (PR) band-aids that patch over serious problems while leaving structural defects to erupt over and over. When companies roll out their "ethics intitiatives" based on this kind of approach, giving everyone a coffee mug with a few "core values" emblazoned on it, people see right through it and become cynical. All the more so when they see that nothing really changes.

For the past 30 years or so ambitious campaigns have been mobilized to clean up the misdeeds of business enterprises. Some governments have crafted mountains of regulations, large companies have created vast networks of consultants and committees, and have made terms such as "conflicts of interest" and "the appearance of propriety" part of our everyday language. Despite all of these efforts, the public's confidence in businesspeople to do the right thing has plummeted to an all-time low.

We can approach corporate reputation with two different mindsets. One looks at the company's image as paramount. It contrives marketing and public relations strategies that get key stakeholders to like the company. Plus, it treats ethical behavior as the kind of conduct that staves off lawsuits. Behavior policies are set up to stop sexual harassment claims, minority worker grievances, and defamation actions from underperforming workers. The conduct of businesspeople becomes driven by what contains litigation costs instead of what is really right. Ethical decision making gets assigned to the human resources and legal departments. Executives compartmentalize. They stop thinking for themselves. Using marketing and public relations gimmicks to get consumers to feel good about the brand name, using management tactics to improve worker productivity and trick the public into believing the firm is a good citizen—while the company's character is corrupt and insincere—does not bring about long-term success. It doesn't matter how slick the talk is. Without trust there is no basis for enduring success. Insincerity ultimately generates distrust. And otherwise well-intentioned ethics initiatives are felt as manipulations.

I coach corporate leaders to adolpt a fresh outlook and follow what I call the eye-to-eye principle: Responses to reputation crises—which arise at the level of character and integrity—must be as deep and as complex as the underlying malady. This means seeing a problem for what it really is rather than trying to divert everyone's attention toward something else. Cosmetic makeovers just don't cut it. Consumers, employees, and investors see right through the smoke and mirrors of image marketing and manipulation schemes. Confidence and trust cannot be obtained at the secondary and derivative (shallow, superficial) level of image. I am amazed at how much effort is put into marketing rather than on just becoming and being what you say you are.

Music Model for Integrity Built by Discipline

In my presentations to businesspeople about the steps involved in building corporate reputation, I like to use the model of musicianship to illustrate some key features.

- *Performing music requires authenticity.* You can't "cook the books" in rendering a live violin performance. There's no separate image to hide behind. Without true technical and artistic mastery, with no underlying primary substance, there can be no genuine musicianship. It cannot be faked.
- *Musicianship is a self-regulating enterprise.* This is an ideal to which we in business should aspire. Think about it. Musicians are not regulated by any federal or state agencies. Technically playing all of the notes correctly— that is, "compliance"—is universally understood by musicians to be merely

the barest of requirements. Superior musical performance is all about the artistry that is added on top of the "minimal" technical execution of the notes.

- *Musicianship takes time to build; there's no shortcut to it.* Your firm's reputational capital cannot be created all at once by some big bang. It needs to evolve.

- *Music follows laws we know little about, but which are real and universal.* Many of the world's greatest composers have professed to having no clue as to either the source of their musical ideas or the rules they followed (in some cases, created) in producing masterpieces that speak to the hearts of people across epochs and cultures.

Trustworthiness is one of the pillars of a good reputation. How do you build trust? Here's the key: *Give trust to get trust.* I get my bagels from a bagel guy in one of those movable stands on the sidewalk. One day I didn't have enough money with me to cover what I'd just ordered. He said, "don't worry, pay me next time." Given that his humble business operates on an extremely tight profit margin, a shoestring really, it's clear that the credit he extended me was not just a ploy to improve image but rather a genuine expression of trust. When a new vendor set up his cart much closer to my apartment, to my surprise I found I didn't go to him. I'm sure there is no difference in quality or price between the two bagel sellers. The new stand is much closer and more convenient. But my loyalty goes to the bagel guy who trusted me.

What is the most valuable part of your business? What part of it could you not afford to lose? Although your firm's physical assets can be insured, so that if they were stolen or destroyed you would be indemnified for the loss, do you have any idea how to protect the invisible, nontangible capital that is so essential to your business?

Have you ever considered the prospect that your firm could have to declare reputational bankruptcy? What if some breaking point was reached, as at Kidder-Peabody and Drexel Burnham Lambert, where nobody trusted your firm enough to want to do business with it anymore? Could anything be done at that point to restore the reputational capital that had been lost?

There is an uncomfortable sense that comes from trying to orient businesspeople toward the ethical dimension of their trade. Most firms I do consulting for prefer that I not use the word "ethics" because of some supposed negative associations with this term. Perhaps "ethics" is viewed to be moralistic—like a Sunday sermon. So instead we agree to use alternative terms such as "integrity." I think the problem is not with the connotations of the words but with the false assumption that corporations are amoral institutions. We all know deep down that ethics is not something you want to trade off for profits. Yet many still believe that companies attain success, that is, profitability, for shareholders only by ignoring ethics. (I'd say there's another false assumption at work here as well: that "success" consists only of material accumulation.) So the reluctance to use the word "ethics" is actually a reluctance to face the truth that today's corporations are moral agents through and through—their character and probity are among the most fundamental determinants of their financial soundness.

Focusing on reputation, from the point of view of business—instead of "business ethics," from the perspective of academic philosophy—was a great illumination for me. I saw that, since the cash value of a firm is intimately linked to its moral character, its authentic reputation really belonged on its balance sheet. Regardless of what country a firm does business in, regardless of what industry it is involved in, whether it produces goods or provides services, whether large or small, labor intensive or technology based, whether it is global or domestic, its very life depends on its reputation. The more I thought about it, I began to discern that the reputation of a business is a special hybrid of economic values and moral values. These two components of reputation are related like yin and yang in Eastern philosophies. They are "complementary opposites." I discovered that, even though the essence of reputation is quite obvious to us all—right under our noses, so to speak—it becomes quite elusive if we attempt to force it to arise or if we insist that all of its properties be quantified. In this way, the quest for reputation is analogous to the quest for happiness: If you try too hard to get it you're doomed to fail. Finally, it became clear to me that if building reputational capital is, as I argue, actually an investment, then money spent on doing it right is different in kind than, say, money that the firm might otherwise just be throwing out the window (though perhaps for noble motives). In other words, there is a return on the investment. The return is to the individual firm (whose good deeds are rewarded by more productive employees, more loyal customers, and more investors), its partners (who "rent" a well-reputed firm's good name), the firm's industry or profession (whose clients become more trusting of, for example, broker-dealers in general), and society (which benefits when a firm finds new ways to be profitable while acting forthright and fair).

A reputation is not something that a person or a firm has in complete isolation. Reputation is relational. A lawyer's reputation will be enhanced—or diminished—by the probity of the legal profession in general. Her reputation is affected by everyone with whom she associates. The practices of even a handful of firms can have a profound effect on a larger group. Consider the political cartoon depicting

"Bermuda Day," which features a parade down Fifth Avenue of executives of corporations incorporated in Bermuda to avoid taxes (it appears in Chapter 1, p. 37 "Switching to a New Paradigm"). So as far as reputation goes, we're all in this together.

Once developed, a reputation is not something that can be locked up and stored. You can't build up a good reputation and then put it in the deep freeze to take out when you have trouble. Reputation is dynamic. Your firm's reputation will always be relative to the level of expectation of social responsibility harbored by key constituencies.

I gave a talk for Life Offices Management Association (LOMA) and Life Insurance Marketing and Research Association (LIMRA), insurance and financial services professionals organizations, about moving beyond compliance to building reputation. I outlined some strategies for building confidence and credibility with key constituencies. Normally this means going past legal requirements to meet clients' legitimate expectations. One of the participants, legal counsel for his firm, pressed me in the Q and A part of the presentation. "All of this sounds great," he confided. "But how do I convince my boss, who's out to slash my department's budget, that these kinds of initiatives are cost-effective? Can we afford to be so ethical?" My response stressed that reputation management—cultivating the company's character—is not a cost-centric enterprise. It's about creating capital and generating value for the firm. Skeptics can always ask how a firm knows whether money spent on doing the right thing really has a payoff. But this problem is not unique to ethics: How do we know whether the latest marketing campaign is going to come back with bottom line improvement? It's often exceedingly difficult to trace specific returns from specific ads. Moreover, despite best efforts to research companies one is investing in or lending money to, there is inevitably risk and uncertainly about the payoff. The same issues of causation and risk—disproportionately brought up to disparage efforts to integrate ethical conduct into business, I believe—apply to marketing costs, investment ventures, and indeed any business activity.

Advantages of a Superior Reputation

> A good reputation is more valuable than money.
>
> —Publilius Syrus, first century, b.c.

Why is reputational capital so important? The business press is flooded with rankings and commentaries about the "most respected" and "most admired" companies. This shows how reputation is becoming a central focus in assessing firms. The prevalence of business scandals are also spotlighting the cost of reputational collapse.

Surveys of corporate reputations are popping up everywhere in the business press. Among the more influential are: *Fortune* ("America's Most Admired Corporations" and "World's Most Admired Companies"), *Industry Week* ("100 Best-Managed Companies"), *Financial Times* ("Europe's Most Respected Companies" and "World's Most Respected Companies"), *Management Today* ("Britain's Most Admired Companies"), *Far Eastern Economic Review* ("Asia's Leading Companies"), and *Asian Business* ("Asia's Most Admired Companies"). The specific criteria used in each differ somewhat. Yet, typically profiles compile a mix of financial and nonfinancial standards. The big ones are:

Ability to change

Management quality

Long-term focus

Degree of innovation

Ability to develop and keep key people

Well-being of workforce

Profitability

Asset use

Financial soundness

Investment value

Customer satisfaction and loyalty

Product and service quality

Community and environmental friendliness

Legal compliance

Corporate citizenship

The respondents used in compiling these profiles vary. For instance, the *Fortune* surveys are based on responses of securities analysts, directors, and senior executives. By contrast, the *Financial Times* derives its surveys from feedback of chief executives, finance officers, and chairmen. Note the constraints here. Viewpoints of important constituencies like employees, customers, and local communities are left out of the picture. Many of the surveys would gain credibility if they incorporated a broader range of constituencies as survey respondents.

Standing alone, no one study is definitive. Yet a critical mass of credible evidence is showing a link between superior corporate reputations and financial performance. Companies with above-average overall corporate reputation scores demonstrate greater ability to sustain or attain an above-average return on assets (ROA). Thus, first, a superior reputation helps a firm attain superior profits. Second, upon reaching that position, it helps sustain superior profits.

Reputational strength brings these advantages:

Draws repeat business

Alerts consumers about the quality of a firm's products

Allows firm to charge higher prices

Attracts better job applicants

Enhances access to capital markets

Attracts investors

Functions as a barrier to entry into markets

All of this makes a formidable toolkit for fashioning strategic advantages.

Getting a Competitive Edge

The comparative advantage theory of corporate strategy says that firms gain sustainable competitive advantage by cultivating intangible and inimitable assets. This is what reputation building is all about. Companies compete for clients, customers, investors, partners, employees, suppliers, and the support of local communities. A good reputation erects an intangible barrier that rivals stumble to get over. You can cut marketing expenses, command top dollar for products or services, erect barriers to competition, and enjoy expanded latitude in decision making.[2] By itself, this competitive advantage ensures stronger long-run returns to better-reputed firms.

The strategies given in this book are especially important for knowledge-centered organizations. Services rendered by consulting firms, law firms, and investment banks are chiefly intangible. They are credence goods. People buy them on faith—on reputation.

- For auditors, consultants, lawyers, and investment bankers, good reputations are themselves marketable products. Clients pay top dollar to lease the reputations of these professionals. Say a new company is having a hard time raising equity capital. To sell an initial offering, it may pay a premium to rent the reputation of a prominent banker. Investors are more likely to buy a public offering underwritten by a leading bank like Goldman Sachs than one sponsored by some no-name. Conversely, companies already enjoying sterling reputations are able to attract investors on their own, without the need of well-reputed bankers or attorneys.

- With a superior reputation you can command premium prices for your products and services. So you can get a return on the investment for the front-end costs of reputation building.

- Reputation gives you more leverage in negotiations with suppliers, creditors, and distributors. Suppliers prefer to deal with credible firms, ones that won't renege on orders. Creditors deal on better terms with firms that provide assurances that they won't be left holding the bag on money lent. Studies show that a good reputation reduces the cost of capital for a firm by improving its ability to raise money in credit markets.

- You get the cream of the crop when recruiting employees. When people are job hunting they solicit the opinions of others. When faced with multiple offers at similar salaries, prospective hires will opt for the firm with the better reputation.

- Your company's good reputation draws clients and customers who may be willing to pay more for your services than those of a less-well-reputed company.

- You get happier, more dedicated employees. Your firm's positive reputation boosts morale and makes associates want to go the extra mile. When associates sense improvement in the ethos of a firm, they get motivated to achieve high-quality standards in day-to-day operations. They will be more likely to support quality initiatives if the organization communicates a commitment to scrupulous conduct. People working in a corporate climate of good character will believe that they should treat business partners respectfully. They will seek to give the best possible value to all customers. Since employees' commitment to quality has a positive effect on your firm's competitive position, a high-reputation work climate has a positive effect on the financial bottom line.

- A good reputation stabilizes customer demand for your company's products or services when the economy's sluggish. Since reputation builds customer loyalty and makes for repeat business, it softens the blows from business downturns. Overall, better-reputed firms have less volatile stock prices.

- If your firm shows it's dedicated to honesty and fair play, it broadcasts its appeal as a strategic partner. Research shows that positive reputations contribute to the success of business alliances. Your firm becomes alluring to other companies that want to polish their own image. Housing Development Finance Corporation (HDFC), which over the years has been held in high regard as India's largest thoroughly professional housing finance firm, with a record of solid governance, exemplary customer service, and a consistent performer in India, recently teamed up with Chubb Corporation, a leading U.S. business insurer. The resulting non-life joint Indian venture, created from Chubb's purchase of a 26 percent stake, is focused on automobile, accident, and household insurance policies.

- Many people have trouble getting enough information before deciding where to invest, from which firm to purchase insurance or financial services. They often turn to reputation to make the selection process easier.

- Firms with outstanding reputations get good publicity when they receive awards or are featured in media stories. Merck and Company gained great international acclaim when it donated and underwrote the costs of distributing the drug Mectizan to poor populations suffering from river blindness in less developed countries. This sort of positive attention cuts marketing, recruiting, and public relations costs.

- Firms with reserves of reputational capital get cut more slack when a crisis hits. It creates a "presumption of innocence" and raises the "standard of proof" needed for those attacking your firm (for instance, activists) to gain credibility. There's more freedom to move around. More time to recover from a hardship.

- A positive reputation is like a healthy immune system. If a reputational virus invades, you will have the strength to fend it off. No firm can be sure that a crisis or scandal will never happen. So it is essential to have your internal defense against it. In response to adverse publicity from a crisis, many companies focus their energies reactively on damage control, often with the help of public relations firms. One benefit of reputational capital is that it helps reduce the risks of damage proactively, before it happens. Following the well-known Tylenol product-tampering crisis, Johnson&Johnson's market share came springing back. The solid reputation of the firm is the reason why. J&J now maintains such immense reserves of reputational capital that when news broke in 2002 about questionable practices in its manufacturing facilities in Puerto Rico, much less damage came about than might be expected. Also, despite getting hammered by persistent criticism about child labor and sweatshops, Nike's sales have not sagged because of its stockpile of reputational capital.

- Business partners may feel comfortable sidestepping costly and time-consuming formalities—to your benefit. And they tend to forgive errors they would otherwise fuss about.

- Reputations create favorable contractual outcomes. Why? Because a good reputation facilitates selection among a range of competitors. Who doesn't feel more confident and secure awarding a contract to a highly regarded firm over its no-name or ill-reputed rival?

- A good reputation improves your bargaining power, authority, and credibility when negotiating with regulators and government authorities. Consider Morgan Stanley's dealings with the Securities and Exchange Commission (SEC) concerning new rules about independence between analysts and investment bankers. Standing on its favorable reputation, the firm could assert with confidence that standards that might be necessary for its competitors were unnecessary for itself. An attorney with a good reputation stands to gain in innumerable ways in dealings with judges and other members of the bar.

- A shiny reputation helps you get customers and keep them. It helps to provide a point of distinction by which customers choose between generic products (like CD players) and common services (like consulting and legal services) that they otherwise find hard to distinguish. Since a good reputation makes customers feel more secure in buying your products and services, you gain an edge with new product and new service introductions. There's a big psychological boost here. This counts with first-time buyers, as well as with products and services whose value is hard to evaluate.

- A positive reputation boosts the impact of your advertising. It makes your sales force more effective. Why? Because they both gain credibility.

Your firm's effort in promoting integrity and fair play not only improves its reputation, bringing the benefits identified above. In addition, forthright and socially responsible conduct also has a favorable direct impact on your key constituencies: clients and customers, employees, suppliers, and investors. So while your firm is undertaking activities aimed at building its reputational capital as a long-term investment, it is simultaneously bringing about more immediate results that also translate into increased profitability.[3]

I

What Is Reputational Capital?

1

Switching to a New Paradigm

[I]n every age there is a turning point, a new way of seeing and asserting the coherence of the world.

—J. Bronowski, *The Ascent of Man*

Tomorrow's successful company can no longer afford to be a faceless institution that does nothing more than sell the right product at the right price. It will have to present itself more as if it were . . . an intelligent actor, of upright character, that brings explicit moral judgments to bear on its dealings with its own employees and with the wider world.

—Editorial, *The Economist*, 24 June 1995

A basic mind change is occurring in business. A new paradigm has replaced one that assumed ruthless activity is the way to beat the competition. The traditional paradigm said good conduct was money lost. "There is only one social responsibility of business," Milton Friedman once proclaimed, "to increase profits." Hard data is suggesting that the old paradigm is wrong.

Reputation Takes Center Stage

In today's business, reputation is *everything*. A recent Hill and Knowlton survey found that almost four in five Americans said that they considered reputation when purchasing a company's product. Thirty-six percent deemed it a significant factor in purchasing decisions. Over 70 percent of investors take reputation into account in decisions—even if it means decreasing financial returns. The study further found that business leaders from the United States, the United Kingdom, and across Europe believe that corporate social responsibility will be more important in the future, especially in building sales and recruiting and retaining employees.[1]

The way people see business is changing. A few decades ago, things were considerably simpler. People just expected firms to produce goods and services at reasonable prices. People esteemed large, well-established companies. AT&T,

General Mills, and Eastman Kodak ruled. Then, gradually, the idea that corporations are moral actors—institutions having a character, if not a soul as well—
began to evolve.

Consequently, companies are under much more moral scrutiny than in the past.
Businesses are being held to higher standards. The paradigm shift is premised on
what we'll term the *business integrity thesis.* According to this thesis people are
expecting solid financial results from business, yet they are also demanding that
companies attain financial returns through fair play and socially responsible conduct. This new emphasis on the company of character is a break from the received
view that corporations are, and should be, fundamentally amoral profit machines—
utterly unable to demonstrate moral character or probity.

A look at the business news media shows how corporations are coming to be
seen more and more as moral agents. Whether you flip through *The Financial
Times,* or *Fortune,* or tune into CNN or CNBC, you find reports on corporate
wrongdoing, workplace dilemmas, the need for MBA programs to integrate ethics
into their curricula, and sagas of success through forthright leadership right along
with reports on interest rates, market trends, and corporate acquisitions.

Not everyone subscribes to the integrity thesis for today's business enterprises.
Disagreements remain about whether corporations even have moral responsibilities, and, assuming they do, the precise scope of those responsibilities. For instance,
many businesspeople believe that since corporations are not literally persons but
rather artificial entities created by law we cannot treat them as moral agents responsible for ethical conduct.[2]

Nevertheless a general consensus exists about the kinds of behavior that reflect
corporate conscience. Among these are:

- Operating on an ethical level higher than the law
- Contributing to civic and charitable causes and nonprofit organizations
- Providing employee benefits and improving the quality of life in the work-
  place beyond conventional levels
- Pursing more socially desirable economic opportunities
- Deploying corporate resources to tackle social problems

Arguments against the business integrity thesis—that is, the case that corporations should be held to these standards—can be grouped into the following
categories: insincerity, amorality, profitability, unfairness, accountability, and
expertise.

Insincerity argument: The movement toward business ethics and corporate social responsibility is basically just a public-relations ploy to shift people's attention
from the pervasive greed, corruption, and cheating in the business world. There's
no real difference between public relations and corporate reputation.

Response: Although some corporations act insincerely, not all do. Paradoxi-
cally, the companies that genuinely appreciate the intrinsic value of ethical conduct,
as opposed to focusing exclusively on its instrumental value in increasing profits
or deflecting attention from misdeeds in other areas of operation, are most likely
to be rewarded financially as people discern that they have a sound reputation
rooted, at least in part, in sincere motives. Making the criticism that corporations
act insincerely actually assumes that it is possible to distinguish disingenuous public
relations motives from sincere moral commitments—that is, the argument assumes
what it wants to deny: that corporations are behaving *badly* when they use ethics
as an attention-deflecting device instead of honoring it for its own sake. If it were
true that *all* corporations *always* acted insincerely, if it were not possible for them
to act on a higher plane, what would be the point of drawing our attention to and
condemning such behavior?

Amorality argument: As artificial entities created by law, business entities are
essentially amoral. Moral considerations are inappropriate in business. Only people
can engage in behavior that can be judged in moral terms.

Response: Granted, corporations are not persons in any literal sense, yet the
attributes of responsibility inherent in corporations allow us to judge corporate
behavior from a moral perspective. There is a huge difference, glossed over by the
amoral entity argument, between regarding the corporation as a legal abstraction
and considering the corporation as an ongoing enterprise. Employees don't see
themselves as inhabiting a legal abstraction for the better part of their waking
hours. Considered purely as a legal form, the corporation is amoral in the same
way all legal concepts—whether contracts, trusts, or whatever—are amoral. If, on
the other hand, we regard the corporation as something comprised of real people,
as something that makes decisions, supplies goods and services—in short, an actual
presence engaged with the world—doesn't it seem natural to attribute moral
agency to it? Of course, even taken as a real, ongoing enterprise, a firm can conduct
itself amorally, even immorally, as some definitely do. Yet it can also assume responsibilities, keep promises, demonstrate respect, and otherwise display character
traits. In the end, there's nothing in the concept of a corporation as such

that dictates the amorality thesis—nor, for that matter, the corporate integrity thesis.

Profitability argument: The raison d'être of corporations is to foster profit-oriented conduct, not to bring about social betterment. The bottom line is what matters to investors and what directly impacts the employees of a firm. Any other concerns distract companies from their central purpose and get in the way of reaching these goals.

Response: Shareholder and employee interests are not quite as narrow as the profitability argument assumes. (This is seen in the rise in socially responsible investing, discussed in detail later on in this chapter.) Corporations are generally expected by their owners to pursue some socially desirable ends.

Unfairness argument: When business managers and executives spend the corporation's money to advance social objectives—developing delivery vehicles with hybrid engines, paying higher wages in developing countries, or donating funds to charity—they're unjustly spending shareholders' money to further their own agendas. It's more equitable to pay dividends and let the shareholders make charitable contributions if they wish. When companies try to become good citizens they stray from their designated role of profit maker—taking unfair advantage of company employees and shareholders. Typically, senior management consults the board of directors about supporting social concerns, yet bypasses getting approval from the company's major stakeholders. So, shareholders are wrongly disenfranchised from decisions that reduce their benefits from the firm.

Response: While a company's executives and managers do have a fiduciary obligation governing responsible use of the firm's assets, the obligation to earn the greatest amount of profit for shareholders doesn't mean disregarding the means used. In addition, the obligation of managers is not simply to get maximum return for shareholders and the highest pay for employees but also to preserve the equity invested in the firm. Obtaining the maximum return for shareholders and protecting the legitimate interests of employees consistent with safeguarding invested capital requires taking a long-term view that promotes the stability and growth of the corporation. Serving the long-term interest of the corporation, in turn, requires satisfying the legitimate expectations of society. Granted, disagreement remains about how extensive society's legitimate expectations for corporations are and how much socially responsible behavior is in a corporation's long-term interest.

Accountability argument: Since firms are private institutions, they are subject to a lower level of accountability than public institutions. A company may opt to support social causes and yet retreat from public scrutiny. But that carries a potential for abuse. Some companies fund causes (for example, pro-life or pro-choice organizations) that its employees or shareholders don't endorse. Others offer money or free products with strings attached—dictating recipients' agendas for less-than-noble purposes. For example, a soft drink company that contributes to a public school might condition its assistance on the school's agreement to put the company's vending machines in the cafeteria.

Plus, corporations can carry tremendous clout. Some, like Wal-Mart, Ford, ExxonMobil and General Motors, have annual earnings surpassing the gross domestic product of many of the world's nations.[3] When these companies advance their own social agendas, their influence overshadows that of some of the governments in countries where they do business. Without clear guidelines and accountability, even well-intentioned corporate pursuits of socially responsible activities might distort the governance process.

Response: Whereas the accountability argument believes it is dangerous to unleash the immense power of corporations from the discipline of the market, it can be argued to the contrary that *not* using corporate power for social betterment itself poses a moral issue. So corporations act unethically by choosing not to get involved in matters where they could have a positive impact.

Expertise argument: Corporations should mind their own business, and leave social and environmental problems to others.[4] Let corporations focus on profit making instead of social agendas. The government can tax corporate profits to fund socially beneficial causes as they are needed. Companies that have expertise with their product or service lines don't necessarily have expertise in identifying and analyzing moral issues or in promoting socially beneficial activities. Corporations attain success in the market by identifying and satisfying customer needs. Yet that ability doesn't necessarily carry over into nonbusiness areas.

Response: While a company certainly doesn't have the expertise to solve every social ill, it has an obligation to at least confront social problems that: relate to the company's conduct, affect significant numbers of people, are close at hand, can be solved with the corporation's resources and expertise, and will continue without the company's efforts. Moreover, many government agencies (especially those in less developed countries) believe that they lack the expertise needed to effectively cure social problems.

Arguments supporting the business integrity thesis are: social contract, stakeholder model, moral minimum of the market, reduction of governmental regulation, power and responsibility, and long-term profitability and financial success.

Social contract argument: We can concede that corporations are artificial entities created by law. But society accords them special status, including the grant of limited liability, which insulates the owners from liability for debts the organization incurs, and other rights, such as the right to use natural resources and the labor force, subject to an underlying responsibility: Corporations, just like other members of society, must contribute to its betterment. Therefore, companies have a moral obligation to contribute to social well-being.

Stakeholder model argument: Executives and managers of a corporation have fiduciary responsibilities to all stakeholders, not just to shareholders. The traditional shareholder view of the firm assumes that a corporation is private property owned by and for the benefit of its owners—the stockholders. But the stakeholder model offers a wider view, holding that corporations are indirectly responsible to society at large and directly responsible to constituencies on which it depends for its survival. Accordingly, a corporation should be managed to benefit all its stakeholders—shareholders, employees, customers, suppliers, as well as the local communities in which it does business.

Moral minimum of the market argument: A measure of ethical behavior is a prerequisite in order for the invisible hand to operate. In fact, business activity would not be possible without basic regard for ethical standards that respect property rights, honor promises, and ensure mutual commitments. Adam Smith argued that humans have a basic regard for others—a sentiment of beneficence—without which the market would not function properly. It's in a company's best interests to operate above the moral minimum of the market. Companies that cling to the moral minimum remain vulnerable to pressure from society and government regulation. A company can maintain greater control over decision making and sidestep costs of regulation by internalizing society's expectations for its behavior.

Reduction of governmental regulation argument: Responsible business behavior reduces the amount of regulation the government must impose. At its worst, regulation is a crude and expensive way of achieving social goals, sometimes imposing inappropriate, overly broad rules that dampen productivity and require extensive recordkeeping procedures to document compliance. If companies can use more flexible, voluntary methods to respect social norms such as pollution control, then government is less prone to impose legislation.

Social involvement by companies also nurtures trust and respect, and that makes government authorities less inclined to interfere in company business. Government agencies tend to be more lenient with socially responsible companies than with those that ignore social plights.

Power and responsibility argument: Corporations are getting to be so large and powerful that they are not effectively restrained by the invisible hand of market forces and government regulation. In order to promote public welfare, companies need to adopt corporate social responsibility as a self-imposed restraint.

Long-term profitability and financial success argument: The strongest case for the business integrity thesis is that ethical conduct in the marketplace actually makes good business sense. Regardless of how you stand in terms of these points of debate, one thing is clear: Insofar as the reputational stakes are much higher for today's companies, the market will dictate the final outcomes. Some firms will commit to higher standards and enjoy the reputational rewards, while others will decline and accordingly miss out on the opportunities. Given the shift toward increasing accountability and transparency, this is a reasonable assumption.

Origins of the Paradigm Shift

When did the moral paradigm for business begin to change? Where is it headed? A survey of the history of its development allows us to draw a few conclusions: It's not a passing fad, it hasn't happened overnight, and it shows no signs of going away.

The corporation's moral status has evolved gradually. Yet we can discern several defining developments that have taken place over the past century.

Corporate philanthropy took root in the early twentieth century with foundations established by tycoons like John D. Rockefeller, Henry Ford, Andrew Carnegie, and John Paul Getty. Many businesspeople and companies of today— good examples are George Soros, Cadbury, and Levi-Strauss—seek to carry on long-standing legacies of civic involvement and charitable contributions. In a seminal case on the development of the business judgment rule, *A. P. Smith Manufacturing Company v. Barlow*, the New Jersey Supreme Court in 1953 upheld a corporate contribution to Princeton University over shareholder challenge. Upholding the corporation's authority to conduct charitable giving on the ground that it creates public goodwill toward the firm—which in the long run benefits shareholders with increased profits—the court pointed to the tendency of the modern era to concentrate private wealth in the coffers of large companies, arguing that modern times dictate that corporations assume both social and private responsibilities toward the communities within which they conduct business.[5]

Codes of conduct began to appear as far back as the 1920s and 1930s. They were at first designed for industries rather than individual firms. The promulgation of business codes by companies picked up in the 1970s, led by multinational firms, and intensified in the 1980s and 1990s.[6]

Ethics programs. Originating in the 1950s as isolated inventions of business leaders, such as General Robert Wood Johnson, who concocted Johnson&Johnson's famous credo,[7] ethics programs have since grown to include a formidable array of contrivances, including moral education schemes, ethics offices,[8] formal agreements on industry standards, social accounting techniques, and social projects.

Confidence-crippling scandals. In the late 1960s and early 1970s issues of corporate responsibility came to the fore. During this time the public began criticizing companies for an array of moral transgressions, such as falsifying records, making misleading communications, shipping defective and dangerous products without warnings or information, undertaking abusive behavior (such as sexual harassment), allowing unsafe workplace conditions, showing unwarranted favoritism (nepotism), maintaining conflicts of interest, bribing public authorities, engaging in unfair and predatory competition, stealing and misappropriating information, polluting the environment, violating election laws, defrauding and misleading investors, interfering with governments in developing nations (International Telephone and Telegraph in Chile), and disregarding civil rights.

Such business scandals took a toll on the public's assessment of the business world in general. In 1968, 70 percent of the public believed business tried to maintain a fair balance between profits and the public interest. By 1977, that number plummeted to about 15 percent.[9] Overseas payment scandals, such as the notorious Lockheed bribery debacle in Japan, fueled sentiments of cynicism. Over several years nearly four hundred major U.S. firms had admitted to making illegal campaign contributions and bribing public officials to gain business abroad.[10] Estimates placed the drop of public goodwill toward U.S. business during the decade of the 1970s at approximately 80 percent.[11]

In recent decades, scandals and misdeeds have continued to appear, with additional practices coming to light: market-timing and late trading in mutual funds; cooking books and falsifying financial statements; "pumping and dumping" securities; "frontrunning;" "churning," "twisting," and "flipping" investments; perpetrating Internet abuses; and giving excessive executive compensation.

Socially responsible investment. Socially active shareholders came on the scene in the 1970s. Their emergence was precipitated by a 1970 federal court decision allowing the proxy process to be used by shareholders to raise social issues.[12] Socially responsible mutual funds grew up in this decade.[13] As we'll see, this trend is continuing.

Legal developments. Especially since the 1990s, the law has been fostering a moral actor view of the firm, embodied in initiatives touching such facets of corporate existence as culpability,[14] governance,[15] culture,[16] concern for nonshareholder consituencies,[17] shareholder resolutions,[18] self-policing and compliance,[19] and risk disclosure policies.[20]

Timeline of Paradigm Shift

1900–1910	Corporate philanthropy
1910–1920	Emergence of corporate codes
1930–1940	Securities and Exchange Acts introduced
1940–1950	Corporate ethics programs appear
1950–1960	Legality of corporate charitable contributions upheld
1960–1970	Public criticism of corporations, especially multinational companies; creation of board-level committees to oversee ethics and social responsibility
1970–1980	Shareholder activism; socially responsible investing
1980–1990	Legal recognition of corporate culture; rise in promulgation of corporate codes

1990–2000   American Law Institute principles of corporate governance; stan-
              dards for corporate culpability
2000–2010   Accounting and governance standards stepped up; self-policing in-
              centives; risk disclosure requirements

Where Has This New Paradigm Taken Us?

Today people admire companies that show concern for all of their constituencies. The most admired companies don't just keep customers and shareholders contented. Today people believe companies are responsible for fairness and quality of life. Race and gender concerns, even tensions between family and job, are now key management matters. The public has moved beyond questioning the making and selling of cigarettes and begun targeting tobacco investors. Investment funds are blasted for owning stock in companies that source from suppliers using child labor, trapping dolphins, or ravaging the environment. On Wall Street many social investment funds apply screens on investment portfolios and control hundreds of billions of dollars in private wealth.

The complexity of today's business world is turning the tasks of executives and managers into an art of forming responsible judgment in complex circumstances. Having rules helps to navigate in murky waters. But to build and sustain reputational capital—and to avoid reputational liabilities—just following the law and settled norms of customary business conduct isn't enough.

The new rule in business proclaims that profits and social responsibility are inseparable. Long-term profits come from a reputation for principle, grounded in integrity and fair play. In the new paradigm, building reputational capital is key. Reputation—not razzmatazz image, not brand identity, not letter-of-the-law compliance—is everything. Your company, its leaders, everyone at all levels of the firm, must change their thinking to this new paradigm.

A fundamental reorientation in values has made it imperative that firms move to the proactive level if they are going to build their reputational capital. The following factors are driving the paradigm shift to new levels:

Increased competitiveness.   Business leaders must seek new strategies for making their companies stand out from others. Integrity and fair play are essential to maintaining competitive advantage.

Globalization.   The world is shrinking and barriers to international business are tumbling. Companies must fulfill their revenue objectives by developing new channels of distribution and entering new geographic markets. If they do so successfully, they strengthen their leadership position, boost productivity, lower their overall cost structures, and pass savings on to their customers around the globe.

Reputation in the international marketplace is a key concern. Multinationals know that good reputations are essential for doing business across cultures. Most well-known companies today have internal mission statements and codes of conduct. Many, including Merck, IBM, Shell, and Hewlett-Packard, have full-time ethics officers who monitor the company's conduct.

Levi-Strauss cancels contracts with suppliers if it finds they employ child labor or overwork their staff. Western chemical companies, realizing in the late 1980s that pollution scandals could put them out of business, became extremely vigilant in policing the industry. Computer companies such as Digital, Compaq, and IBM have pushed for higher environmental standards. Accountancy firms such as Price Waterhouse are helping post-communist countries set up modern accounting systems. Oil companies such as British Petroleum and Arco guarantee that they will build schools and airports and act as green watchdogs in return for permission to drill for oil in places such as Siberia and Alaska. Being a good corporate citizens makes eminent business sense.

24-hour media. It is a CNN world. Business behavior everywhere is increasingly subject to exposure by the media and special-interest activists.

Shortly after Stanley Works announced its plans for reincorporating in Bermuda, I was asked repeatedly by TV journalists to examine the ethical implications of the move. I received similar requests following disclosure of questionable arrangements in private placement memoranda for brokerage firms selling investments in Enron-related partnerships. Television brings otherwise remote ideas and problems like child labor, famine, and global warming into the living rooms of consumers and the general public. A firm's malfeasances can instantly be spread around to news affiliates and brokerages all over the world.

And it's not just the traditional media. Fervent special-interest groups are becoming increasingly adept in leveraging the web and the media to relate companies' conduct to social and environmental ills. Activists use the Internet to attack companies.

Consider Burger King. The Rainforest Action Network called for an international boycott, alleging that the chain used cattle that grazed on pastures formed by denuding South American tropical forests. The company initially ignored the charges. In two years Whopper sales dropped about 17 percent. While it's impossible to know precisely how much of the decline was attributable to the boycott, the company eventually changed its suspect habits.

Rise in legal/regulatory standards.   Widespread proliferation of laws along with
stepped-up enforcement initiatives are ratcheting up risk of legal—and reputational—liability for both companies and individual businesspeople. Some noteworthy examples:

- An international pact negotiated in 2003 under the auspices of the United
  Nations Economic Commission for Europe (ECE) forces companies from
  over 30 countries in Europe, Central Asia, and North America to disclose,
  factory by factory, their output of toxic waste and pollutants such as carbon
  dioxide, acid rain generators, heavy metals, and carcinogens such as
  dioxins.
- In 1999, listing requirements for the London Stock Exchange directed disclosure of a company's policies for managing risk. Extending beyond financial and legal risks, it covers risks touching on business probity and
  reputation.
- In June 2002, in response to pervasive accounting scandals in the United
  States, the Securities and Exchange Commission (SEC) voted to impanel
  the Public Accountability Board to reform oversight and improve accountability of auditors of public companies. The idea was to enhance the credibility of the financial reporting process. A month later, U.S. Congress
  cooked up its corporate oversight bill, designed to deter dubious accounting and management practices, by increasing penalties for corporate fraud.
  Then the SEC rolled out rules requiring CEOs and CFOs of the largest 947
  companies in the United States to sign off on the accuracy of their financial
  statements. On top of it all, at the end of August, the Senate began rein-
  forcing the Sarbanes-Oxley Act, which steps up corporate accounting and
  governance standards.[21]

Even the reputations of credit rating agencies are getting called into question
with a rash of new regulatory initiatives:

- The SEC is pledging a sweeping overhaul of the regulation of credit rating
  agencies following criticism of their role in the collapse of Enron and the
  telecommunication industry crisis. Critics of the agencies are calling to
  open the business to competition. Three agencies dominate—Standard and
  Poor's, Moody's Investors Service, and Fitch Ratings. They are the only
  agencies accorded the SEC's lucrative Nationally Recognized Statistical Rating Organizations (NRSRO) recognition, making them the official arbiters

of credit quality. The SEC says it will consider opening the ratings business to other players. The key area of concern is conflicts of interest arising when companies pay for ratings, which are opinions of a company's or government's creditworthiness. Pressure for change has been turned up by the Sarbanes-Oxley Act.

Increased public scrutiny and mistrust of business ("Enronitis").   People sense a general downturn in business ethics. Consider this: A 1996 poll found a majority of respondents agreeing with the claim that most people on Wall Street "would be willing to break the law if they believed they could make a lot of money and get away with it" and that Wall Street workers were concerned with "making money and absolutely nothing else."[22] Employers are getting skeptical about job recruits.[23] They can't take it for granted that new employees will have the right values for the firm. There is widespread cynicism that white-collar crime is not sufficiently punished. A recent cover story in *Fortune* urging jail time for corporate criminals blasts: "Enough is Enough."[24]

The public is aware of a kind of structural and systemic disease in financial systems that some have dubbed "Enronitis."[25]

Expectations of leadership are shifting from government to business.   Privatization worldwide is switching power from governmental to commercial sectors. In the last two decades, governments of more than 100 nations have implemented such changes as the issuance of shares in state-owned enterprises, sales of government assets, opening competition in state-contolled sectors, and contracting out public services to private interests.

Consequently, bit by bit, the public is shifting its expectations of leadership in tackling social and environmental issues from government to business. In the United States, the failure of federal programs and partisan gridlock has exacerbated public demand for action against society's lingering ills. So, as legislators hesitate, commercial firms pressured by consumers' mounting concerns are enacting social policies.

Escalating influence of corporations.   Today's corporations have a towering presence in peoples' lives. A lot of folks spend the bulk of their waking hours working for corporations. Corporations touch—some would say invade—virtually every aspect of human existence: entertainment, financial security, education, health care, food, clothing, housing, transportation, and so on. Corporate advertisers aim to influence how people dress, eat, spend vacations. They persuade people what medications and cosmetics to use, what cars to drive, and what appliances to acquire.

By means of campaign donations, lobbying, and public relations efforts, corporate advocates shape policy and public discourse.

Given the mounting influence of corporations, in everyone's face so to speak, it's no wonder people are prompted to expect them to exhibit moral character.

Development of worldwide human rights standards for global corporations. Transnational business has global influence and bears global responsibility. In a growing trend, the public expect business to be a supporter of human rights as more companies expand overseas. Firms need to incorporate into their global strategies a standard by which they respect human rights in the global workplace, require compliance from their vendors, and integrate human rights into their decisions when selecting a country in which to do business.

This standard of behavior has special applications in countries where the human rights of employees are not protected by domestic law. Respect for the human rights of workers imposes certain obligations on multinational companies that may exceed what local laws require and what local industries actually practice.

Socially conscious investing.   As noted above, socially conscious investing began in the 1970s, when activists urged institutions and investment funds to divest their holdings in South Africa. During the past decade, the value of U.S. socially aware investments has risen from $50 billion to over $500 billion. According to Social Investment Forum data, it is one of the financial industry's strongest areas of growth.[26]

Socially responsible investing involves choosing investments in companies that are considered to do business under ethically sound operations. This concept of ethically sound operations is very broad, especially when applied to the global investment market. It can mean everything from manufacturing goods that are not harmful to people or the environment to hiring with nondiscriminatory employee policies. The socially responsible investment movement has created unique opportunities as well as concerns in the global marketplace.

There are several approaches. Individual investors can research the companies they purchase and measure them against a subjective set of parameters—qualities the investor deems important. Investors can also buy mutual funds that apply this discipline. There are investment management companies being introduced worldwide that concentrate on socially responsible investments. The companies range from individual firms created to focus solely on socially responsible investment opportunities for their clients to more mainstream investment companies that are simply adding socially responsible mutual funds to the collection of products they offer. These actions are a direct result of an increasing demand for these kinds of investments. The funds seek to provide alternative investment options to those investors who want to ensure that their money is used to promote businesses they deem appropriate. And socially responsible investments provide the added bonus of returning to the shareholder the satisfaction of using his or her money to support only ethically sound companies.[27]

The different approaches to socially responsible investing lead to another investment theme prevalent with this concept: shareholder activism. While exclusion may keep out investments of unethical companies, the concept of inclusion, that is, including controversial companies in a portfolio, allows for investors to exercise their rights as shareholders in an effort to make change. In effect, they are investing in companies they do not believe to be ethical. However, they hope to be able to work with the corporation in order to elicit change, as they are often large institutional investors and therefore may be entitled to numerous voting rights.

The concept of the socially responsible investment has become so popular globally that there are now indices available in several countries whereby the performance of mutual funds can be compared to the performance of an index of socially responsible investments. In 2001, the *Financial Times* and the London Stock Exchange jointly introduced the FTSE4Good, a series of indices created to benchmark the funds that invest in socially responsible investments in the United Kingdom.

Last year, the U.K. government introduced a requirement for pension funds to state in their investment policies the extent to which they take ethical issues into consideration in their investments. Germany followed suit with a law introduced in 2002. Other European countries, including France, Austria, and Switzerland, are considering similar legislation. The creation of these indices has also brought to light the issue of consistency in the investment selection process.

Asia does not yet have a social index, but investors are becoming more conscious of the companies in which they invest and are requiring corporations to increase their standards on the environment and the workplace. In the past two years, Japan, Hong Kong, and Singapore have introduced socially responsible funds to their investors. Singapore residents can purchase shares in a prowomen and profamily fund.

There is a well-established movement in Canada. Currently about 3.2 percent of all investment assets in Canada are held in ethical investments. Acuity Funds, Ltd. in Toronto has a series of funds that specifically target the environment, including the Clean Environment Equity Fund, the Clean Environment Global Equity Fund, and the Clean Environment Balanced Fund. However, larger diversified investment management companies, such as Caisse de Depot in Montreal, must pick and choose their issues more carefully. As the largest institutional investment company in Canada, the company has to be sure that the issues they pursue are those with a large consensus, such as child labor, human rights, and environmental issues, so as not to risk relationships with their large numbers of clients.

One concern that has arisen with the creation of such funds and indices is the subjective measure with which some decisions are made and its attendant inconsistencies. Upon the FTSE4Good indices' commencement and the release of the names of the companies they included, there was discussion about decisions regarding both exclusion and inclusion. For example, the index excluded Royal Bank of Scotland and Tesco, a U.K. supermarket company, mainly because they failed to sufficiently publicize the socially responsible investment initiatives they were undertaking, but included British Petroleum (BP) and Shell oil companies (seen as "good guys" by many because of their environmental initiatives) as well as WorldCom and Global Crossing (recently exposed as "bad guys" because of massive accounting irregularities).[27] Although Royal Bank and Tesco were later added, such decisions raise concern from current or potential shareholders that have an interest in socially responsible investing. This has led to another concern of such screening—that the reputations of the companies that are omitted may be jeopardized, even if the companies are acting in a socially responsible manner by most standards. These indices and selections have received much attention in the media and in financial news, and the corporations that might have been included under a different set of circumstances may be unfairly criticized if the selection criteria is based on too narrow a set of parameters.

Consumer conscience.   Today's consumers seek information concerning health, safety, and environmental risks associated with their purchases. Consumers form more positive impressions of companies that back causes they themselves endorse. Consumers are more prone to buy from companies they view as ethical and socially responsible. Decades ago, companies regarded manufacturing automobiles with exploding gas tanks or dumping banned pesticides in Third World countries in financial terms. Consumers judge companies nowadays holistically. Social performance—how the company impacts on the environment, whether it worsens or alleviates social problems—matters right up there with financial performance.

Consumers indicate by their purchases not only the value of your firm's products or sevices but how they view your firm's role in the community. The implication is clear: Since uprightness shapes consumer choices, your company's deportment is a bottom-line priority.

The Message

The message to business is clear: To survive in this new paradigm you must develop the ability to increase reputational capital. This means being proactive. But equally important, your firm's reputation must be real. A reputation is only as good as what it's based on. It won't come about from image manipulation (public relations techniques) or from legal compliance techniques (formal ethics programs).

What does it mean to do business in the new paradigm? To build a solid, resilient, and lasting reputation, your firm's managers need to invest heavily in establishing rapport with key constituencies. This entails keeping a hand on the pulse of expectations of chief constituencies, in particular: employees, investors, suppliers, customers and clients, and communities. In the long run it all pays off, since positive reputations generate the auspicious results outlined earlier in the introduction: more leverage in negotiating and contracting, lower advertising costs, successful alliances, enhanced employee loyalty, more leeway in decision making, and an immunizing effect from scandals and crises.

Where Will It Go from Here?

Because expectations of corporate conduct are in continual flux, there's no sure yardstick for measuring changes in the levels and types of misconduct—and exemplary behavior as well—that transpire over time. Behavior seen as ethical in one era becomes unacceptable as expectations rise and laws change. For instance, in the early 1900s child labor was accepted business practice in the United States, yet is now prohibited by law and considered immoral. Nevertheless, debates continue about whether various kinds of child labor found in developing countries around the world are acceptable or not.

Novel issues will continue to crop up as a result of innovations in technology and changes in society and politics. For instance, data privacy was not a major concern until the late 1980s and 1990s, when companies began to exploit newly available information technologies to track consumer purchasing patterns without the consumers' knowledge or consent. Recent advances in biotechnology, such as cloning and stem-cell research, are raising ethical issues that have never before presented themselves.[29] Globalization is posing cross-cultural dilemmas that remained submersed back in the 1970s.

But despite these changes and uncertainties, it's necessary to pay attention to the kinds of expectations bearing on your firm's conduct.

Sources of Reputational Liability in the New Paradigm

There are three sources of reputational liability: the court of law, the court of key constituencies (employees, suppliers, business partners, clients, investors), and the court of public opinion.

- The letter of the law is applied in a court of law. The frequently overlooked spirit of the law, however, is applied in the court of public opinion and the court of key constituencies.

- No due process rights exist in the court of public opinion. No right to confrontation of witnesses. No right to a presumption of innocence. No right to an appeal. In today's Internet and CNN world, a firm's conduct—whether it is exemplary or unscrupulous—is subject to instantaneous broadcast to everyone, everywhere.

- In the court of key constituencies, employees, business partners, clients, investors, and suppliers care about a firm's reputation. If these groups form negative judgments about a firm's comportment they will withdraw support and give it to competitors to whom they ascribe a more favorable reputation.

Ask yourself: How is your company's reputation impacted (favorably and unfavorably) by compliance with the letter of the law, compliance with those you work with, and compliance with public expectations?

Illustration: Corporate Inversions

Bermuda is becoming a favorite offshore financial location for a variety of companies, including some insurance and reinsurance firms. Benefits include quick reincorporation, tax avoidance, and lax regulations. Most operations and jobs stay in the United States. The practice is (in some circumstances) legal. But it is perceived as an instance of corporate irresponsibility. Consider the outrage expressed by the American public upon learning that firms such as Ingersoll-Rand, Stanley Works, Tyco International, and Global Crossing were reincorporating in offshore tax havens like Bermuda to cut tax bills. Although technically legal, these moves were perceived as unpatriotic, tax-dodging tactics, especially in the wake of the World Trade Center attacks of September 11, 2001.

NEW PARADE: BERMUDA DAY

TOP EXECUTIVES MARCH DOWN FIFTH AVENUE TO CELEBRATE THE ISLAND WHERE THEIR CORPORATIONS ARE REGISTERED TO AVOID TAXES.

Source: *The New York Times*, 18 June 2002.

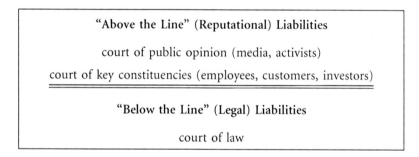

"Above the Line" (Reputational) Liabilities

court of public opinion (media, activists)

court of key constituencies (employees, customers, investors)

"Below the Line" (Legal) Liabilities

court of law

Although legal liabilities damage reputations, most reputational loss comes from "above the line" liabilities:

- The majority of the drop in stock price after corporate misconduct (whether proven or not) goes public is comprised of *reputational* injury.

- Anticipated legal sanctions (fines and damages from lawsuits) make up only about 6 percent of the decline.

In the "above the line" region, the applicable "law" is unmanifest. It consists of implicit contracts, and standards of integrity and fair dealing. These standards flow from the raised expectations in the new paradigm. The "above the line" liabilities are ignored by Alpha- and Omega-type firms.

In the "below the line" region, the applicable "law" is manifest. Below-the-line liabilities are often the motivating force for Omega firms adopting "ethics programs."

We know the sources of law that are applied and enforced by courts of law. But what sources of "law" are applied by the court of key constituencies and the court of public opinion? Consider O. W. Holmes's dictum (delivered in a lecture to incoming Harvard law students) that "prophecies of what the courts will do in fact, and nothing more pretentious, are what I mean by the law."[30] This *predictive theory* of law helps us understand the elusive nature of the "law" of the court of key constituencies and the court of public opinion. The idea is that the law resides in the actual judgment given, not in any crisp prexisting formulation in a statute or case precedent. The big challenge is to forecast/predict what these courts will expect from your business. Yes, they expect much more than they used to. But acknowledging this is the key to gaining your competitive edge in today's business.

How Can I Predict What the Court of Key Constituencies and the Court of Public Opinion Will Demand of My Company?

Before we look at what the nonlegal "courts" demand, keep one basic point in mind. Customers, employees, and investors are, first and foremost, people. Just like you and me. Being mindful of that obvious, yet often overlooked, fact is the best guide to understanding the expectations they have for your business.

Studies bear out that most people believe businesses share the same moral and ethical standards as individuals do. And a sizeable percentage think we ought to hold companies to even more stringent standards than we hold people to, because businesses' size, resources, knowledge, and impact are bigger than individuals.

- Don't fall into the trap of thinking your own values, opinions, and judgments are the same as those of the key constituencies and public opinion.
- Don't ask the legal department to make this kind of prediction.
- Compliance with the spirit of the law matters just as much as—often more than—compliance with the letter of the law. (See the example of Stanley Works which failed to anticipate that using legally available offshore reincoporation techniques to lower their company's taxes might be interpreted by many as a dubious slight-of-hand.)
- Human rights matter in countries where legal protections accorded to workers and others impacted by your firm's operations are thin. (See, for

example, Shell in Nigeria, Pepsi in Myanmar, Microsoft in China). Ignoring the firm's responsibilities for actively promoting basic rights triggers strong adverse judgments from shareholders and other constituents.

- Consider local culture and extend a high level of respect to it. (See, for example, H. B. Fuller and EuroDisney, firms which underestimated the negative perceptions generated by their foreign operations.)

- Use context-rich surveys and public opinion polls to plumb the level of expectations that key audiences in countries your firm is entering will hold your firm to.

Making Responsible Judgments about Reputation

Just because expectations for firms are rising doesn't mean that all of those expectations are legitimate. Are some firms getting unfairly condemned? How to separate the wheat from the chaff? Here are some guidelines for the courts of public opinion and key constituencies:

- Is this a universal standard or something that's relative to a culture (for example, nepotism)?

- Look at the total picture. In the totality of circumstances, does the firm's conduct show a pattern of misbehavior, or is this a one-shot event? What kinds of constraints and pressures is the firm under? Do these excuse their conduct? (For example, some companies, which reicorporated offshore to cut their worldwide tax bills, were prompted to do so because of overly burdensome U.S. tax laws).

- Is the violation a significant one or is it trivial? The law (both civil and criminal) makes distinctions about degrees of offenses. The more severe the offense, the weightier the sanction. Shouldn't informal norms for corporate reputation judgments reflect similar nuances?

- Is the criticism based on a firm's breaking a pointless law or regulation—one that is without a rational basis or fails to serve any social purpose?

Finally, learn to recognize these reputation risk triggers:

- Does the board of directors set an ethical tone—or does it give a seal of approval for unscrupulous practices?

- Does the firm merely follow the law? Or does it strive to go beyond compliance?
- Are standards different in home and host countries?
- Is there risk of potential "guilt by association" by dealing with firms of dubious repute?
- Do leaders "walk the talk"? Are they personally committed, credible, and willing to take action for the values they espouse?
- Do people take ownership of their actions? Do they pass the buck or deflect accountability?
- Are members trustworthy and conscientious? Are they are fair? Do they stand by promises and carry out responsibilities in a competent way?
- Do colleagues have a strong organizational identity? Are they committed to the firm's aims and ideals, and do they strive to achieve them in a responsible way?
- Does the company fulfill responsibilities to its stakeholders? Is it a good corporate citizen? Does the firm rely on self-governance mechanisms to achieve this aim?
- Do the values and principles espoused by corporate leaders mesh with the firm's day-to-day practices? Is the gap between practice and principle getting so wide that it undermines credibility of your firm and its leaders?

2

Getting a Handle on Reputational Capital

> Look, and it can't be seen.
> Listen, and it can't be heard.
> Reach, and it can't be grasped.
>
> —*Tao Te Ching*

Corporations' reputations are based on people's judgments. Reputations also respond to the identities and images companies create for themselves as an attempt to improve sales. But images differ from reputations in important respects. We need to get clear about the differences between identity, image, and reputation. It's important to know what reputation is so that it can be protected and enhanced.

Don't Mistake Reputation for Image or Identity

It is common to use the terms "corporate identity," "corporate image," "brand image," and "corporate reputation" interchangeably. But these concepts are not at all the same.

Corporate identity, as typically understood, encompasses various symbols—a corporation's name, logo, advertising slogans—the kind of things that let people recognize it. Wherever you are in the world, it's easy to find a Starbucks when you're looking for their familiar green mermaid emblem. Managers commonly—and mistakenly—assume that changing a company's identity symbols by itself will magically improve the company's image and reputation. Identity changes rarely improve image and never elevate reputation. Immediately following a parade of scandals with the sale of many of its financial services products, I noticed that the color and font of Prudential's name, emblazoned on the side of its headquarters in Newark, NJ, were charged. WorldCom recently announced plans to change its name. Surprised, anyone?

Corporate image is an overall evaluation, a set of beliefs and feelings people form about a firm. The feelings are normally tied to short-term "personality" values like excitement and enjoyment. Disney is adroit at cultivating the images of fantasy and family fun.

The advertising world knows that customers aren't just out to purchase products or services. People are also buying personalities or brands. So marketers craft *brand images* matching the "self-images" consumers desire. Successful brands, like the Subaru Outback, make a short leap between brand image and customer self-image.

The idea that brands have a basic personality or image captures the fact that people buy products and services not just for what they can do but also for what they mean. In marketing parlance, products and services give customers functional benefits and psychological boosts. Clothing fashions can put wearers in an "in crowd," or they can express wearers' moods and emotions. All this brings competitive advantage. Faced with functionally similar offerings—most shirts do a similar job of covering us—consumers choose products and services carrying symbolic meaning. Some advertisers—the ones that came up with the Marlboro Man spring to mind—are legendary for cooking up brand images that tap into people's self-image and desired lifestyle.

A positive corporate identity can uplift corporate and brand images. People link the identity symbols to the company. Meanwhile the identity symbols call up peoples' image—their mental picture and feelings—of the company and its brands. Recall the hapless Maytag repairman, who symbolized the reliability of the company's appliances. Some corporate identity symbols trigger enhanced images. Merrill Lynch's bull, symbolizing a rising stock market, triggers upbeat feelings for potential client investors.

Corporate reputation is a value-based composite that ranges from commerce (Dell has built a reputation for effective direct marketing) to compliance (PPG enjoys a reputation for respecting not just legal but ethical standards) to conscience (Merck's philosophy places people before profits). The most admired firms attain financial success, obey the law, and act responsibly. The corporate image is subjected to judgments by the courts of key constituencies and public opinion concerning acceptable conduct for the kind of organization in question. The court of key constituencies includes a broad audience of stakeholders: consumers, employees, investors, and shareholders. The court of public opinion includes other audiences offering assesments of the firm: analysts, news reporters, propagators of the rumor mill. Reputations crystallize from these audiences' evaluations. These are judgments of policy and principle, analogous to those made by law courts, except that they are tied to a broader set of values than those captured in legal and regulatory standards. The expectations of corporate behavior are continually ratcheting upward. In today's world of business, the principles/values that matter are integrity and fair play. (As we'll see in chapter 5, integrity involves reaching the right balance of virtues like authenticity, honesty, responsibility, and steward-ship of the environment, employees, and economy.) These are long-term concerns.

From my work in China while stationed at Peking University, I learned that the concept of reputation I was exploring in connection with modern business strategy resembled the notion of "face" in traditional Chinese culture. There are two senses of face: *lian* and *mian-zi*. *Lian* stands for society's confidence in the integrity of one's character. A firm or person can't operate successfully in the society if they have lost face. *Mian-zi* denotes distinction earned from having achieved success in life. Having attained high status, one acquires dignity and deserves respect. The values a company shares with its stakeholders drive trust, confidence, and support, just like the reputation held by a person.

The concepts of identity, image, and reputation are contrasted and compared in table 2.1 below:

Table 2.1 Different Facets of a Firm's Deportment

Corporate Attribute	Outlook/ Duration	Linked most directly to what attributes?	Within province of which areas of the firm?	Which constituencies targeted?
Identity	Mid-to long-term	Personality of firms	Marketing, public relations	Consumers
Image	Short-term	Personality of brands	Marketing, public relations	Consumers
Reputation	Long-term	Character, conscience, credibility of firms and their associates	All departments of the firm	All key constituencies

While the concepts of corporate image and corporate reputation may overlap, it is important to keep them separate. Corporate reputation runs deeper than surface impressions. Like image, reputation has to do with what people think and feel about a company. But unlike image, reputation:

- Is long-term, meaning it requires consistent behavior over a period of time to change;
- Is based on the firm's character, not its focus groups. This means reputation is hard-wired into the firm's values, its culture, its conduct;

- Is associated with all aspects of the firm, cutting across all departments and divisions;
- Impacts all constituencies—not just consumers but investors, shareholders, employees, business partners, suppliers, local communities.

Note that although the images of the Marlboro Man, Joe Camel, et al. seem to be as strong as ever as marketing gimmicks, the reputations of the companies behind these logos have suffered great damage, especially as a result of disclosures that tobacco companies intentionally hid information about the addictive properties of nicotine for many years from the public. When it comes to reputation, in other words, a popular logo doesn't cover up bad decisions.

Corporate reputation matters because it builds reputational capital. A reputation is built by demonstrating integrity, being known as honest and forthright, and playing fair. Reputational capital, on the other hand, comes when the power of a good reputation is harnessed to improve the relationships on which successful business depends.

You build reputational capital by catering to the respective expectations of your firm's key constituencies while remaining true to the firm's inner integrity. Reputational capital is a form of intangible wealth that bears some resemblance to—yet is quite distinct from—the accounting concept of goodwill and the marketing concept of brand equity. The problem with identifying reputational capital with goodwill is that goodwill has a narrow accounting function tied to evaluating a firm when it gets purchased by another. Likewise, the problem with associating reputational capital with brand image is that brand image refers to the personality that only one category of constituents—consumers—ascribes to a company's products.

Your company's reputation stands apart from its identity and its image, although reputation is related to both of these. A firm's reputation has its roots in a management discipline that promotes a fair and favorable workplace, quality products and services, an attractive investment for shareholders, and good citizenship in local and more extended communities.

To What Do Reputations Attach?

Reputations are associated with the business conduct of people, the firms they work in, as well as an entire profession or field. Not only does a fund manager have a reputation tied to his behavior, but so does the brokerage firm at which he is a partner, and the securities industry at large.

Country reputation: Countries acquire reputations as attractive or unattractive places for investors and businesses. Transparency International, a nonprofit organization headquartered in Berlin, publishes an annual "Corruption Perception Index" that reflects impressions of businesspeople about prevailing levels of corruption among nations.

Industry-wide reputation: A reputation is a partly cognitive, partly emotive feature that grows up within an entire industry or profession. It signals the overall credibility, reliability, and appeal that an industry or profession holds for clients and customers. It is influenced by the self-image held by its own participants as well, whether lawyers, analysts, or accountants.

Firm-specific reputation: A firm's reputation is established as its key constituencies—employees, consumers, investors, suppliers, and local communities—pass judgment on its past and present conduct, perceived intentions, and projected future prospects. The judgments embody a mixture of commercial, compliance, conscience, and citizenship criteria. Over time, the judgments crystallize to form a company's perceived ranking relative to rivals in its field.

Person-specific reputation: A person's reputation is a character portfolio that captures the multiple images of his or her business probity held by colleagues, clients, subordinates, and superiors. The assets in one's character portfolio are diversified, spread across an array of virtues like honesty, loyalty, and fairness. Occasional losses in one can be offset by large reserves held in the other. A person's reputation signals his or her overall level of integrity in business dealings.

Taking a Holistic Approach

From my research and consulting work, I am convinced that we need to reexamine some basic assumptions about the nature of the firm and its internal functioning. The standard separation of financial and social aspects of corporate behavior is no longer tenable. The key to success in reputation management is merging the firm's financial mandate with its social imperatives. And there are now compelling reasons for unifying the frequently fragmented functions of finance, marketing, human resources, public relations, investor relations, government relations, and compliance. Giving corporate reputation the prominence it deserves requires forging closer bonds—exploiting latent shared interests—among disparate departments in your firm. From a reputation perspective, the human rights ramifications of the labor practices a firm undertakes are related to the credibility of its high-buck celebrity endorsements—and both hook up with shareholders' concerns. A common cause unites the segmented functions of the firm. That cause is to capitalize on a company's untapped reserves of reputational capital.

We can visualize the essential nature of reputational capital with figure 2.1. The figure, which in ancient Eastern thought symbolizes the complementary nature of the intuitive and the rational, is a suitable vehicle for expressing the complementary nature of tangible and intangible wealth that our analysis of reputational capital inspires. The diagram depicts a symmetric arrangement of the dark yin and the bright yang. However, the symmetry is not static but captures a continuous cyclic movement.[1] This is appropriate to the cyclical, dynamic nature of corporate wealth creation: quarterly earnings, valuations of current and future cash flows, the flux of stock price over time, bull and bear markets.

The two embedded dots in the diagram incorporate the insight that whenever one of the two forces reaches its extreme, it contains within itself the seeds of its opposite. This corresponds to the findings of my research that ethical conduct and the discipline that fosters it lies at the heart of superior financial performance, and that good corporate citizenship is not absolutely unbridled and open but rather constrained by the firm's economic resources.[2] The interplay of yin and yang, the

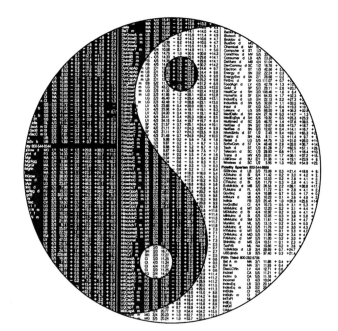

primordial pair of opposites, is accordingly an apt representation of my conception of reputational capital as an embodiment of both economic and ethical components—commerce and conscience—long thought to be polar opposites, but essentially complementary attributes of successful firms. Reputational capital is a manifestation of the dynamic interplay of the polar opposites of "soft" intuitive, complex character assets captured in ethics (yin) and "hard," clear, rational financial assets studied in economics (yang).

Wealth Generator

A corporate reputation is a productive asset. It generates wealth. Reputations create a form of capital—reputational capital—that goes unrecorded on corporate balance sheets. In chapter 3, "A Fresh Economic Concept with Strategic Significance," I set out the provocative thesis that creating shareholder value extends beyond exploiting the traditional kinds of financial and organizational capital to leveraging value from the company's reputational capital. To build and safeguard reputational capital, corporate leaders need to pay keen attention to the expectations of key constituencies. Keeping abreast of the changing perceptions and interpretations of constituencies is integral to staying competitive. In the new paradigm, you need to pay attention to *who* matters to your business and to *what* matters to them.

Competitive Advantage

Reputation is a source of competitive advantage. A reputation has significant economic value for your company because, like a snowflake, no two are exactly the same. The special and subtle ways your firm's reputation crystalizes can't be replicated by your competitors.

For firms that have become leaders in their industry and for celebrities, service companies, and enterprises whose operations make people vulnerable (for example, the pharmaceutical industry), sustaining competitive advantage requires a commitment to the ongoing management of the company's reputation.

Inside-out, your company can implement managerial practices that foster a corporate ethos that treats associates with respect and compassion. Outside-in, your company can be proactive in broadcasting its most appealing characteristics to customers by providing exemplary service, to communities by undertaking social and environmental projects, and to investors by maintaining solid financial performance. The firms that compete with integrity—that treat employees better, provide better products and services, offer better investments, operate with greater environmental sensitivity, act more responsibly—end up with superior reputations.

3

A Fresh Economic Concept with Strategic Significance

Reputational capital is not only among the most important strategic assets your firm has (it helps you compete in surprising new ways), but it is also a potent new economic concept (it lends recognition to the financial value of the firm's moral character). As a *strategic* concept, reputational capital holds promise to: (1) give firms a way to achieve competitive advantage in a business environment characterized by unprecedented expectations of corporate social and environmental reponsibility; and (2) provide a means for firms, leaders, and governmental authorities to restore credibility and trust in a business environment of deep suspicion and mistrust. As a key *economic* concept, reputational capital holds promise to (1) account for neglected economic growth; (2) account for how productivity is linked to ethical corporate behavior—making the case for why, in business, ethics often pays in the long run; (3) help guide better governmental policies concerning corporate self-governance and autonomy; and (4) help inform nation-states on policies that encourage investment and promote economic development.

In this chapter I will show:

- What kind of wealth reputational capital represents. This involves relating the concept of reputational capital to the traditional economic account of capital.

- How reputational capital links integrity and fair play to the bottom line. What considerations bear on whether or not reputation pays.

- Why building and preserving reputational capital is a fundamental concern of several key constitutents of the firm, namely those bearing risk and having a stake in the firm's financial performance: shareholders, board of directors, executives, managers, and employees. This entails integrating the concept of reputational capital into prevailing financial models of the firm (institutional, contractual, and stakeholder).

• How the coordinated efforts of the above constituents in forming reputational capital unleash and stimulate corporate self-governance—a preferred alternative to stepped-up governmental regulation and control.

Reputation as a Variety of Capital

You may have learned about the aggregate production function if you took Economics 101. Basically, it shows how growth relationships among a company's inputs improves the bottom line. Here's a simple production function:

$$Q = f(K, L)$$

The Q stands for output. K denotes capital input. L represents labor input. Capital is assumed to be something that's tangible and nonhuman. When we increase capital (K) and/or labor (L) inputs, we increase the output. But what if we acknowledge, as recent research bears out, that productivity grows not just from increasing inputs but from cultivating capital formation as well?[1] Let's expand our thinking. In reality, there's not just one but several different kinds of capital that generate wealth. The list below illustrates what I'm saying: We ought to be giving reputational capital its due, along with the other varieties of capital identified by economic theory:

Reputational Capital

Knowledge Capital

Human Capital

Organizational Capital

Financial Capital

To get these additional types of capital into the production function, let's use a slightly jazzier equation:

$$Q = f(L, K_1, K_2, K_3, \ldots)$$

Here, all those Ks ($K_1, K_2, K_3 \ldots$) stand for the different varieties of capital (listed above) that can make up the entire stock of your firm's capital.[2] In line with the insights developed in this book, we find that one of the Ks in the aggregate production function is reputational capital.

In terms of market capitalization, a firm has a certain value. A good portion of that value is made up of physical capital. If you take all the company's assets and liquidate them, you'll get a certain value. It turns out to be, on average, about 40 to 45 percent of the value in the books of the companies. The rest of the value is intangible.

Why is this significant? Simply put, increases in reputational capital—intangible assets that are not fully captured on the balance sheet—will make your firm's output grow. Think of it as a goodwill bank account. Notice that growth in output happens both from growth of capital inputs and from the magnitude of the stocks of capital.

How Reputational Capital Links Ethics to the Bottom Line

Does building the firm's reputation really pay? Say a company begins behaving better—acting with integrity and fair dealing—and its bottom line improves. How do we know whether its financial gain is a reputational ripple effect or whether it comes from some other factor? Maybe the company's profitability is being caused by an upturn in the economy, improved efficiency, or something else.

The causal jump from acting with integrity and fair play to growing economic value from reputational capital is difficult to trace for three primary reasons. First, there's sometimes significant lag time between good conduct and the reputational benefits that come of it. The economic value you generate from being honest about the downside of a deal for a potential client is apt to take time to be realized. The payoff might not occur until you get subsequent business from the client—when he ends up choosing you over competitors because he knows he can trust you. Second, some of the wealth-generating connections are indirect. Your good deed might fetch rewards in the form of positive referrals—made in recognition of your scrupulous traits—that spread throughout your client base. Third, there may be short-term costs that offset eventual financial gains from fair dealing. For instance, being honest and upfront about the negatives of a deal for the prospective client creates a cost seen from the short run—say, that particular sale doesn't go through. But long-term it might turn out to be a wise investment in your good name and credibility as the client ends up becoming your loyal customer on bigger, more lucrative deals.

It's impossible to precisely pinpoint which and how many acts of integrity and fair play will actually produce economic gains sufficient to offset the opportunity and other costs incurred. So, especially for some small firms, there is always a risk that the financial rewards for forthright conduct may arrive too late. This is not to suggest that moral behavior be taken as a purely economic effort. Rather, this underscores why it's important to gauge the kind of strategies used in generating reputational capital to your firm's specific capabilities, size, and financial resources. In other words, building reputational capital raises "suitability" issues: What's a reasonable investment in reputational assets for one business (a real estate firm) may be disastrous for another (a machine parts manufacturing company). Considerations such as time frame for anticipated return on the reputational investment, riskiness of the investment (risk adverse or not), and diversification of reputational assets are all legitimate and essential concerns. Your company may consider balancing an especially risky investment in reputation capital (say, funding a controversial cause that may incite an activist backlash) with a more conservative initiative (say, a tried-and-tested method).

To fully appreciate how reputation pays we need to adopt a broad view and look to long-term results. Refraining from making an illicit payment might mean the loss of a government contract today, creating short-term losses for the current quarter—yet further down the road not only does the company avoid a public scandal and legal convictions, both of which impose huge long-term costs, but it can build a reputation for refusing to acquiesce in demands for bribes, which can save the firm from having to incur such costs when dealing with public officials.[3] Realizing financial gains from the values of integrity and fair play requires disciplining patterns of thought, conduct, and human interaction for many years. Over time, a Zeta firm's orientation triggers the following factors, which can directly or indirectly improve the bottom line. The structure of reputation:

strengthens competitive advantage

improves risk management

raises employee creativity and effort

builds trust among key constituencies

enhances access to resources and opportunities

cuts complaint, monitoring, and compliance costs

stimulates knowledge sharing

improves product and service quality

solidifies brand equity

opens access to talent

generates opportunities for creating partnerships

With so many potentially positive financial effects, is it fair to say that Zeta companies will necessarily attain superior overall financial performance? The problem is, it's hard to predict since there are so many factors bearing on the profitability of a firm. Currency devaluations, changes in consumer tastes, technological innovations, departures of key clients, shifts in the political climate, revisions in government policy, natural disasters, and wars all have the potential to turn a good company's gains into losses overnight, rendering simple equations of integrity and profitability dubious. Plus, since even experts disagree about how to go about defining and measuring things like "ethics," "integrity," "social responsibility," and "outstanding financial performance," it's best to approach the problem with a healthy amount of discretion and humility.

Despite all of this, research is beginning to lend credence to the linkage between forthright conduct and financial success. Keep the following findings in mind to counterbalance skepticism about the payoff of reputation-enhancing actions:

- A 2002 survey of eight hundred CEOs from Europe and North America reports that a majority believe that the most important outcome of a positive reputation is an increase in sales.[4]

- An analysis of 95 studies of the linkage between corporate social and financial performance, using 70 different measures of financial performance and examining 11 areas of social performance, showed more positive than negative correlations between social and financial performance.[5]

- Another study, which summarized 52 research projects, found that 33 of them demonstrated a positive correlation between corporate ethics and financial performance, 14 proved inconclusive or indicated no effect, and only 5 indicated a negative relationship.[6]

- The Sustainable Asset Management Group, which monitors the Dow Jones Sustainability Index, found that the three hundred companies comprising the index outperformed other global indexes from 2000 to 2003.[7]

- A study of 160 CEOs, directors, vice presidents, managers, and analysts, conducted in 2002, found that 91 percent believed effective corporate social responsibility management creates shareholder value. Forty percent were from international firms with over 1,000 employees located in the United States, Canada, Europe, Asia, and Africa. Eighty percent of the respondents agreed that nonfinancial indicators, including environmental and social performance metrics, are essential in predicting future financial performance.[8]

- Numerous empirical studies document systematic positive correlations between corporate citizenship and business performance.[9]

- A recent study of the 500 largest U.S. companies appearing on the *Business Week* 1,000 list found that those with a defined commitment to ethical principles outperformed their peers.[10]

How Reputational Capital Squares with Received Models of the Firm

The concept of reputational capital fits nicely into the standard economic models of the corporation. These are: (1) the social institution model; (2) the contractual model; and (3) the stakeholder model. Regardless of which model of the firm we consult, the main idea we arrive at is this: The concept of reputational capital supports the ideal of free-market capitalism, upgraded by a recent value shift toward corporate social and environmental responsibility.

SOCIAL INSTITUTION FRAMEWORK: BUILDING REPUTATIONAL CAPITAL ENGAGES MANAGERS IN UPHOLDING PROFESSIONAL STANDARDS FOR BUSINESS

The Social Institution Picture of the Firm

According to the social institution model, a firm is a quasipublic organization. Because the state grants the privilege to incorporate in order to promote the general welfare, corporate property has an inherently public quality. Managers use resources at their disposal to advance the welfare of customers, employees, and the public. Managers balance the conflicting interests of key constituencies. A manager belongs to a profession carrying public responsibilities. So managers and the board of directors which oversee their day-to-day operations don't just serve shareholders. They are both public leaders and business leaders.

Analysis: The "sanction" for noncompliance with these standards is reputational loss. The "reward" for honoring them is reputational gain. The public responsibilities that corporate managers comply with—or violate as the case may be—are set by the three "courts": the court of law, court of key constituencies, and court of public opinion.

CONTRACTUAL FRAMEWORK: BUILDING REPUTATIONAL CAPITAL
ACTS AS AN INTERNAL (SELF-GOVERNING/POLICING) CHECK ON THE
GAPS LEFT BY A WEB OF CONTRACTUAL RELATIONSHIPS AMONG
CONSTITUENCIES

The Contractual Picture of the Firm

The so-called contract view of the firm looks at the firm as a package or cluster of contracts spread out among the firm's constituencies.[11] Under the contractual view, investors, employees, suppliers, and customers enter into mutual agreements with a firm. These constituencies give it some essential resource and get something valuable in return. The manager's job is to balance the contracts among all the different groups.

Analysis: Acknowledging the power of reputational capital in the corporation lends support for the contractual model of the firm. Reputational capital acts as a self-correcting force for defects, or drawbacks, connected with the purely contractual conception of the firm. The firm's reputation operates as a built-in internal incentive for the firm to initiate its own measures (self-imposed standards of integrity and fair play) in order to protect against drawbacks commonly associated with the contractual theory of the firm: (1) negative externalities (for example, if the firm pollutes, its reputation is damaged—witness what happened with the Exxon *Valdez* incident—and customers choose another firm, the value of the stock drops, and talented employees leave to work elsewhere); (2) breaches of implicit contracts (for example, if the firm violates important implicit contracts, the same result); (3) burdens of nonshareholder groups bearing residual risk (for example, because the potential for reputational liability forms a large part of the firm's residual risk, not only shareholders but other constituencies, such as employees and suppliers, bear some risk for the firm's reputation); and (4) unequal distribution and bargaining power of weak and disempowered groups (for example, gross unfairness in distribution, such as excessive CEO compensation, or grossly underpaid workers in sweatshops in underdeveloped countries, reflects poorly on the firm's reputation, so there is a disincentive to allow such policies).

How Shareholders Figure In

For those steeped in finance, the purpose of the firm is clear: maximize shareholder wealth. But wait a minute. Why should shareholders' interests be the end-all-and-be-all of business? Consider this: Shareholders are not owners of the firms in which they invest.

Shareholders, bondholders, and other investors provide capital. Yet what is more important, shareholders undertake the *residual risk* of doing business. Residual risk is the risk left over after a firm meets its legal obligations. We might conceivably spread residual risk out over each and every one who contracts with a firm. But we don't. We assign the bulk of risk bearing to one group. Today's large, publicly held corporations confer the title of residual risk bearer on the shareholders. It's being a residual risk bearer—not capital provider—that sets shareholders apart from other constituencies in the cluster of contracts that comprises the firm.

It's hard to protect residual risk bearers with the kind of contract provisions extended to bondholders, employees, customers, and other constituencies. You get some protection from being able to diversify and from having the limited liability that shareholders enjoy. Shareholders are blessed with prospects of higher returns than are extended to secured creditors like bondholders. But the biggest protection for shareholders is corporate control—that bundle of rights that encompasses the right to choose the board of directors and approve key changes. Plus, shareholders enjoy special attention from management. Managers have fiduciary duties to maximize shareholder wealth, to run the firm in line with shareholders' interests. A basic tenet of the contractual model is that society is better off when shareholders hold the reigns of a corporation. Wealth-maximizing decisions are most apt to come from residual risk bearers. After all, they shoulder the marginal costs and reap the marginal benefits flowing out of new ventures. The contractual model proclaims that firms generate the most wealth when decisions are made by keeping the shareholders' interests paramount. Keep in mind that the ultimate objective of the firm is to maximize wealth for the entire society. The objective of shareholder wealth maximization is just a way to bring about that broader objective. So it's not that constituencies other than shareholders—employees, customers, suppliers, and the larger community—are left by the wayside. These groups secure protection from other kinds of contracts. All in all, they are well served when shareholders have control.

Gaps in the Contractual Model

Recognizing the key roles played by reputational capital fills in several gaps left open by the contractual theory of the firm.

Externalities. Externalities happen. Society's welfare takes a dive when corporations reap profits for shareholders by dumping toxic wastes into rivers. Recall the infamous dumping of toxic waste by Hooker Electrochemical Company into the Love Canal. One way to deal with this problem is by assigning property rights so that firms have to internalize cost they otherwise externalize. Letting third-party victims of pollution sue twists the arms of firms to list compensation costs in their profit calculations. This internalizes pollution costs. The government, through agencies like the Environmental Protection Agency, can also make firms internalize pollution costs by leveling fines and other penalties against them.

Implicit contracts. The contractual model takes for granted that nonshareholder constituencies like customers and employees are well-served by their own contractual arrangements. That's fine as far as explicit contracts like sales agreements and employment contracts go. But implicit contracts—sometimes portrayed as social contracts rather than ordinary contracts you go to court to enforce—often require management's goodwill to be respected. Practices like downsizing and hostile takeovers can amount to breaches of implicit contracts. Witness the attacks mounted against Wal-Mart based on the complaint that the proliferation of its retail chain alters tax and job bases and forces small locally owned stores to close because they cannot compete against the retailer's economies of scale. Nevertheless, many laws help to buffer nonshareholder groups from rampant violations of their implicit contracts.

Residual risk. Problem: The contractual model says that shareholders carry all residual risk. That's why it grants them control over the firm. In reality, though, other constituencies, such as employees and suppliers, shoulder risk too. If you think about it, savvy shareholders with well-diversified portfolios bear comparatively little risk. The idea, though, is that they lay claim to the firm's residual returns. Following the standard rationale for letting shareholders control the firm, groups bearing residual risk should have a voice in key corporate decisions. Consider the plight of highly skilled employees, such as product specialists, who develop valuable firm-specific human capital. They are carrying significant residual risk. What if the firm lays them off? Start-up companies can lure employees only by promising higher salaries going forward. The promised salaries depend on the firm's performance. So these kinds of employees are also residual claimants. They share the risk. That's why many start-up companies offer employees shares of stock or stock options. And groups besides shareholders that carry residual risk sometimes win a seat on the board of directors.

Wealth and power imbalance. Contracting groups have unequal bargaining power. The imbalance shakes out in the unfair distribution of the wealth that a firm generates. Powerless, disenfranchised workers can't bargain well in a cluster-of-contracts firm. Inequality of bargaining power is a big problem, especially in developing countries.

The Stakeholder Theory of the Firm

According to the stakeholder theory, corporations are run to benefit anyone with a stake in the firm. This includes customers, employees, shareholders, suppliers, and the local community. A stakeholder is any individual or group that affects or is affected by the firm's conduct. Each stakeholder has a different relation to the firm. But each constituency matters to the firm's operation, so its interests must be taken into account by managers.

Analysis: A firm's reputation is not just a single reputation but rather the result of many assessments linked to many relationships between the firm and its constituencies (stakeholders). The firm should attempt to satisfy the interests of all those who have a stake in the firm, since those constituencies together contribute to the bulk of the firm's wealth, which is its intangible reputational capital. In the new paradigm for business, the firm's own interests are promoted by taking an "outside-in" viewpoint—that is, advancing the legitimate interests of its key constituencies. The concept of a stakeholder is central to understanding how firms build reputational capital—and how they lose it. The stakeholder model lets us track the wide array of obligations corporations owe to various constituencies. Neglecting or deliberately disregarding these obligations triggers attacks on the firm—punching holes in the storage tanks of reputational capital. On the other hand, the satisfaction of obligations and interests across key constituencies is what builds corporate reputations.

Just What Kind of Wealth Is Reputational Capital, Anyway?

By far the most common gauge of shareholder wealth is stock price, not accounting profits, which can be manipulated. Yet stock price is also influenced by many nonfundamental factors: investor psychology, economic trends, and market irrationality. These are all outside of management's control. Insofar as stock price captures the risk preferences of shareholders having little stake in the firm, it's not always the best guide for managing a firm in the long-run. In other words, managing to maximize stock price doesn't always produce maximum firm value.

An Extended Balance Sheet

We get the picture of corporate wealth that our concepts and assumptions provide for. So, if you're accustomed to thinking that the real measure of wealth maximization is by accounting profits or stock price, let me suggest a better way. Throughout this book we will see that, based on emerging trends in today's markets, the real value of a firm lies much deeper than just its financial state. We need to acknowledge forms of wealth that slip through the cracks of ordinary financial accounting methods. So what's my proposal? Along with the normal assets and liabilities, we need to include—via an extended balance sheet—the value added to the firm by intangibles running to and from various constituencies (employees, customers/clients, suppliers, strategic partners, investors) and the costs incurred by the firm from damage to these intangibles. The intangibles include things like corporate culture, trust, integrity, perception of fair dealing, credibility, dignity, pride. These make up *reputational capital* and *reputational liabilities*, respectively. The difference between them is *net reputational capital*, a breed of wealth not captured by ordinary financial accounting practices. This proposal reflects the view that the value of a firm consists not merely in its financial state but in its strategic, financial, and operational abilities in building reputational assets.

The idea of shareholder wealth maximization is not fixed—it varies according to a range of alternative interpretations. Deciding which interpretation you opt for involves making value judgments. It involves choosing whether the interests of just the shareholders, or of all constituents of the firm, or of all groups impacted by the firm's activities, matter most. And it also involves deciding whether short-term or long-term interests are more important. In other words, if the value of a firm is assumed to be its value as an ongoing enterprise able to create wealth for society indefinitely into the future, then managers should not lump all the attention on the interests of individual shareholders and on current stock price. Instead, they should weigh the interests of all of the groups that make up the firm, or balance the interests of all groups affected by the firm, and focus on long-term performance.

Business decisions that generate short-term profits benefit well-diversified shareholders with a strong risk tolerance and a short-term outlook. On the other hand, those that cultivate long-term prospects of the firm—that is, making the commitment to building the firm's reputational capital—advance the long-range interests of risk-averse shareholders as well as various constituencies having a stake in the firm.

The long-term value of a firm is recognized by courts in some cases to encompass the value it brings to employees, consumers, and society at large.

Social Return to Reputational Capital

Macroeconomic theory holds that when a firm enjoys growth in capital, the private return is the increase in that firm's output. But the output increase enjoyed by the individual firm may extend further: It can increase the productivity of other firms. Economists call this spillover effect the social return to capital.[12] This downstream effect (or loss, as the case may be) of reputational capital is evident in the collateral damage effect a scandal may have on the credibility of an entire industry, such as the accounting professions in the United States following the imbroglios with Enron, WorldCom, and Arthur Andersen, and, in Europe, in the wake of accounting irregularities disclosed in connection with the Dutch retailer Ahold.

Business behavior grounded in integrity and fair dealing generates credibility and trust. This greases the machinery of contracting among a firm's constituencies. Scrupulous conduct permits informal commitments to flourish. This brings about more flexibility and less suspicion and red tape than you get with formal agreements. If bondholders are suspicious of management they might demand restrictive bond covenants. Employees distrustful of management might look to unions to draw up a collective-bargaining agreement. Contracting can't fly without trust. So even if we assume that the end all and be all of the firm is shareholder wealth, that treasure doesn't show up unless a firm competes with integrity and fair play.

Reputation Building Inspires Corporate Self-Governance

My account of reputational capital provides an integrative answer to the question "whose interests does a corporation serve?" Your firm's reputation building is *everybody's* business, from the board of directors to the small investors, from the chief executive to rank-and-file employees. Indeed, for many firms, the formation of reputational capital brings benefits to more extended audiences, such as suppliers and potential business partners. The task of building reputational capital creates a common mission linking shareholder and stakeholder interests. Because building, safeguarding, and leveraging the firm's reputational assets involves maintaining a positive reputation across all key constituencies, the stakeholder model is essential. Yet, at the same time, successfully balancing competing stakeholder interests in order to build reputational capital ultimately leads to the creation of wealth for all who have contracted with the firm, so the contractual theory is also essential.

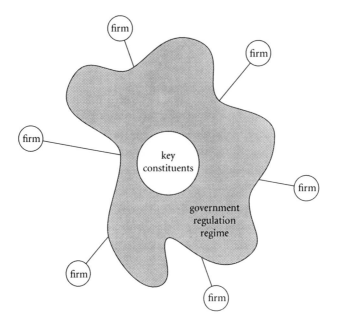

- Trigger: Corporations behave amorally—indifferent to opportunities for preserving and generating reputational capital with their key constituencies.
- Result: Government increasingly intercedes—forcing compliance with legal rules and regulations that specify exactly how corporations must deal with their key constituencies.
- Trend: Diminishing corporate moral autonomy; fewer opportunities for self-imposition of moral standards; darkening of pathways for reciprocity, respect, and trust between firms and employees, shareholders, investors, suppliers, and customers.

Figure 3.1   Government Regulation Regime

Who Is Responsible for Forming and Safeguarding Reputational Wealth?

When we start to look at the firm's conduct through the reputation lens, it brings the responsibilities owed by various consituents into sharper focus.

Board of directors.   The firm's shareholders elect a board of directors, who serve as corporate policy makers. Since accountability for what the corporation does or fails to do rests ultimately on the board of directors, it follows that the board bears responsibility for the firm's reputation. After all, the members of the board oversee management. Directors normally set up audit, nominating, and compensation

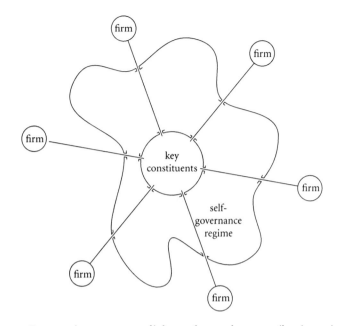

- Trigger: Corporations act as enlightened moral agents (business integrity thesis)—mindful of mandate to build reputational capital to promote welfare of both the firm (increasing shareholder wealth and enhancing employee well-being) and society (advancing legitimate interests of both immediate and remote stakeholders).

- Result: Reduced need for government to intervene in relationships between corporations and key constituencies by means of coercive sanctions. Corporations are guided and rewarded in adopting self-imposed moral standards by reputational weslth incentives.

- Trend: Formation of genuine, transparent, noncoercive relationships between corporations and constituents. The relationships are built on reciprocity, respect and trust.

Figure 3.2   Self-Governance Regime

committees to deal with more routine matters of running the company. The board members are responsible to the shareholders for choosing honest, credible, effective managers and especially for selecting the corporation's president. They may also be responsible for choosing the executive vice president and other officers. The cumulative weight of all of these actions impacts the firm's reputation. Officers and directors are fiduciaries of the corporation. As such they should act in the best interests of the corporation and not profit at the firm's expense. They are morally responsible for the overall ethos of the corporation and its major policies; they can set a tone for integrity or they can overlook unscrupulous business conduct. They can and should ensure that the firm is managed fairly and honestly and that the interests of the shareholders are given proper attention, not ignored by management. According to prevailing legal standards set by the business judgment rule, officers and directors are allowed to make mistakes. Yet they must show that their decisions were made pursuant to careful study, deliberation, and discussion. In those decisions, they may consult experts, such as attorneys, accountants, and financial analysts. Here is yet another point of contact with responsibility for reputation, since officers and directors need to show that these experts were well-chosen—that is, that they had a reputation for credibility and reliability in their professional services.

Management.   Management bears responsibility, through the board, to the shareholders. It is responsible to the shareholders for managing the firm honestly, fairly, and efficiently. Management is also responsible to the firm's employees. It both hires them and provides for the conditions of work. When hiring practices are fair, and favorable conditions of employment maintained, the company's reputation will get a boost.

Management is responsible for setting the character and moral tone of the firm, which drives the firm's reputation. Unless those at the top insist on maintaining high standards, unless they reward exemplary conduct and punish misdeeds, the corporation as a whole will tend to grind on heedless of the reputational dimensions of its behavior.

Employees.   Employees are responsible for doing the jobs they are hired to perform. Within the guidelines of their job description, employees are expected to carry out their tasks as directed by superiors. Since the behavior of even rank-and-file workers impacts the firm's reputation, it is important that job requirements be spelled out to communicate to employees the fact that the firm considers reputation as an asset comparable to other tangible assets and that reputable behavior is an essential requirement of their position. It is equally important to demonstrate how conduct that may not ordinarily be seen by employees as being linked to the corporation's reputation—such as treating clients and customers with respect—in fact is.

4

How to Gauge Reputational Capital

Some Preliminary Reflections

Please take a moment to read through this age-old folktale, even if you're already familiar with it:

There once was a man who had been traveling for a long time. Having run out of food, he was weary and hungry from his journey. When he came upon a small village, he thought, "Maybe someone could share some food."

When the man knocked at the first house, he asked the woman who answered, "Could you spare a bit of food? I've traveled a long way and am very hungry."

"I'm sorry, but I have nothing to give you," the woman replied.

So the traveler went to the next door and asked again. The answer was the same. He went from door to door and each time he was turned away.

But then one villager said, "All I have is some water."

"Thank you," the traveler said smiling gratefully. "We can make some soup from that water. We can make stone soup."

He asked the man for a cooking pot and started building a small fire. As the water started to boil, a passing villager stopped and asked him what he was doing. "I'm making stone soup," the traveler replied. "Would you like to join me?" The curious villager agreed.

"First, we must add a special stone," said the traveler. "One with magic in it." He reached into his knapsack and carefully unwrapped a special stone he'd been carrying with him for many years. Then he put it in the simmering pot.

Soon people from the village heard about this strange man who was making soup from a stone. They started gathering around the fire, asking questions. "What does your stone soup taste like?" asked one of the villagers.

"Well, it would be better with a few onions," the traveler admitted.

"Oh, I have some onions," he replied.

Another villager said, "I could bring a few carrots," Someone else offered, "We still have some potatoes in our garden. I'll go get them."

One by one, each villager brought something to add to the pot. What had started as just some water and a magic stone had now become a delicious soup, enough to feed the whole village. The traveler and the villagers sat down together to enjoy their feast, and the miracle they'd help to create.

The story contains an insight connected to our concept of reputational capital that I'd like to draw your attention to. When it comes to assigning value to reputational capital, what's key is not any independent or intrinsic value, but rather value relative to other business assets. Consider the folktale: Is the stone really magic? Believing that there's something special about the stone is what motivates the villagers to join in. Looking at the stone in isolation—asking what the "fair market value" of the stone is by itself—misses the point.

Reputational capital is analogous to the stone's value as a sort of *strange attractor*—it generates a whole-is-greater-than-the-sum-of-its-parts arrangement for the common good. The story is a metaphor for the power of reputation to motivate constituents to do business: to contribute, to partner with you, to invest with you. The folktale is, of course, subject to multiple interpretations. Cynics tend to see the traveler as a trickster who dupes the villagers while contributing nothing of his own. But this overlooks the unique properties of the stone in the wider context, which includes trust, reciprocity, and goodwill. I think a better reading of the tale acknowledges the special value the traveler adds by inspiring and mobilizing the townspeople. The question of motivation—whether the man with the stone is really just interested in himself or whether he wants to make everyone better off, is not especially important. After all, at the end of the day, they share in a commonwealth that would not be possible without the element of collective goodwill. It is by believing and trusting in the power of the stone that its power gets activated and realized. In this way, appreciating the magic of the stone—and, by extension, the unique value of reputational capital—sets in motion a dynamic of wealth creation.

Measuring Reputations

Measuring and quantifying corporate reputation is a tricky business. More often than not, what's being diagnosed is brand and corporate image rather than deeper character traits. Yet nurturing those deeper traits holds the keys to building reputational capital.

So you need to be careful not to confuse corporate image with corporate reputation. That's hard because a lot of people use the two interchangeably. To help clarify matters, let's pull apart two distinct senses of reputation. There is a weak (shallow) sense and a strong (rich, deep) sense. The weak sense of reputation is the one people use when they are really talking about brand and corporate image. By analogy, a company's "reputation" in this weak sense is like an individual's "personality." Managers directing their energies toward this sense of reputation set about to directly manage impressions. This is public relations and marketing stuff. All the books on corporate reputation and the current measures of reputation used by analysts, accountants, economists, and marketers deal with this superficial aspect of brand and corporate image. Moreover, most accountants confuse short-term reputation assets with long-term reputational capital. Finally, they do not factor in anticipated future accumulations of reputational capital, which are of key strategic importance.

A robust sense of reputation—the focal point of this book—deals with the underlying character of the company. The company really is more than just the sum of its images. This sense of reputation is the one worth singling out because it is directly linked to the firm's moral character and its virtues.

Here's a first step to getting a handle on reputation reality. Ask these questions:

- Who counts? Which constituencies does your firm need to build a solid reputation with? In the reputation checklist provided in table 4.1, principles are grouped according to their relevance to key constituencies.
- What counts to your firm's key constituencies? The principles given in the checklist canvass core concerns.
- What aspects of reputation matter in your firm's sector (line of business)? In the checklist, some principles may not be relevant for your industry. If so, just indicate n/a (not applicable).
- Going forward, what are your firm's priorities in building its reputation? At the end of the checklist, set out the top three reputation drivers your firm needs to focus on.
- What's going to matter most in the future? In five years? In ten years?

Then, work through the checklist below. When done, see how many "No" responses there are. Each "No" signals a potential reputational pitfall that needs to be addressed.

I recommend setting stretch targets against which to set your firm's business goals. This enables you to measure progress over time. For instance, one target can be to change two responses on the checklist from "No" to "Yes" every eighteen months.

Gaining a clear understanding of your company's reputational strengths and weaknesses compared to your rivals, and setting measurable goals to address them, affords a sound rationale to rollout a reputation management program. Ultimately, you can leverage the knowledge to your firm's advantage.

Use this checklist to benchmark your firm's reputation against rivals.

Table 4.1 Reputation Checklist

Reputation Driver	Is it met?		
Overall			
Generates value for all constituencies	Yes	No	n/a
Follows the spirit as well as the letter of the law	Yes	No	n/a
Combats corruption and bribery	Yes	No	n/a
Respects human rights in all countries of operation	Yes	No	n/a
Promotes economic and social development in the Third World	Yes	No	n/a
Is environmentally friendly	Yes	No	n/a
Vision and Leadership			
Has credible leadership	Yes	No	n/a
Has leaders with clear vision for future	Yes	No	n/a
Has leaders who recognize and seize market opportunities	Yes	No	n/a
Clients and Customers			
Offers quality that meets/exceeds customer expectations	Yes	No	n/a
Offers good customer service	Yes	No	n/a
Ensures health and safety of customers, discloses risks	Yes	No	n/a
Doesn't create products that harm the environment	Yes	No	n/a
Shows respect for people in products, marketing, and advertising	Yes	No	n/a
Employees and Associates			
Provides jobs and compensation that allow good living conditions	Yes	No	n/a
Preserves employee health, safety, and dignity	Yes	No	n/a
Listens and responds to employee concerns	Yes	No	n/a
Handles workplace conflicts/negotiations in good faith	Yes	No	n/a
Accords equal treatment and opportunity regardless of age, gender, race, religion, disability	Yes	No	n/a
Helps employees develop transferable skills and knowledge	Yes	No	n/a
Sensitive to unemployment and dislocation problems	Yes	No	n/a
Shareholders and Investors			
Shows prospects for future growth	Yes	No	n/a
Maintains strong record of profitability	Yes	No	n/a
Obtains a fair and competitive return on investment	Yes	No	n/a
Discloses accurate, relevant information	Yes	No	n/a
Conserves, protects, and increases investors' assets	Yes	No	n/a
Respects investors' input (suggestions, complaints, formal resolutions)	Yes	No	n/a
Deploys corporate assets for business, not personal, use	Yes	No	n/a
Business Partners			
Has valuable attributes worth "renting," (e.g., expertise, loyal customer base)	Yes	No	n/a
Honors promises	Yes	No	n/a
Is candid and honest	Yes	No	n/a

(*continued*)

Reputation Driver	Is it met?

Suppliers

Is honest and fair with pricing, licensing, rights to sell	Yes	No	n/a
Avoids coercion and needless litigation	Yes	No	n/a
Builds stable, long-term relationships in return for supplier value, quality, competitiveness, reliability	Yes	No	n/a
Shares timely information, integrates suppliers into planning process	Yes	No	n/a
Makes payments on time and on agreed terms	Yes	No	n/a
Gives priority to suppliers and subcontractors whose conduct respects human dignity	Yes	No	n/a

Rivals

Shuns collusion with rivals	Yes	No	n/a
Promotes open markets for trade and investment	Yes	No	n/a
Refrains from illicit payments or favors to win competitive advantage	Yes	No	n/a
Respects property rights, both tangible (e.g., physical ownership) and intangible (e.g., patents, copyrights, trademarks, trade secrets)	Yes	No	n/a
Refrains from espionage, using forthright means to obtain commercial information	Yes	No	n/a

Local Communities

Avoids improprieties with government officials	Yes	No	n/a
Minimizes social and environmental harm caused by company activities	Yes	No	n/a
Works alongside community groups to better health, education, work-place safety, the economy	Yes	No	n/a
Respects local culture	Yes	No	n/a
Supports good causes and backs employee involvement in civic activities	Yes	No	n/a

General Public

Promotes security and peace	Yes	No	n/a
Fosters social integration and diversity	Yes	No	n/a
Upholds democratic institutions and the rule of law	Yes	No	n/a
Is respected and admired	Yes	No	n/a

Sector-specific drivers: (e.g., for the insurance industry, compliance with new Patriot Law requirements; for the fast-food industry, consideration of health impact of products)

1. _____

2. _____

3. _____

(*continued*)

Table 4.1 (*continued*)

Firm-specific drivers: (e.g., possible adverse effects of our new product/service on customers)

1. _____
2. _____
3. _____

Our top reputation priorities going forward (e.g., getting known for taking a robust stance against bribery in our foreign divisions):

1. _____
2. _____
3. _____

Corporate reputations impact the bottom line. A favorable reputation improves your firm's profitability along several fronts: It lures investors to securities, draws customers/clients to products and services, and binds employees to their jobs. Granted, a good reputation alone will not accomplish all this in the absence of profitability. Nevertheless, for publicly traded companies, being in a state of favorable repute ratchets up the price at which securities trade. The economic value of a corporate reputation can be measured at least in part by the excess market value of the firm's securities.

The economic value of corporate reputation is especially pronounced for service providers, who find themselves hard pressed to reveal any other noteworthy assets in their portfolios. Actually, all companies—whether in services or in manufacturing—lean not just on tangible assets like people, plants, and equipment but also on intangible assets such as patents, trademarks, servicemarks, copyrights, brand names, and reputation. Being thin on material products, service companies rely heavily on their reputations to keep afloat.

Ways to Calculate Reputational Capital (and Their Limitations)

Let's tour through the different methods for quantifying reputational capital.

Intellectual Capital Approach

Advocates of this approach claim that the value of a firm's intellectual capital is an accurate gauge of the company's reputation. Consider Johnson & Johnson and Union Carbide. These companies each have an immense cache of brand names, patents, and trademarks. Revenue streams for a company's patented products can be projected based on patent protection periods afforded by the firm's respective countries of operation. (Periods for patent protection vary from jurisdiction to jurisdiction.) The costs connected with obtaining the patent are compiled, capitalized, and amortized on the balance sheet in a straightforward way. The economic value of a corporate reputation that is bound up in patents can be measured with some precision. What about the dimensions of brand value extending beyond patents, such as trademarks and brand and corporate image? Here, it's a little trickier. On the revenue side, although trademarks are protected indefinitely, so long as they continue to be used, it's uncertain how much strength a brand will maintain, how long it will keep its cachet, and what future revenues it will fetch. Plus, accounting rules of some countries let companies capitalize and depreciate only the administrative costs tied directly to securing a name. They don't let companies capitalize indirect costs incurred in building and maintaining a name. In other words, the advertising, service, and support costs that build brand equity—the principal drivers of the corporate reputations (in the weak sense)—don't appear on the books.

The big problem with the intellectual capital approach lies not so much with what it measures as with what it ignores. No firm—even those whose main source of wealth appears to be derived from patents or trademarks—can avoid acquiring reputation in the deeper sense. Consider that although Union Carbide's stock price initially plummeted when news spread of the methyl isocyanate leak from its plant in Bhopal, India, the company eventually rebounded from the catastrophe. Recall how resilient Johnson&Johnson's reputation was in the aftermath of the Tylenol product tampering fiascos. Both companies scored highly on the Reputation Checklist. This shows the kind of broad, character-based criteria that constituencies use in assessing a firm's reputation.

Accounting Approach

Some accounting methods ignore the value of intangible assets altogether. And accounting rules of some countries prevent firms from capitalizing the costs of projecting images and protecting names. Consequently, advertising and research and development costs—outlays that contribute heavily to building a company's reputation—are simply expensed and routinely vanish into thin air. The method of immediately expensing costs that build reputation brings about this undesirable result: Balance sheets habitually undervalue companies. Estimates of a company's true worth become speculative. Think about an independent insurance agency. The bulk of its assets are intangible. They consist of customer lists and client contacts—

which are maintained through reputation. On paper, the company is worth almost zilch. But it will likely sell on the open market for hundreds of thousands of dollars. Its reputation is obviously worth something. Yet one can only venture a guess as to its value. Keeping on the safe side of this assessment problem, U.S. accountants recognize goodwill only when a firm is sold. They measure goodwill as the excess of the company's purchase price over the fair market value of its tangible assets. Goodwill typically incorporates the value of all intangibles, including brand names and reputation.

If it all looks like creative accounting, at least it's backed by a sound economic rationale. The balance sheet basically reflects only historic numbers. So it can fail to capture current market value. In circumstances where a company is bought for more than its balance sheet value, it helps to show why the surplus is being paid. Restating various asset items to reflect their current market value does this. After restating all assets based on their market values, an increment may remain that cannot be explained in terms of physical assets. This increment is goodwill. It represents the value of buying an ongoing concern with a viable production technology, qualified people, and a market—as opposed to a dead collection of assets. Under the purchase method, asset values are restated based on their market values on the day a business combination deal is struck. Under the pooling-of-interest method there is no restatment of the cost of the assets—the accounts are simply added up and no goodwill is created. (The default method of accounting for business combinations is the purchase method, and the pooling-of-interest method may be applied only if certain criteria are met.)

Some debates among accountants center around the complexities of measuring the elements of goodwill and the hardships posed by associating costs with future benefits.

Other accounting controversies arise about whether goodwill should be capitalized on the balance sheet and depreciated or written off against a merged company's equity (retained earnings). Most international accounting standards do not permit reporting internally generated goodwill or the value of brand names on the balance sheet. But changing the rules to explicitly capitalize reputations in financial statements would bring about a positive result. It would make managers more cautious in safeguarding these intangible assets.

Disputes about intangibles in accounting are apt to continue unless some reliable and comparative estimate of reputational capital emerges that can be accounted for somewhere within a firm's financial statements, if not squarely on the balance sheet.

Marketing Approach

Marketing specialists provide an array of ways to measure brand equity—the value of a corporate brand. One received method asks how much sales royalty a third party must pay for the right to use the brand name. The limitation of this approach is clear from the distinctions we made previously among corporate identities, reputations, and brand images.

Finance (Market-Based) Approach

One way to tabulate the economic benefits flowing from a positive reputation is from the excess value investors are willing to pay for the company's shares.

This method of calculating a company's reputation assumes that stock price incorporates all known information about a brand and fully reflects a company's future prospects. This market-based approach points out that, when assessing a company, investors don't look at liquidation value but probe deeper to the firm's capacity to generate future profits as a going concern. Accordingly, the market value of a public company should reflect its value as an operating enterprise. The excess market value over the liquidation value of its assets roughly corresponds to the overall esteem in which the company is held by key constituencies. In sum, this approach views the reputational capital of all public companies as a form of additional worth derived from both undervalued historical assets and from goodwill. Taken together, they add up to investor confidence in a company's future prospects.

But looking at the excess value investors pay for shares has its limits. Using the stock price as a measure of reputational capital does not work for private companies that are not publicly traded, and it does not work for law firms, accounting firms, solo practitioners, and financial services professionals.

Also, the distinction between market price and intrinsic value must be noted. Assets can be mispriced. The traditional efficient markets formulation claims that an asset's market price is the best available estimate of its intrinsic value. But a more recent approach, the rational efficient markets formulation, recognizes that no investor will rationally take on the expenses of gathering information without an expectation of being rewarded by higher gross returns compared with the free alternative of accepting market price. Modern finance theorists recognize that when instrinsic value is hard to determine, as with common stock, and when trading costs exist, there is yet more room for price to diverge from value.

Table 4.2 Comparison of Approaches to Measuring Reputational Capital

Method	Criteria Used	Limitations
Intellectual Capital	Value of patents, trademarks, service marks, copyrights	Some firms' reputations are not derived from these
Marketing (brand equity)	Market value over and above liquidation value of a brand	Reputation is broader than brand name
Accounting (purchase method)	Goodwill (excess of firm's purchase price over fair market value of tangible assets)	Goodwill recognized only when firm is sold; valuation is speculative
Finance (market-based)	Excess value investors are willing to pay for the firm's shares	Non-public companies excluded; market price divergence from intrinsic value
Extended Balance Sheet	Extra-balance sheet reporting of reputational ratings and rankings. Assessment of how key constituentcies (other than financial analysts) evaluate the firm.	Exact measurement difficult

Extended Balance Sheet Approach

Stock price primarily reflects the perspective and interests of shareholders. But the perspectives of other consituencies, such as employees, suppliers, competitors, and news media, can be quite different from that of shareholders. For instance, employees make their own assessments of a firm's reputation when deciding to sign on to a company and at what time to leave. Most people would not consider a company's current stock price as the key factor in deciding whether or not to accept a job offer.

The actual value of a firm extends beyond its financial state. Together with assets and liabilities, one can look to an extended balance sheet to determine the value to the firm of intangibles running to and from a broad range of constituencies, and costs triggered by damage to such intangibles. The intangibles encompass corporate culture, trust, integrity, perception of fair dealing, and credibility. These comprise reputational capital and reputational liabilities. Under this approach, calculating the difference between capital and liabilities yields net reputational capital.

Losing It

Obviously, scandals and misdeeds seriously impugn your firm's reputation. As a result, companies typically hemmorage market value when in the throes of such crises. For publicly traded companies, a declining stock price reflects the market's appraisal of the damage sustained from shots to the firm's reputation and credibility. When the firm's integrity is maligned, its future profitability is at risk. In fact, in the wake of revelations of illegal corporate conduct, the bulk of a drop in stock price embodies the firm's reputational harm. The likelihood of incurring legal sanctions like fines and civil damages from the misdeeds amounts to a scant 6 percent of the decline in stock price.[1]

Short-Term Reputational Capital

Short-term reputational capital is like a snapshot of a firm's reputation. A company's short-term reputational capital is gauged by current market value. It captures the immediate investor perceptions of a company. It fluctuates with the daily rise and fall of a company's share price.

Take a look at the short-term loss sustained by Martha Stewart Living Omnimedia, Inc. (MSO) when, initially, allegations emerged that Martha Stewart acted on inside information when she sold her Imclone common stock, and, later, when she was indicted for making false statements to federal authorities. MSO's business was heavily dependent on Stewart's public image and reputation, as indicated below:

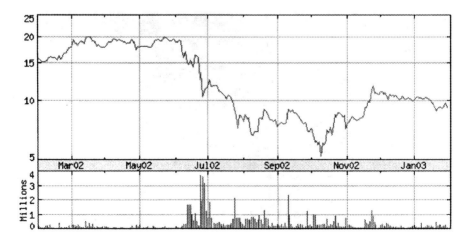

Chart 4.1: Martha Stewart (NYSE: *MSO*)
http://finance.yahoo.com/q?s=mso&d=ly. Copyright © 2002 Yahoo! Inc.

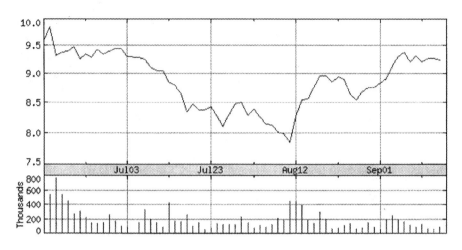

Chart 4.2: Martha Stewart (NYSE: *MSO*)
http://finance.yahoo.com/q/bc?s=MSO&t=3m&l=on&z=m&q=1&c=.
Copyright © 2003 Yahoo! Inc.

A similar picture can be shown for Johnson&Johnson, after a former employee from its Puerto Rico factory said that he was pressured to falsify records in connection with a spate of illness among users of the firm's anti-anemia drug, Eprex.

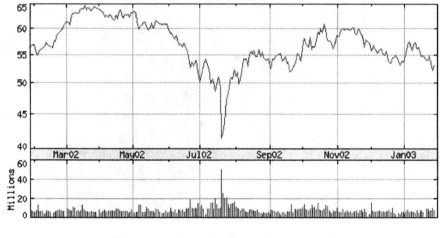

Chart 4.3: Johnson&Johnson (NYSE: *JNJ*)
http://finance.yahoo.com/q?s=jnj&d=ly.
Copyright © 2002 Yahoo! Inc.

Long-Term Reputational Capital

As the chart reveals, in the short run, Johnson&Johnson's stock lost value. However, short-term vissisitudes tend to dampen out over long-term calculations of a firm's reputational capital based on average market value and book value across a time span of many years. Look at this long-term record of Johnson&Johnson:

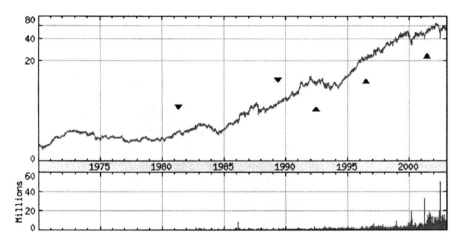

Chart 4.4: Johnson&Johnson (NYSE: *JNJ*)
http://finance.yahoo.com/c/my/j/jnj.gif.
Copyright © 2002 Yahoo! Inc.

The chart shows a steady incline of stock performance for this AAA company. This is one of the clearest depictions of how reputational capital has the power to carry a company through crises. The company faced product tampering episodes with its Tylenol brand in 1982 and 1986. On Septermber 30, 1982, reports of five deaths from cyanide ingestion were traced to a production lot of Tylenol capsules. Worried about losing its reputation for gentleness and safety, J&J's McNeil consumer products division promptly pulled all Tylenol capsules from retail shelves. Within days, the company took aggressive action to block reputational loss: (1) All capsules were scrapped and the safe tablet version was offered as a replacement; (2) an intensive ad campaign was launched portraying J&J as a victim of sabotage; (3) tamper-resistant packaging was introduced, and more than 80 million new samples were distributed free of charge at a cost of some $30 million to J&J. The actions would prove remarkably effective in rebuilding Tylenol's premier position in the marketplace as well as J&J's long-term stock of reputational capital.

Long-term reputational capital is like a lengthy biography of a firm's reputation.

It portrays a company's reputation for a sustained time frame of several years. In the long term, corporate reputations are more stable.

Stimulating Competition for Credibility

I don't intend to settle the disagreements about the optimal method for systematically measuring the dollar value of a reputation. In truth, focusing too much attention on just the physical, measurable, short-term aspects of reputational capital is barking up the wrong tree. Why? Because it overlooks the distinctively qualitative nature of corporate character, which takes a long time to develop. Whichever approach we adopt, one thing is clear. A corporate reputation is a prized asset—one that has been woefully underrated and, insofar as the deep linkages between ethical behavior and credible reputation have been passed over, misunderstood as well.

I do believe that extended balance sheet reporting of reputational ratings and rankings can—and should—be undertaken. The overall effect would be to encourage firms to compete for greater reputations. Auditors could assess and report on how key constituents besides financial analysts evaluate a firm. Some movement in this direction is discernable. A growing number of firms report in their annual statements the results of employee surveys in the belief that investors care about the company's human capital. The same could be done with customers, suppliers, dealers, and other constituencies. If well-regarded companies reported their relative reputational standings in their annual statements, they might inspire others to do so. Prospective employees, investors, and other constituents would pay heed to these ratings as an indicia of the company's reputational capital. This, in turn, would press lesser-ranked rivals to follow in the footsteps of reputable firms, burnishing their own reputations.

At the end of the day, a superior reputation enhances the value of a company's potential licenses, partnering arrangements, products, and services. This, in turn, raises revenues. And over time better revenues lead to superior market value.

5

Integrity and Fair Play: Wellsprings of Reputation

What is integrity in business? Here's a time-worn tale I like to deliver when I speak about cultivating organizational character. It concerns a professor of business ethics framing a problem for the class: Two merchants are running a shop. A customer comes in and buys an item, paying with a $100 bill. When the customer's gone, one merchant is startled to see he was handed not one but two $100 bills. What's the right thing to do? A student's hand shoots up and he eagerly blurts out, "the merchant should return the second bill to the customer." The professor retorts, "Young man, I'm teaching a course in business ethics here. If you want morality you have to go over to the theology department. The question I'm wrestling with is, does he tell his partner?"

I think that little joke sums up nicely what I've been saying throughout this book about what distinguishes the Zeta firm from the rest of the pack: linking so-called business ethics with morality, that is, principles of integrity and fair dealing.

Reputational capital grows—it spreads out in a ripple effect as your firm is perceived by key constituencies to act with integrity and fair play. Those key constituencies respond favorably to your firm because you have earned their trust and credibility. Here's the basic dynamic: Reputation is built by character. Character is formed by integrity and fair play. These are the roots of character in both business and in personal life. What results is a signature of your firm's credibility that can never be forged or replicated by rivals. Many companies take the wrong path by attempting to base reputation on superficial images of themselves. After Enron, Arthur Andersen, WorldCom, Adelphia, Global Crossing, Tyco, HealthSouth, and Royal Ahold, it's clear that some managers routinely manipulate and put a positive spin on presentations made to financial analysts and reporters.

In the final analysis, corporations are institutions of our own creation. They will never be any better than the people that run them and work in them.

Some Common Misconceptions

Let's take a look at four of the most pernicious myths about integrity and fair play commonly assumed, believed, and practiced in many corporations.

Myth #1: Right and wrong are learned "at mother's knee." You can't teach an old dog new tricks.

Reality: All available research shows this myth to be wrong. Studies reveal that adults show more change than youth in moral education programs, and that moral development continues with age.[1] The ability to use moral reasoning and enter moral judgment progresses with the help of social interaction and educational programs, including MBA ethics courses.[2] Research in moral psychology finds that people pass through three levels of moral development. In childhood, the focus is on the self, on "what's in it for me." People at this stage respond to punishments and rewards. At the second level, the focus is on group norms, what "everybody else" is doing. Some people never get past the first or second level. But a third level is reached by some people. Here the focus is universal. One reasons about dilemmas using general principles and rules, arguing by analogy from similar cases. People are most likely to get to this third level if they engage in reasoned debate with others who do not share their own personal viewpoint

One survey found that 49 percent of workers thought that their business ethics had improved over the course of their careers. The belief was strongest in firms conducting ethics programs.[3]

Myth #2: Integrity is personal, you can't bring it to work with you.

Reality: As it turns out, contextual factors have a strong impact on behavior, both good and bad. The Milgram experiments showed that people conform to expectations of authority figures.[4] Many instances of business misdeeds stem from organizational factors like unrealistic performance expectations, faulty performance systems, inadequate controls, poor training, sloppy hiring practices, and bad leadership. Organizational culture is a prime contributor to business crime. On the other hand, the Tylenol decision at Johnson&Johnson shows that a firm's ethos can lead to good behavior.

Myth #3: People are basically honest and upright, so it's unnecessary to worry about encouraging integrity and fair play in your company.

Reality: Research demonstrates that people who rely on conscience alone can make radically divergent judgments about what's fair dealing. Employees at one firm were queried whether it would be appropriate to have a copy of a competitor's proposal in hand in a bidding arrangement. Responses covered the field, from "looks fine to me" to "highly unethical." Answers like "OK so long as the proposal is freely given" and "could be a problem if the proposal carried proprietary information" popped up in the middle.[5] Even forthright, well-intentioned people slip up. Plus, a lot of people are unfamiliar with cultural traditions other than their own. In some countries, multimillion dollar bank loans are effectively secured with nothing more than an oral promise and a handshake. Not being sensitive to the many different ways of interpreting right conduct in business can cause problems and misunderstandings when crossing borders.

Myth #4: Business is lean, mean, and ethics free. Firms that try to be ethical won't survive. Nice guys finish last.

Reality: Studies of successful service companies show that most people want to do business with someone who is honest and trustworthy. And they prefer to transact with those who respect their needs and interests. Nobody wants to work for, invest in, or do business with a company or person lacking integrity. With the increasing demand for transparency, it's harder now for people to ignore dishonest behavior or assume it won't come to light.

Integrity

Integrity itself is not a virtue. It's a composite of virtues. Collectively, in the right balance, the virtues work together to constitute a harmonious whole. The term *integrity* means "wholeness." Integrity in a corporation's culture is similar to the moral character of a person. Since integrity means being complete, undivided, an important goal of your company is to align its financial mandate as closely as possible with your company's moral imperatives. As for members of the firm, the goal is to bring individuals' multiple ethical selves together, so that an associate has the same moral outlook in the office as she would at home. Many people mistake the state of integrity for the pursuit of isolated virtues, such as honesty. But integrity requires an adroit give-and-take across various virtues, which conflict with one another in the complexity of business settings. Depending on context, integrity might require withholding the whole truth from someone, for instance, in the interest of protecting them from severe emotional harm or protecting the confidentiality of some third party.

I have had occasion to interact, sometimes on a deep personal level and in high-pressure, out-of-the-ordinary situations, with business leaders from many different industries and across numerous cultures. I find that the overwhelming majority of managers and executives take their personal integrity—and that of their organizations—very seriously. There are exceptions, of course. But people are everywhere more alike than different. They seek the best from and for themselves, and they seek the best from and for their firms and associates.

The voice of integrity speaks clearly and deeply within each of us. It is a silent voice—fearless and focused. It is a voice we all trust to do the right thing, to honor commitments, to follow the rules of the game. Sometimes integrity commands behavior that goes against conventional or narrow understandings of doing the right thing.

There are numerous pathways to integrity. No one of them is necessarily the correct route. Some people take a rules-and-principles approach. Others focus on consequences, aiming for conduct that promotes the collective welfare of all those affected. Some people adopt a compassionate viewpoint as their compass. There are those who lay stress on rights and obligations, while still others are guided primarily by intuition. Yet whatever path you take, in the final analysis it is reputation that serves as the overall assessment—the bottom line—in judgments about our own and others' integrity.

Fair Play

The philosopher John Rawls said that justice—which he takes to mean fairness—is the "first virtue" of social institutions.[6] I believe the same holds for corporations and other financial institutions.

Having a reputation for fair play opens doors in business. Let's face it, business just wouldn't work if each part of every financial transaction needed to be spelled out expressly in writing or delineated in a contract. We'd never get anything done. Since it's virtually impossible to shepherd most living, breathing business deals through within the straightjacket of a written contract, parties prefer to do business with people they believe are not out to shaft them. By sticking with people you can trust to play fair and square, you make gains by cutting down on transaction costs, like those for attorneys, auditors, and inspectors. The vast majority of disputes between businesses get settled without going through contracts line by line or bullying with lawsuits and sanctions. While attorneys certainly have their place, those that persistently threaten to sue tend to sour negotiations. Many lawyers fail to grasp the give-and-take needed in business. The point I wish to make here is that there's no substitute for trust in making deals run smoothly. Along with integrity, fair play forms the basis for that trust.

A Question of Motivation

I am often asked: If a firm is motivated to do things to improve its reputation purely by the wish to make a profit, can it grow reputational capital?

First, I believe that profitmaking itself can be a source of doing good. It protects the legitimate interests of many consituencies. There is no necessary contradiction between a company doing good and doing well.

Yet getting reputational rewards from good deeds requires genuine motives. One hundred percent purity isn't necessary. People know your for-profit company is not Mother Theresa, Inc. But people deplore corporate marketing and PR campaigns masquerading as citizenship and social responsibility initiatives, especially when interposed to divert attention from a firm's own misconduct. When employees discern that ethics training is being rolled out as litigation proofing for senior management or the board, it dampens any positive outcomes that would otherwise be produced.

It's hard to reap the full financial benefits of integrity and fair play unless your company has an explicitly stated commitment to doing right. Attitude matters. Since reputational capital is generated from moral action backed by sincere motivation, companies that too aggressively promote an instrumental "it pays to be ethical" attitude work at cross purposes. Taken from a completely financial perspective, you might say that it pays to appreciate the intrinsic value of good business conduct, and that it's most prudent to guide one's actions by this premise.

Admittedly it's often hard to know what is really fueling a company's apparent good conduct. Intel lost goodwill by refusing to replace defective Pentium microchips. Intel said the chips would fail in only a small percentage of cases—typical users might, as a result of the flaw, get a wrong answer once every 27,000 years. But people didn't want to get defective chips, period. Initially hit by a wave of negative publicity, Intel eventually changed its stance, agreeing to replace at no cost any Pentium chips. The company also rendered a public apology both for problems caused by flawed chips and for its own lack of concern for its customers. However, since the concessions came about only after customers complained, was its motivation really all that noble in the first place? The hitch is that the company's actions come across more as an exercise in crisis management than as an expression of day-to-day integrity.

Integrity and Fair Play for Individual Businesspeople

So far we've been talking about corporate behavior. What about the conduct of individuals? Here are some common workplace behaviors that compromise integrity and jeopardize personal reputations:

Gaining unfair advantage

Letting false impressions form

Misrepresenting facts

Entering conflicts of interest

Sidestepping legitimate rules

Failing to disclose material facts

Leaking proprietary or confidential information

Being emotionally abusive

Failing to report wrongdoing

Taking credit for another's work or ideas

Backstabbing colleagues

Misappropriating property (taking office supplies, padding expenses)

Abusing otherwise legitimate processes (using business loans for personal use)

Common rationalizations people offer for their misconduct in business contexts include:

Everybody's doing it

If we don't do it, somebody else will

Nobody's hurt by it

Just following orders

It's perfectly legal

No one's going to notice

They mistreat me here so I deserve this

The whole system's so corrupt anyway

It's dog eat dog

The big danger with self-serving rationalizations is that you can become so convinced you're right that you overlook the behavior's negative reputational impact. You don't think the behavior is so bad. And it may well be that your misdeed isn't high on the scale in terms of actual harm done. But other people—clients, colleagues, the media—won't see it the same way if your behavior comes under scrutiny. To them, your conduct may seem inappropriate. So your reputation— and that of the whole organization—can take a dive even from acts that are moral misdemeanors. In other words, there is a persistent tendency to rationalize away both the wrongdoing itself and the negative reputational harm, especially when there's some anticipated short-term payoff.

Credibility and Trust

Unfortunately, in the aftermath of the Enron implosion and the attendant flood of accounting and corporate-governance scandals, corporate credibility is viewed with some skepticism. It's no longer enough just to have a great brand, sparkling financial returns, and a charmed chief executive. Now more than ever, integrity and fair play—and the trust and credibility they generate—are the linchpins of corporate reputation.

Credibility and trust lets us place confidence in the conduct of others while, at the same time, taking some risk that the expected behavior won't come about. When trustworthiness becomes part of your character, you are able to cultivate trust-building relationships.

Research shows that the ethical tone set by senior and lower-level managers is a central factor in shaping employees' overall perceptions of integrity and fairness at work.[7] Employees' perception of the relative level of their firm's reputation leads to performance-enhancing—or, as the case may be, performance-sapping— outcomes within the organization. If the boss leaves work early or calls in sick when he's really not, subordinates are tempted to do so as well. If employees see leaders making personal long-distance phone calls at work and charging them to the company, or padding their expense accounts, then the employees are be more likely to do so, too.

One study found that companies seen by their employees to have a high level of honesty and integrity enjoyed an average three-year total shareholder return of 101 percent. For firms perceived to have a low degree of honesty and integrity the three-year total return was merely 69 percent.[8] To improve productivity and teamwork, it's important that employees throughout the organization feel bound together by trust. A trustworthy work climate lets people rely on decisions and actions of coworkers and enables them to be treated with respect and consideration. Trusting relationships between managers and subordinates generate decision-making efficiencies.

Apart from the effect trust has on bottom line results like profits, earnings per share, and other factors traditionally thought to determine a company's success, think about other impacts. When trust is low, organizations decay and relationships deteriorate, resulting in politics, infighting, and general inefficiency. As ethical conduct decreases, employee commitment to the organization falters, product quality declines, customers leave, and employee turnover skyrockets. In the 2000 National Business Ethics Survey, more than three-fourths of all employees indicated that their "organization's concern for ethics and doing the right thing" was an important reason for continuing to work there.[9]

The powerful gravitational pull of trust holds your organization together. It enables it to stay efficient and productive, and to make profits. Absent credibility and trust, it is exceedingly hard to forecast outcomes of human interaction. Credibility and trust are strong motivators that draw out the best in people. But building them demands time and patience. The National Business Ethics Survey produced a noteworthy finding: When employees see values like honesty, respect, and trust applied frequently in the workplace, they feel less pressure to compromise their own beliefs, observe less misconduct, are more satisfied with their organizations, and feel more valued.[10]

6

—————

Tallying Up Reputational Effects

So far, we've been talking about organizational design features that tend to build
corporate reputations. You may be wondering if there's some way to predict
and evaluate the reputational impact of your firm's business activity to help guide
specific business decisions. This chapter sets out a method, or calculus, that allows
you to estimate reputational effects. The process is straightforward: You consider
the probable positive reputational effects a business decision will bring to everyone
concerned and subtract the anticipated negative reputational impacts. You compare
that total with the amount resulting from alternative courses of action. Although
business decisions are normally quite complex, involving a consideration of many
factors, the calculus helps you hone in on the target, choosing the course of action
that maximizes favorable reputation and minimizes unfavorable reputation. Like a
utilitarian moral analysis that calculates the "greatest good for the greatest number"
by comparing the amount of pleasure versus pain generated by alternative courses
of action, you consider all the projected consequences of business decisions that
bear on your organization's probity: both immediate and remote, direct and indirect, short-term as well as long-term.

A direct tallying of the reputational impact of business decisions is, to some
extent, more relevant to the actual world of business than using conventional
models of ethical decision making, that is, those that evaluate conduct according
to its tendency to maximize community welfare, promote justice, conform to social
contract-based norms, or display moral virtue. This is so because businesses operate principally out of self-interest, making decisions that maximize the wealth of
the firm.

Pundits might worry that directing our efforts toward reputation-maximizing
decisions instead of, say, pursuing rights-respecting or welfare-maximizing conduct
may sometimes lead to unethical choices being made. I disagree. The action that
promotes a firm's reputation (civic involvement motivated by a genuine concern
for the plight of the urban poor)—as opposed to its image, which indeed often

can be at odds with the firm's authentic character (civic activity cynically under-taken to divert attention from accounting improprieties)—will almost always be the one that touches the hearts and promotes the welfare of people. I have yet to find a single instance where behavior that benefits a company's reputation does not at the same time amount to doing right, all things considered. The defense Lockheed president Carl Kotchian gave of his decision to bring suitcases full of cash to Tokyo to bribe the prime minister of Japan in order to win approval for a jet contract[1] was premised on a utilitarian moral analysis, albeit an attenuated one. He argued that paying a bribe would keep his company out of bankruptcy, benefit the prime minister, create wealth for the company's shareholders, and allow employees of the firm to hold on to their jobs. While it has been pointed out that his reasoning stopped short of factoring negative consequences for other stake-holders, such as competitors and the citizens of Japan[2]—I believe it is significant that the probable long-term reputational ramifications of the decision to pay a bribe were utterly absent from Kotchian's analysis. Indeed, most business ethics textbooks offering a utilitarian model glide right over such considerations.[3]

On the other hand, the "front-page-of-the-newspaper test"—which asks how a decision would be portrayed in a headline—is widely promoted as a quick test for ethical decisionmaking in business precisely because it captures the reputation dimension.

Suppose, for instance, your company faces these business decisions:

Decision #1:
downsizing the workforce with no regard or assistance for terminated employees
versus
downsizing with compassion for terminated employees

Decision #2:
reincorporating the company in an offshore tax haven to cut worldwide tax bill
versus
staying put

Standard business ethics evaluations of these situations, although certainly sensitive to the reputational aspects, would center around asking questions such as: What is your firm's obligation in this case? Which choice promotes the greatest good?

I believe that those are important questions for businesses to consider. But business is not just about being ethical. (Not to mention that pinning down exactly what's "ethical" and what's not is often exceedingly difficult.) It's also about being profitable. And it's hard for businesspeople to make the linkage between their conduct and ethics directly. This is why I believe that reputation is the missing link between business and ethics. Making decisions that build your company's reputation (and your own reputation as well) serve to improve the bottom line directly, which is what businesspeople are trained to do. The decisions that build reputation turn out to also be decisions that promote ethics and demonstrate respect for the letter and spirit of law. But what's so important to recognize is that choosing to build reputation is making the right *business* decision—it's as much a business decision as allocating money for advertising and capital improvement. In fact, reputational capital is itself a form of capital, an intangible asset. If it bothers you that it seems difficult to quantify and track down the benefits that will come from undertaking practices that enhance reputation (for example, from building goodwill in relationships with key constituencies), consider that in advertising, you don't necessarily know in advance exactly what impact particular ads will have on target audiences. Certainly, surveys and market research guide decisions, but neither one lends itself to precise, certain predictions of outcomes. Once I came to this realization, all of the analysis I had done on business ethics started to appear in a totally new light. With the fresh perspective of *building reputational capital* we see that, in truth, there is no fundamental contradiction between ethics and economics. Steps your company takes to build its reputation are at the same time the soundest long-term investment it can make in terms of satisfying its objectives of wealth maximization for shareholders and other key constituencies.

Granted, measuring reputation is not totally precise, but at least it is more measurable than something as effusive and endlessly disputational as "ethics."

So, let's see how the reputation calculus addresses these decisions.

Remember, the key question is not: What is your firm's duty? Nor: What action will bring about the greatest good for the greatest number of those affected? Rather, it is: Which course of action—downsizing brutally or with compassion—will maximize the reputation of the company and accordingly lead to the formation of reputational capital? Granted, this depends on whether word of the firm's behavior gets out, and whether it is criticized to the point where its reputation suffers. For small, unknown companies, this is probably not a key issue.

Now, I believe, we are in a position to make a rational business decision without bringing in such obscure and unmeasurable concepts as duty or obligation. Let's walk through some sample reputation calculations. We'll assign numbers to represent relative gains and losses to reputation (for example, "plus five" or "minus two") with the understanding that all this is meant to be illustrative only, so no matter if people form different opinions about the specific magnitudes that should be assigned for these problems. Since everyone will bring different numbers to the equation, depending on their own values, I encourage you to assign your own numerical values based on your best estimate of positive and negative reputational impacts in each of the scenarios we are analyzing. The point of all this is to sketch out a method for you to adapt to your company's own circumstances. And bear in mind that such rough assignments of value to reputational effects don't occur in a vacuum. In other words, many specific conditions (such as the size of the available labor pool in the downsizing example and the degree of notoriety of the company in the reincorporation example), all of which cannot be taken into account in our simplified examples, will impact outcomes. Also, any given behavior may be taken to be highly inappropriate for one type of firm (say, a large investment bank or asset manager) yet deemed acceptable for another (a small manufacturing company, for instance).

Example: Downsizing the Workforce

There are some short-term costs associated with providing generous severance packages and displacement assistance (minus 3), but surviving employees' morale is boosted, keeping their productivity high (plus 10). Longer-term, word will get around that this is a decent, fair place to work at, so down the road, when cash flow improves and it's time to beef up the workforce again, you get the pick of talented recruits that want to sign on to your firm (plus 5). The local chamber of commerce takes note of your commendable behavior and awards the firm a good citizen certificate, which is reported in a leading newspaper. This is, in effect, free marketing that casts favorable light on the company's name (plus 3). On the other hand, making sweeping cuts with no assistance creates a perception of meanness and cruelty, leading to a sullied reputation as a bad place to work and substantial negative publicity propagated through the rumor mill (minus 10). One employee is angry and feels that you discriminated against her, so she sues the firm, requiring you to mount an expensive legal defense (minus 7). However, if you downsize by simply letting employees go swiftly, with no regard for assistance, there are some lower short-term costs (plus 5).

Downsizing brutally results in -12, while downsizing compassionately results in $+15$. The results point to the kinder, gentler option.

Example: Reincorporating Offshore (Corporate Inversion)

Your firm can reincorporate in an offshore tax haven like Bermuda. This would be legal, at least currently, although tax laws might be changed to penalize the move since you're not the only company pursuing this strategy. So, your firm's action has contributed to government mobilization for stepped up corporate taxation in the long run (minus 2). Short-term gains enjoyed by shareholders will make shareholders subject to a hefty capital gains tax. The fact that even if their shares rise they will barely break even after taxes gives the shareholders a dim view of the company's decision (minus 2).

The public perceives the move as a tax-dodging trick that erodes respect for tax law, and establishes the nominal postal-drop headquarters as a sham, and they will consider it an unpatriotic gesture to boot. In top newspapers op-ed commentary reflecting such sentiment specifically references your company's name (minus 10).

The firm's worldwide tax bill will be cut (plus 8), which would otherwise lift the overall reputation of the company, were that not offset by news that the chief executive will get higher pay, bonuses, and profits on the sale of stock options. This kicks up sentiments of resentment and an impression of unfairness (minus 8).

Pursuing the alternative of staying put means the tax liability remains substantial (minus 6). However, the op-ed piece that otherwise would have lambasted your firm instead praises its forthrightness and patriotism, generating substantial good-will and publicity (plus 10).

Reincorporation results in −14, while staying put equals +4. All in all, the reputational gains of staying put outweigh the reputational losses of reincorporation.

7

Becoming a Zeta Firm: A Company of Character

Companies fall into three distinct categories, according to which of the "worlds" we looked at earlier—Flatland, Lineland, or Realland—they live and move in. Table 7.1 summarizes the basic attributes of Alpha, Omega, and Zeta firms.

Let's examine these alternative orientations in greater detail.

An Alpha firm reacts to crises and scandals by putting out fires. Everything's ad hoc. Only a few related work units stand up and get involved. The firm tries to unwind the damage done to its reputation by channeling energy toward containing legal liabilities and putting the right spin on things. After the fire is put out there is no carryover. The firm returns to hunting down profits and success in cold blood. The law is understood only as a series of trip wires that keep the firm from going where it wants. So the dominant strategies become: Exploit opportunities and cut corners whenever feasible. The driving ethos is summed up in J. P. Morgan's dictum: "I don't hire lawyers to tell me what I cannot do. I hire them to help me do what I want to do." The trust factor is zip. It's "dog eat dog." Background philosophy: "Business is business."

At their worst, the Omega firm's implicit ethos is enshrined in the cynical adage "The secret of life is honesty and fair dealing. If you can fake that, you've got it made." Companies at this level wait for norms of public expectation of social responsibility to emerge and crystallize, and then mobilize to present the image of meeting them. They adopt "ethics compliance" systems that are really just microcosms of formal legal systems. Such business ethics programs confuse ethical standards with legal standards. The firm promulgates excessively detailed rules that tell people exactly what to do and what not to do. Over time, members immersed in this kind of corporate culture can no longer think for themselves. The Omega firm uses business ethics as a tool for commanding its employees to stay out of trouble or, failing that, to plug holes in the dike *ex post facto*. But the reputational crises

Table 7.1 Three Kinds of Firms

Type of Firm	Characteristics	Outlook	Focus	Opportunity for Building Reputational Capital
Alpha	Respond ad hoc to external sanctions (formal and informal). Avoidance of legal norms sought when advantageous.	Short-term financial	Self-interest	None
Omega	Effort spent on developing positive image. Compliance with letter of legal norms sought mainly for economic reasons; compliance with ethical standards pursued for marketing benefits.	Mid-term financial; limited social	Stakeholder interests	Limited
Zeta	Integration of self-imposed principles and values into all levels of organization. Pursuit of letter and spirit of the law sought as a matter of principle and obligation per social contract.	Long-term financial; expansive social	Universal interests, values, and rights	Substantial

will eventually come washing over. In such a corporate culture, the low trust factor that prevails can be expressed as follows. Suppose someone says "I trust *that* the figures in your financial statement are true." Here, the "trust *that*" the numbers are accurate basically conveys a warning: "If your financial statement is false, then you will be punished by legal authorities." Bottom line: Trust for the firm comes from knowledge that it will do such-and-such *or else*. But this is only conditional, not genuine, trust.

Here are the wrong turns that Omega companies take:

Treating reputation primarily as a marketing, PR, and legal matter. This obsession with quick results, with sending the right stories to the press, manipulating images, and dodging bullets, can fetch palpable short-term results, yet fail in the long run. From the public relations perspective, reputation only matters *ex post facto*, after a scandal or crisis hits. At that point all that can be done is damage control.

Writing codes of conduct that boss people around. Ethics programs often become excessively legalistic. Some of them resemble miniature legal systems in themselves. The danger of establishing too many rules for your firm is that the rules leave no room for the exercise of judgment and common sense. The result is a deadening effect. It can lead to a culture in which members cannot make decisions for themselves. I know of one firm that states in its code of conduct that employees are prohibited from eating garlic during lunch. That kind of rule-obsessiveness inclines members to become "ethical prigs," constantly criticizing and judging others for violations of rules without regard for the deeper rationales and values that support the rules. This undermines trust rather than promoting it.

The over-rule approach obscures the importance of human values. The ethics program becomes like a huge machine that avoids—even interferes with—the exercise of human judgment and common sense.

Getting rid of unnecessary rules makes the firm's culture more open and flexible and helps unleash human potential for creativity and productivity. Housing Development Finance Corporation consciously opts not to have a code. They feel it is more important to live out the principles their firm is based on.

Breaking stupid and unimportant rules—whether they are legal rules or ethical rules—should not form a basis for a loss of reputation of either an individual or a company.

Treating legal standards as if they were ethical standards. This gives an *appearance* of building ethics, but it misses the mark. Omega companies may pour tons of money into so-called ethics programs. But my perception is that an inordinate number of Omega company leaders care mostly about image and cosmetics. Many of their ethics programs get launched in reaction to public outrage or regulatory investigations. Ethics officers become a magnet for powerless, clueless employees groping in the dark for some way to tackle a special problem. I've been approached more than once by ethics directors looking to hire me as an external consultant to render "independent advice" that they had cooked up in advance. (I always decline the invitation.) What this turns out to be is a way of outsourcing especially questionable judgment calls to deflect responsibility or cover rear ends. People know what's up when leaders try to justify the means by the ends. Actions speak louder than words. People know exactly who gets promoted and rewarded and who gets called on the carpet. And why. Granted, ethics programs can sensitize people to harassment, diversity, and similar hot-button compliance issues but very few of them even make a dent in deeply rooted, systemic-based misconduct. I've seen ethics programs that just push unscrupulous behavior deeper underground, making already sinister operations yet more so.

Zeta firms take a holistic approach to link citizenship and commerce, ethics and economics. The firm seeks success within the letter of the law, yet reaches beyond that to embrace its spirit as well. The law is understood to set the minimum. But Zeta firms stretch way beyond what the law dictates.

This mindset is captured in a code provision of PPG Industries, Inc., which proclaims that "[c]ompliance with the law is the absolute minimum expected of a PPG associate, no matter where he or she works. All PPG associates are expected to behave in a manner which is not only lawful but also morally acceptable to all of the constituencies with whom we have dealings."[1] A one-time CEO of the firm, Vin Sarni, mused "It is not enough to simply say that our conduct is lawful. The law is the floor. Compliance with it will be the absolute minimum. Our ethics go beyond the legal code. That's not just waving the flag. We live that. And I personally believe that we have a competitive advantage from being that way."[2]

In a Zeta firm culture, you're more likely to hear someone say "I trust your figures." By contrast to the Omega's threat-based "trust *that*," the meaning here is: "I know your character for honesty."

Sunbeam and Enron: Paragons of Alpha Companies

While under the reign of CEO Albert ("Chainsaw") Dunlap, Sunbeam Corporation exhibited classic symptoms of an Alpha firm. Dunlap acquired a worldwide reputation as a ruthless executive by slashing thousands of jobs and making deep cuts across operations. He was known for his ability to restructure and turn around companies that were failing financially. Attracting monikers like "The Shredder," and "Rambo in Pinstripes," Dunlap had a penchant for boasting—highlighted in his book, *Mean Business*—that maximizing shareholder wealth was his polestar. Sunbeam brought Dunlap on board to save the ship. Its earnings had been heading south since December 1994. By 1996 the stock was down 52 percent. Earnings had fallen 83 percent. The day Dunlap was named chairman and CEO, the company's stock jumped 49 percent. The share price increased from 12½ to 18⅝, adding $500 million to Sunbeam's market value. The stock climbed to a record high: $52 per share in March 1998. Although Dunlap's reputation influenced the initial stock increase, he knew his reputation alone would not hold the stock price up. Dunlap laid plans to eliminate half of the company's twelve thousand employees worldwide. The job reductions would touch all levels. Upon learning of Dunlap's draconian job elimination plans, Labor Secretary Robert Reich exclaimed, "There is no excuse for treating employees as if they are disposable pieces of equipment."[3] Managerial and clerical positions were reduced from 1,529 to 697. Headquarters staff was cut 60 percent, from 308 to 123 workers. Dunlap fashioned ambitious financial goals backed with big stock options for top executives. Managers' careers hinged on making the numbers. Obliterating 10,500 stock-keeping units (SKUs)—individual variations of product lines—let Dunlap shed factories and warehouses in a massive cost-saving measure. He dumped 18 factories worldwide, and cut the number of warehouses from 61 to 18. Dunlap achieved his financial objectives at Sunbeam. But all that shareholder wealth would be short-lived.

Within two years, the SEC had Sunbeam under the microscope for accounting irregularities. Auditors exposed tricks used to boost sales and inflate earnings while Dunlap was at the helm. Shareholders flocked to court, charging the company with making misleading statements about its finances and luring them to purchase artificially inflated stock. A class-action lawsuit was filed on April 23, 1998. Sunbeam and Dunlap were codefendants. The lawsuit alleged that Sunbeam and Dunlap violated the Securities Exchange Act of 1934 by playing fast and loose with material information about operations, sales, and trends. Dunlap's modus operandi is called "channel stuffing." The ploy boosted Sunbeam's revenue—on the balance sheet, that is. The strategy entails selling products at large discounts to retailers, then holding them in third-party warehouses for later delivery. By booking sales in advance of shipment or billing, the company reports higher revenues as accounts receivable. This inflates quarterly earnings. Essentially, sales get moved from future quarters to the present one. In a single quarter, Sunbeam added $50 million in revenues.

On June 13, 1998, the board of directors, the executive vice president, and firm attorneys conducted an extensive review of Dunlap's odious oeuvre. Concurring in their lack of confidence in Dunlap to turn Sunbeam around, the board decided to lose "The Shredder." A one-minute conference call alerted Chainsaw Al that he was history.

In January 2001, the New York Stock Exchange "de-listed" the company's common stock. The next month, Sunbeam filed for bankruptcy. The company settled out of court civil fraud charges mounted by the SEC.

What does the Sunbeam story illustrate? From an Alpha firm perspective, Dunlap's leadership—from the massive layoffs to the illegal conduct—is business as usual, a success story, albeit a short-lived one ending with the implosion of his reputation, which wiped out his career. From the vantage point of an Omega firm, which recognizes that corporate image suffers when the chickens come home to roost from illegal behavior, Dunlap strayed from the path in that regard, but aren't layoffs sometimes necessary? A Zeta firm's concern for reputation gives us grounds for pause. Even when layoffs are warranted, how a company does them matters. It matters not just in order to maintain a good image but because brutal downsizings are an affront to the dignity of employees. Long after an unscrupulous leader has left, misdeeds such as Dunlap's generate negative reputational effects—a legacy of treachery the firm will carry around its neck like an albatross—that can make transitioning from an Alpha firm to a Zeta firm more difficult.

Of course, an Alpha firm's neglect of its character may be so widespread as to wipe it out, making the question of the impact its legacy has on its future moot. Witness the notorious Enron case.

Congressional hearings and investigations by the SEC and Justice Department have unmasked the many ways the recently collapsed Enron Corporation cooked its books. A myriad of misdeeds involved hiding losses and debts, enriching inside executives, and inflating profits by nearly $1 billion.

The fault lines underpinning the energy trader's demise developed within a complex network of off-balance sheet vehicles run by its chief financial officer, Andrew Fastow. The full board of Enron undertook a critical step to waive the firm's code of ethics to permit Fastow to run some of these special purpose entities (SPEs).

The SEC deemed that Enron's debt-laden SPEs belonged on the company's balance sheet. So the company rejiggled its financials, which eventually led to the company's bankruptcy—the largest in U.S. history. Enron's failure cost investors and employees billions of dollars.

Sherron Watkins, a vice president of Enron Global Finance, detected improprieties in the company's innovative transaction structures. In a letter to then chairman and chief executive Kenneth Lay, she wrote "I am incredibly nervous that we will implode in a wave of accounting scandals. My eight years of Enron work history will be worth nothing on my resume, the business world will consider the past successes as nothing but an elaborate accounting hoax."[4]

Taken together, the misdeeds underlying the Enron collapse happened not just from improper accounting and the character flaws of inside executives. Enron's corporate culture was a key contributing factor. Too much emphasis was laid on earnings growth and individual initiative. And checks and balances were missing. The culture increasingly relied on unethical corner-cutting. Too much discretion was handed over to inexperienced managers without backup controls to reduce failures. Performance reviews were handled by the very people whose deals needed to be signed off on. The firm's risk assessment and control group answered directly to the CEO—who himself encouraged excessive risk taking—not the board of directors. Another essential check—the legal staff—was compromised in its reporting relationships. It was not centralized in-house but spread out among business units. In this way it was readily co-opted by hard-driving executives.

Performance review methods fed a culture in which people were scared to cross those who might mess up their reviews. Bit by bit the culture transformed into a "yes-man" environment. Andrew Fastow acquired a reputation for deploying the review system as a weapon to retaliate against those voicing opposition.

The intricate web of questionable business practices involved not just Enron but also the active cooperation of many firms and professionals in the accounting, legal, and financial industries.[5] Arthur Andersen, Enron's auditor, systematically shredded documents, and hence got black eyes through their dealings with the firm. Major clients such as Merck and Company and Delta Air Lines abandoned Arthur Andersen in pursuit of more reputable firms.

Another firm tainted by Enron association, Merrill Lynch, placed its reputation at risk by preparing the prospectus for LJM2, one of Enron's hundred-odd special purpose entities (SPEs)—partnerships set up to hide potential losses or debt from public view. Although technically the LJM2 partnership between Merrill Lynch and Enron may have been valid—current rules permit firms to remove SPEs from their balance sheets if investors contribute only 3 percent of the SPE's capital—those rules are not acceptable to investors.

As Sherron Watkins's letter to Mr. Lay intimated regarding a similar arrangement: "It sure looks to the layman on the street that we are hiding losses in a related company and will compensate that company with Enron stock in the future. The overriding basic principle of accounting is that if you explain the accounting treatment to a man on the street, would you influence his investing decisions? Would he sell or buy the stock based on a thorough understanding of the facts? If so, you best present it correctly and/or change the accounting."[6]

And Enron's LJM2 created a conflict of interest. How could Mr. Fastow, who received $30 million for managing LJM, reconcile the contradiction between the low earnings LJM2's assets would yield for Enron and the high returns promised to LJM investors in the prospectus? Although Merrill Lynch's prospectus mentions the potential conflict of interest, the degree to which it favorably promoted an arrangement in which Enron and Enron-created SPEs function as both buyers and sellers raises questions about Merrill Lynch's integrity. The very legitimacy of the exchanges and the prices at which they were struck is dubious. Plus, the partnerships were barely visible to Enron's shareholders.

Some who were invited to invest in Enron's SPEs—but declined—expressed disapproving perceptions of the deal. The chief investment officer of the Houston Firefighters Relief and Retirement Fund believed the partnership arrangement posed "a pretty blatant conflict of interest. . . . It was kind of a stinky deal."

From one perspective, we may say that Enron embodied the traits of an Alpha firm. Yet a plausible case could be made that Enron was a kind of cross-breed, displaying some characteristics of Omega firms, too. After all, the company worked hard to portray the image of an ethical company. As for the Omega firm's obedience to legal requirements, it is notable that attorneys engaged to look over the company's accounting practices determined they were, technically speaking, "not inappropriate," Although they acknowledged that certain transactions might lead to "bad cosmetics," lawyers nonetheless found the practices to be "reasonable" from Enron's standpoint and in line with the firm's "best interests."[7]

Whether we classify Enron as Alpha or Omega, however, one thing is clear: The company systematically failed to assume the vantage point of integrity and fair play. And that failure seems to have been the predominant factor in the firm's demise.

Profiles of Omega Firms

The Body Shop

Here's a firm that crafted an image of social responsibility that had little substance behind it. Advertisements appearing in the 1980s for this British-based body-care company depicted cofounder Anita Roddick sitting in rain-forest clearings bartering with indigenous peoples to acquire their renewable products. The promotions vouched that The Body Shop products never involved animal testing. Catalog covers touted progressive causes. Together, Roddick and her husband Gordon became the very model of conscience-driven CEOs.

An article[8] in *Business Ethics* magazine exposed them as something else. The 1994 article made startling allegations showing how the cosmetics maker secretly undertook business practices that belied its highly trumpeted claims: Charitable contributions and environmentally friendly initiatives fell far short of what the company took credit for; indigenous people supplied less than 1 percent of the firm's raw materials; product ingredients were tested on animals (though not directly by the company); The Body Shop's "natural" cosmetics contained a good deal of preservatives; and relationships with franchisees were getting sufficiently dysfunctional to trigger a Federal Trade Commission inquiry.

The piece essentially averred that the company's glitzy concerns for social improvement were motivated not so much by conscience as by greed. Public perceptions of the gap between rhetoric and reality sent the company's stock prices and sales travelling south.

Dow Corning

Having been one of the first companies to set up a lavish formal ethics program in 1977, Dow Corning was something of a pioneer in corporate ethics. In that year CEO Jack Ludington instituted a business conduct committee. Reporting directly to the board of directors, six executives each devoted up to six weeks per year to committee tasks. Two members audited each business operation every three years. Lengthy review sessions were conducted with groups of associates who were encouraged to raise ethical issues. Results of the audits were passed on to an audit and social responsibility committee of the board of directors. John Swanson, a manager–business communications specialist, spearheaded the initiative. Ludington boasted that company managers "would not intentionally do anything questionable and would even blow the whistle if they learned of any actual wrongdoing within the company."[9]

Such comments prompted critics to accuse the company's ethics program as, ironically, fueling a culture of arrogance when humility would have been better. The elaborate ethics program didn't keep the firm out of hot water. First, critics alleged that the company allowed plastic surgeons, who had a vested interest in having women perceive themselves as inadequate, pressure the company into developing a product of dubious value. Second, breast implants were rolled out despite warnings from a company engineer in 1976 that intimated that the implants could rupture and cause serious medical problems.[10] Third, critics complained that the firm was providing implants to surgeons while the company was still conducting initial safety testing on animals. Fourth, after legal claims began piling up, the company enlisted public relations firm Burson Marsteller to create ersatz grassroots groups, dubbed "astroturf," to lobby government and talk to the media.[11] A 1991 memo from CEO Dan Hayes intoned: "The issue of cover-up is going well. Obviously this is the largest single issue on our platter because it affects not only the next 2–3 years profitability of DCC, but also ultimately has a big impact on the long-term ethics and believability issues."[12]

So, even though the ethics program was designed to cultivate a forthright culture, it gave employees mixed signals. Upon departing the firm, Swanson complained about company's "good time"[13] ethics program—one that worked only so long as expeditures were not too big.

Pursuing the Path of a Zeta Firm

In my research and consulting stints around the globe, I find that the most successful Zeta firms seek creative new ways to integrate economic and social considerations into their competitive strategies. This means doing things right—maintaining solid financial performance—while doing right. Acting like good citizens. What they do reflects their core values. One of Merck's initiatives provides a particularly striking illustration of the possibilities for accomplishing this.

Merck & Company

Millions of people in the African and Latin American tropics suffer from a malady called river blindness. Parasitic worms, transmitted by black fly bites, burrow under the skin, releasing millions of microscopic offspring, microfilaria, that move throughout the body. When the microfilaria invade the eyes, victims go blind.

Prior to 1979 there was no safe treatment for river blindness. But that year, a Merck researcher discovered that one of the company's best-selling animal drugs, Ivermectin, killed a parasite in horses similar to the worm causing river blindess in humans. Company scientists asked Merck's chairman to let them concoct a human version of the drug.

But this presented a conundrum. The victims of river blindness would not be able to afford a cure at a price that would recoup costs for research and testing, which could top $100 million. Even if it was affordable, handing out the drug would be a nightmare. Victims lived in remote areas, meaning no access to clinics, hospitals, physicians, or drug retail outlets. If the drug carried side effects or was misused, bad publicity might hurt sales of the animal version of the drug, which ran at about $300 million a year. Suppose cheap copies of the drug were made. They might be sold in black markets for animal treatment. That would cannibalize the company's lucrative Ivermectin sales to veterinarians.

Management remained undecided. Even though Merck enjoyed worldwide sales to the tune of $2 billion a year, its net income as a percent of sales was declining because of rising development costs for new drugs, increasingly restrictive and costly government regulations, fewer scientific breakthroughs, and declining productivity of company research programs. Facing such worsening conditions in the drug industry, Merck managers were reluctant to take on expensive projects with scant economic promise, like this one. But without the drug, millions of people would continue to suffer.

Merck management concluded the potential benefits of a cure for river blindness couldn't be ignored. Many managers believed the company was morally obligated to proceed despite the costs and the slim chance of economic reward. In late 1980, company managers approved sizable funding to develop a human couterpart of Ivermectin.

Following seven years of costly research and extensive clinical testing, Merck developed Mectizan, a human version of Ivermectin. A pill, taken once a year, eliminates all traces of the river blindness parasite and prevents new infections. Yet no buyers stepped forth. Merck asked the World Health Organization (WHO), the U.S. government, and governments of nations afflicted with the disease to buy the drug to protect some 85 million people at risk. Getting no response, Merck decided to give the drug away for free. But the plan was hard to put in place. Adequate distribution channels were nonexistent. Working with the WHO, the company underwrote an infrastructure for distributing the drug safely and preventing its diversion to the black market. By 1996, with the help of government and private voluntary organizations, the drug was finding its way to millions of people, ending suffering and transforming lives. Finally, in 2000, river blindness had been added to the list of eradicated diseases, according to the World Health Organization

Why did the company spend so much money and effort on researching, developing, manufacturing, and distributing a drug that made no money? When the company saw that one of its animal drugs might cure such a serious human disease, they felt the only responsible option was to develop it. People will remember this and have high regard for the company in the future. The company knows the strategic importance and long-term advantages such actions bring about. In the aftermath of World War II, Merck brought streptomycin to Japan to treat tuberculosis. Although they didn't make money from the donation, today Merck is the largest U.S. pharmaceutical company in Japan. George W. Merck, son of the company's founder, says "we try never to forget that medicine is for people. It is not for the profits. The profits follow, and if we have remembered that, they have never failed to appear. The better we have remembered that, the larger they have been."[14]

This case shows how a company can build goodwill and reputation that enhances opportunities for long-term bottom line results. In the short term, Merck's managers knew that tens of millions of dollars were being spent to develop a product with a slim chance of bringing in profit. But by taking an outside-in viewpoint that happened to mesh with its inside-out mission for helping people, Merck achieved long-term worldwide acclaim for its strategic decision to invest in a reputation for ethical behavior.

Can we conclude that Merck is a Zeta firm? Not necessarily. Some critics of the firm accuse it of effectively bribing doctors to use their products. The concept of a Zeta firm is an ideal; it provides a benchmark by which to evaluate and compare your firm's conduct. And the behavior of any individual company is typically inconsistent, falling short of moral perfection. So no single example of good conduct, or even a string of saintly noble deeds, would suffice to make a business a Zeta company in an idealized sense.

Your firm does not have to be as sizable and well-established as Merck to build long-term reputational capital and reap the results in terms of superior financial success. No matter how big, no matter what line of work, the basic laws of reputation in business are the same. And the new paradigm of today's business means you cannot afford to lose out on strategic opportunities everywhere for doing well by doing right.

II

How to Build and Sustain
Reputational Capital

8

Generating Reputational Capital

If you must choose between a good reputation and great wealth, choose a good reputation.

—King Solomon

Let's begin with the most basic question prompted by this book: How can a firm build reputational capital? Zeta companies build reputational capital by staying focused on these fundamental objectives:

- Demonstrate integrity and fair play—"rightdoing"—in all business dealings to build the character of the firm and its people.
- Discern what really matters to the firm's reputation, given the size of the firm and the line of business it's in.
- Link the values your firm molds for itself—inside-out perspective (what do we want to be?)—to the values of key audiences like clients, associates, shareholders, investors, local communities—outside-in perspective (what do we want our reputation to be?).
- Instill in all employees the wish to do the right thing to ensure the long-term success of the firm. More than emphasizing to members of the firm the need to appear ethical, it's necessary to generate a commitment to the intrinsic worth of a sound reputation.
- Pursue superior operational performance conjointly with ethical soundness. There is a demonstrable payoff for forthright business conduct. But that doesn't ease the hard choices that competitive and volatile market conditions impose. Compliance and citizenship are essential, but they're no substitute for market responsiveness. A Zeta company's enterprise model must integrate commerce, compliance, and citizenship. Your company cannot maintain reputation-generating practices like good citizenship without being grounded in a viable economic model.

• Find creative ways to build reputational assets by harnessing the firm's special identity (what the company is about) and core competencies (what the company does best).

Fair play and integrity—the wellsprings of your company's reputation—are a mix of moral character, fidelity to law, quality in producing goods and delivering services, and financial discipline. The trick is to move from establishing reputation and credibility to building reputational capital. Your firm's reputational capital expands as it pursues pathways of fundamental virtue that cut across all of its constituencies (stakeholder relationships) over time. It takes time to build trust. Reputational capital is built and sustained over the long term.

Reputation building is dynamic. You need to keep up with the expectations of key constituencies as those expectations continue to inch upward. (The expectations also vary depending on which cultures your firm is engaged with across the globe. Attitudes in Bangkok about employee relations are much different from those in Stockholm.) But don't look at these new expectations as Alpha and Omega firms do—as a costly burden. See them as a golden opportunity for gaining competitive advantage.

"Fine," you may say, "but in choosing to build the firm's reputation aren't we going to be sacrificing some of our potential for financial success? Can we afford to be ethical?" Luckily, you can avoid Solomon's dilemma. Have your cake and eat it too. Building a good reputation is the route to sustainable wealth in today's business.

That's not to say no risks or costs are involved. But, from another perspective, any business investment carries costs and risks—so why should investments in reputational capital be any different?

The following chapters proceed step by step with ways to build and sustain reputational capital. We'll begin with some general principles and considerations and follow with a three-step method: (1) forging reputation from the inside-out, (2) deploying outside-in strategies, and (3) marshalling resources toward the firm's special attributes.

General Principles and Considerations

SEEK FORTHRIGHT AND HONEST PEOPLE TO WORK WITH; LOSE THE UNSCRUPULOUS CLIENTS AND BUSINESS PARTNERS

Reputation building (or, as the case may be, reputation devastation) is interdependent. If you and I do business together—whether you are my colleague, partner, client, employee, or investor—our reputations, and those of our firms, are engaged with one another.

The reputations of many professional service advisors were burned by servicing the byzantine debt-hiding schemes of their client, Enron Corporation. Among the victims of reputation deflation by association were law firms Vinson and Elkins; Akin, Gump, Strauss, Hauer, and Feld, and Shearman and Sterling; accountants Arthur Andersen[1] and Deloitte and Touche; and investment bankers Deutsche Bank, Bankers Trust, and Chase Manhattan. Working with an unscrupulous client in the professional services industry can cast a cloud of suspicion about a firm as surely as using sweatshop suppliers does for companies in the manufacturing business.

There are exceptions. It's expected that lawyers will defend people and corporations charged with crimes. That's necessary to protect their right to the presumption of innocence and due process. But increasingly, people deplore news of law firms that proactively assist corporate scoundrels in designing fraudulent financial vehicles.

KEEP THE JOB OF BUILDING THE FIRM'S REPUTATION INSIDE YOUR FIRM

You don't want to leave the job of building reputation to an external consultant. And definitely do not leave the task to the public relations and marketing people. This reduces reputation to image, which it's not. Your firm's senior management needs to lead the way. Why? Because the key drivers of reputation—vision, mission, culture, policies, strategy—are right inside your own firm. Outside experts will be out of touch with your firm's culture and internal dynamics.

Reputation is also too precious to remain solely within the CEO's clutches. After all, if the firm's reputation is centered entirely around the CEO, what happens when the CEO moves on to greener pastures? At the same time, the CEO needs to rally behind the effort. The point is this: Reputation management is the responsibility of senior management, and its implementation is the responsibility of every associate. After all, employees have the most to lose if the firm loses reputation.

Some companies name a chief reputation officer or a chief reputation advisor. The chief reputation officer's (CRO's) job is to protect the company's intangible reputational assets, similar to the way the chief financial officer is charged with oversight of financial capital, the chief information officer keeps tabs on corporate data, and the chief operating officer controls operations.

The CRO's responsibilities entail oversight of advertising; corporate contributions; employee, customer, and media relations; quality; legal compliance; investor relations; and public affairs. Instead of single-handedly performing each of these tasks, CROs usually work with specialists from each field, helping them to acknowledge the reputation consequences of decisions. The CRO aids in underscoring the importance of reputation and making the otherwise hidden value of reputation explicit.

So, should your firm use a chief reputation officer? Generally, I would advise against it. The CRO role can be more effectively handled by the CEO. The main problem with setting up a distinct CRO function is that it puts up walls when what you really need to do is integrate the firm's character into its actions. For smaller firms it's normally not necessary to establish a CRO position. Whether you do or not, make everyone in each department of the firm a guardian of the company's reputation.

The board of directors has legal and fiduciary duties toward shareholders. Since reputational capital is a significant form of wealth from a stock growth perspective, the board should also bear responsibility for promoting conduct that builds and safeguards this precious asset of the company.

MAKE THE FIRM'S REPUTATION EVERYBODY'S CONCERN

Every associate in your company must be directed toward building and maintaining the firm's long-term reputation. In a profound way, corporate reputation is analogous to a hologram. Every part of a hologram, in a sense, contains the whole. Illuminate any part of a hologram and the entire image is reconstructed. Blake wrote, "To see the world in a grain of sand." A company's reputation embodies the same principle. The entire organization's reputation is enfolded in each of its parts. The conduct of each member of your firm, from the lowest to the highest rank, reflects the reputation of the entire company. When your secretary declines to make appointments for clients, turning them away on the grounds that his or her "shift is over for the day," the act speaks for your whole firm. The business lost from those now disgruntled clients, and that of others who learn of your firm's reputation for poor customer service, directly impacts your bottom line.

So you want to incorporate systems that reward and encourage reputation-enhancing behavior. Also set up procedures for discouraging and punishing reputation-dimming behaviors. Every member of the firm must be guided to see the reputational consequences of their decisions and actions. The challenge is to recognize and execute the many different tasks that build and maintain the firm's reputational capital.

An employee's misconduct that damages your firm's reputation is as bad as and probably worse than their outright embezzling of tangible assets. Seen another way, reputation bashing is tantamount to a tort that causes economic injury to the firm. Conversely, conduct that enhances the firm's reputation adds economic value to the firm. So, the reputation-enhancing conduct of even low-level employees may be as significant in terms of value creation as senior salespeople winning lucrative contracts for the firm.

STRIVE TO MAGNIFY AS WELL AS MAINTAIN REPUTATION

The lists below illustrate varieties of ethical practices and how they impact on the company's reputation. The second list represents conduct that generally must be observed if the firm is going to keep from losing reputation. Let's call the kinds of behavior that sustain reputation "silver deeds." Norms governing conduct within this category are often (though not always) backed up by authoritative sanctions in a country's own legal orders. The first list represents behaviors that tend to magnify reputation beyond normal levels. We'll term this type of conduct, which is normally above and beyond legal requirements, "gold deeds."

Conduct that Magnifies Reputation (Gold Deeds)

Following the spirit of the law

Keeping promises and commitments

Being honest and fair

Being trustworthy

Being compassionate

Actively helping others

Improving the environment

Improving the community

Conduct that Maintains Reputation (Silver Deeds)

Following the letter of laws and regulations

Honoring contracts

Dealing in good faith

Not lying, cheating, or stealing

Doing no harm

Respecting human rights in overseas operations

In formulating strategies that will serve to *build* the firm's reputation, probe these questions:

- Given the firm's core competency and identity, what specific gold deeds can we undertake to build our reputation?
- What gold deeds can we set out to accomplish on a regular basis to maintain healthy relationships with customers, partners, investors, and suppliers?
- Do our associates grasp the value and importance we place on our reputation? What about our clients, suppliers, and competitors? The local government and community? The public?

In looking to *preserve and maintain* the firm's reputation, pay attention to these issues:

- Given the firm's degree of vulnerability to reputational attack and loss, what specific silver deeds should we accomplish to sustain our reputation?
- What might go wrong? Are there any minefields in our business operations?
- Are we equipped to foresee rogue behavior, unethical acts, scandals, or crises that can imperil our reputation?
- Are we poised to handle unanticipated events, such as a sudden switch in public attitudes toward our product or service, or stepped-up regulations of our business activities?
- What kinds of behavioral controls and monitoring systems are in place to reduce the likelihood of a crisis?
- What sorts of compliance programs do we have to safeguard the integrity of our conduct? Are they working?

Practice humility

It's risky to hold yourself out as high and mighty. This raises expectations. People will hold you to an impossibly high standard that can't be met. So the more you promote and market yourself as a reputable firm, the more vulnerable you will be to attack when mistakes/malfeasance happens. Critics charge that Dow Corning Corporation became so arrogant and complacent with its ethics initiatives in the early 1980s that they never stopped to consider whether the silicone breast implant—which put them in the middle of a legal and reputational disaster by 1989—

was a legitimate product to begin with or whether it was introduced to the market prematurely.[2]

For this reason, it's best not to make absolute claims. Wal-Mart said all its products were made in the United States; Tom's of Maine and The Body Shop boasted that all their products were "natural." The credibility of these companies was weakened when the truth came out that these claims were false.

DON'T TRY TO PLEASE EVERYBODY

Any activity your business undertakes to do good will raise someone's ire. U.S. West contributed to the Boy Scouts and they were hammered by gay-rights activists. When Levi-Strauss stopped funding the Boy Scouts, they unleashed venom from some religious leaders. By trying to satisfy all of the people all of the time your company will come out as spineless and wishy-washy in the end. It's better to exercise autonomy, following the firm's own moral lights.

Focus on people and groups with legitimate, justifiable expectations. Decide what groups are most important to your firm. Above all, don't change your tune mid-song. Retailer Dayton-Hudson was engaged in long-standing donations to Planned Parenthood. Angry anti-abortion demonstrators lined up outside Dayton-Hudson stores cutting up credit cards. So, in an abrupt about-face, the company began contributing to anti-abortion groups. Pro-choice protests erupted, taking the company to task for abandoning their cause. Overall reputational effect? Abysmal, because funding diametrically opposed groups is hypocritical.

EXCEED THE LEGAL

Don't turn over the ultimate decision making on reputation-sensitive matters to lawyers. They are there to protect the company from first-dimension financial risk and second-dimension legal risk. That gets you up to letter-of-the-law compliance measures. But safeguarding the company's integrity in the long run mandates cogent conduct in the third dimension. We're talking spirit-of-the-law, and beyond.

It's really hard to ignore the lawyers, of course. They're persuasive. They know how to argue and they talk with authority. Truth be told, when faced with a crisis, the instinct of most executives is to check with legal. See if you have the fortitude to say, "I don't care what the lawyers say. This is the right thing to do."

Here's the problem with disregarding the spirit of the law. Companies are judged for violations of the spirit of the law in the court of public opinion. That's what happened when Stanley Works opted to reincorporate to cut its worldwide tax bill. Compliant with the letter of the law, yes. But a major felony in the court of public opinion. And the sanctions imposed by the court of public opinion are the most severe by far. It cannot be appealed. For some firms, the death sentence has been imposed.

Be transparent and open

People tend to form impressions and opinions before becoming fully informed about situations and context. But in matters of ethics, context is vital. It can be debilitating when people's rush to judgment before all the facts are in. Even if what you disclose is controversial and sparks criticism, that is better than suffering the ill effects of concealment and wild rumors.

Ford Motor Company issued its first-ever "corporate citizenship report" at its annual meeting on May 11, 2000. The company confessed that its profitable sport utility vehicles (SUVs) pollute the air, contribute to global warming, and guzzle more gas more than ordinary cars. The company also admitted that SUVs endanger other motorists. But—the company did *not* pledge to stop making SUVs, which make up about half of the company's earnings. So Ford will keep making them. However, the company announced that it planned to improve its SUV's gas efficiency 25 percent within five years. Demand for SUVs is still going strong. And even though they're three times as likely as cars to kill the other driver in a crash, legally they're not deemed "inherently unsafe."

So why did the company point out all the problems with the highly popular, high-margin vehicles?

It's all about reputation. William Ford, Jr., the company's chairman, is laying a foundation of trust. This is a smart move. Auto makers could get reputations like those of tobacco companies in the court of public opinion if they ignore the social problems. Mr. Ford's statement was altruism mixed with long-range business planning.

Clearly, Ford has extensive data showing that SUV safety and environmental risks are significant. As with the tobacco industry, if it sits on this information, it risks getting sued down the road. By being honest and straightforward, the company hopes to build credibility.

Similarly, in the midst of recent disputes about how companies should be handling stock options, Coca-Cola announced directly that it would treat them as expenses. The news was met with a generally favorable response from a public filled with post-Enron suspicion. Soon after, Intel's CFO declared that his company would *not* treat stock options as expenses. But he gave specific reasons backed by sound financial rationales for this decision. After all, the real source of debate over the expensing of stock options is not so much about which method is used per se as it is about being up front about the procedure the firm is going to be using.

Guide your firm's social orientation by financial self-interest

In choosing from among alternative works to fund, select projects that are likely to benefit your firm financially.

Suppose your company is considering creating an on-site daycare center, implementing a flextime program, or building an employee gym. It's easier to make the case for these initiatives with evidence that they will reduce turnover and absenteeism sufficient to pay part of their own way.

The hotel industry typically pays maids low wages. Many live below the poverty line and are difficult to retain for more than a year. Marriott was unable to increase wages to reduce turnover among its approximately 150,000 low-income workers. Seeking a way to retain employees, and to lower costs of training and supervising new hires, Marriott found that workers are often torn from their jobs by personal problems. Supervisors reported investing up to half their working time helping employees with personal hardships. The company deployed a 24-hour, multilingual hotline, staffed by trained social workers who assist employees with problems involving child care, homelessness, substance abuse, domestic violence, and immigration and naturalization. The project reduces the hotel's turnover, tardiness, and absenteeism.

The hotline processes over 2,000 employee calls annually. Although it costs more than $1 million a year to operate, it saves over $3 million a year in hiring, training, and related costs. The company documents heightened worker productivity and morale, as well as improved relations with managers and co-workers, as results of the hotline.

If your company is privately owned you gain a bit more flexibility. But even here, try to gear social programs to profitability. And remember that "profitability" includes positive reputational outcomes that may take some time to come to fruition.

Strike a balance between social and financial imperatives

Profiting from a reputation for integrity and fair play means, as Dr. Phil would say, you need to get *real*—three-dimensional, that is. The first dimension, that of cash flow, is basic. But commerce is ruled by law. So the second dimension, compliance, comes into play. To get out of "Flatland" your firm needs the third dimension:

character. What you're aiming at is the right balance within this triad. The key here is balance. Blindly pursuing integrity for its own sake in business spells disaster. After all, the third dimension is just that—third in a linked series that builds on the first and second dimensions. The best-seller *A Civil Action* portrays the plight of a three-attorney personal injury law firm investing too much of its time, energy, and resources in pursuit of conscience.[3] A blind resolve to win for a noble cause at all costs, involving rejections of numerous offers to negotiate and settle with opponents—which would maintain its cash flow—in litigating a massive personal injury lawsuit sends the firm in a downward spiral to bankruptcy.

The story of Consumers United, an insurance company, teaches a sobering lesson. It's dangerous to spend too much energy on altruism while neglecting the bottom line. Consumers United wanted to take a progressive tack. They covered policyholders' unwed domestic partners and offered unisex insurance rates. The company's founder passed the firm's ownership to employees. They dictated corporate policy and could overrule him by majority vote. The firm also built low-income housing on vacant acres it bought in Washington, D.C. It funded a local youth group, promising to pay for each member's college education

This generosity caught the eye of insurance regulators. Would altruistic moves like footing poor kids' college expenses ensure sufficient reserves to cover future claims? Eventually industry regulators obtained a court order that pulled the plug on the company.

9

Forging Reputation from Inside

Successful reputation building begins at home. The firm's vision, mission, and leadership guide business decisions and member's conduct. Your firm's strategy, culture, and workplace incentives need to be aligned with these guideposts.

Setting the Right Tone at the Top

Cultivating a great reputation starts at the top of an organization. Your company's top team establishes a clear vision that they transmit throughout the company. This shapes the firm's overall culture—its ethos. This lends leadership and direction for associates to create an organization that's meaningful and authentic for the constituencies that dictate its destiny. And vision is contagious: It reaches external audiences as well.

Employees look first to the example set by their immediate supervisor for signs of their firm's culture. Leading by example is most important in day-to-day situations unseen by the public. Executives and managers establish standards for following or ignoring rules simply in how they handle routine pressures of business life.

The CEO's Role

In the end the CEO bears responsibility for your firm's growth. By growth I mean financial performance, adaptation to change, and character.

People squabble about who's accountable for a company's reputational ups and downs. CEOs in the United States are prone to accept acclaim for gains. The losses? Oh, that's somebody else's fault. In Japan, on the other hand, a CEO in the midst of a profit-sapping scandal normally steps down.

Over the last decade of the millennium, CEOs came to personify their companies. Warren Buffett hit the nail on the head when, speaking about the firms that made *Fortune's* top ten list, he quipped "People are voting for the artist, not the painting." Is anyone surprised by the recent release of best-sellers by (General Electric's) Jack Welch (*Jack: Straight From the Gut*) and (IBM's) Louis Gerstner (*Who Says Elephants Can't Dance*) in the years they left the office of CEO?

While General Electric took only sixth place in shareholder returns among *Fortune's* top ten list for 1998, it took first place overall. Jack Welch was the reason. With regard to the "most admired" companies, much of their corporate reputations are driven not only by operational, financial, and social performance but also by the leadership of the CEO. These are the attributes that are valued by the managers and company analysts who rate Fortune 500 companies: To achieve a good ranking in this poll, a company must have superior financial performance and an exceptional CEO to trumpet the company's activities. Examples: Jack Welch—General Electric, Bill Gates—Microsoft, Michael Dell—Dell Computer, John Chambers—Cisco Systems, David Glass—Wal-Mart, Herb Kelleher—Southwest Airlines, Warren Buffett—Berkshire Hathaway, Craig Barrett—Intel, Arthur Blank—Home Depot, and Richard McGinn—Lucent Technologies.

Currently it's sort of a mixed bag. So long as stock prices are cranking up, it seems the CEO can be "cellophane man" for all anyone cares. But CEO divas are still quite an item in the business press. One thing is clear: Credibility and character count. Post-Enron, integrity and fair play matter more than the old gung-ho. Press reports about the lack of executive integrity are everywhere. One notable media story exposed the rise of companies conducting extensive background checks, complete with credit reports and neighbor interviews, for prospective CEOs. Ronald Zarrella, Bausch and Lomb's chief executive, was found to have shaded the truth about his credentials, saying he had an M.B.A. from New York University. Actually, he left prior to graduating. The board responded by cutting him out of a $1.1 million year-end bonus.

Today CEOs are getting slammed for hoarding huge bonuses as they terminate legions of mid-level managers and production workers in the face of recession fears. Dennis Koslowski, CEO of Tyco, siphoned off millions from the firm by granting and forgiving employee relocation loans. He used the wealth for such essentials as a $15,000 umbrella. A banking executive I know joked, "some of these CEO's are worse than leaders of the mob. At least the mob bosses take care of their own people."

Leadership is key in forging corporate values and growing a network that nurtures organizational integrity and fair play. Leadership centered on strengthening values among employees creates consensus on standards of conduct. It forms patterns of shared relationships. Leaders create culture. Because leaders occupy highly visible positions, they play a key role in spreading values, norms, and codes. Leaders provide a structure for integrity and fair play by putting both formal and informal ethics training programs in motion. As we've seen, they must not be quick-fix or overly legalistic programs.

Leaders can change culture. Jack Welch changed the staid, bureaucratic GE into a lean and highly competitive organization. The details are set out in his recent book *Jack: Straight From the Gut.*[1] Welch got the ball rolling by clearly articulating his vision: GE would be number one or number two in the world in each of its businesses. Any businesses failing to measure up would get sold off.

GE employees liked the job security of the pre-Welch GE. But Welch aimed to encourage competitiveness, risk taking, creativity, self-confidence, and dynamism. He recruited managers interested in shining. If GE no longer needed the managers, they'd move on. Welch proved to be adroit at finding and eliminating unproductive work. He directed managers to eliminate reports, reviews, and forecasts. He urged them to speed up decision cycles, to transmit information through the firm quickly by peeling off unneeded bureaucratic layers. All of this led to the "leaner and meaner" GE culture.

Leadership is the single most important element of a firm's ethos. Integrity and a sense of fair dealing—or the lack thereof—are like a mountain stream. They flow down from the top. Associates watch what leaders do. They make sense of the ethos based on what the leaders say and, more than that, what they do.

Robert Haas is chairman and chief executive of Levi-Strauss. From its birth in 1850, the company has enjoyed a reputation for extraordinary success coupled with commitment to social responsibility. Haas, himself the great-great grand nephew of the company's founder, pursues a revered company tradition that he dubs "responsible commercial success"—merging profit making with making the world better off. When he took the helm in 1984, the company was obese and bureaucratic. Haas steered the company in the waters of private ownership through a $2 billion leveraged buyout of nonfamily stockholders. In announcing the buyout, Haas stressed the financial benefits, yet added that the move would free up management to focus on long-term interests and ensure that the company could implement its values and traditions. Haas has a guru reputation, known within and outside the company for fostering diversity, openness, empowerment, and ethical conduct. He refuses to engage with suppliers that violate Levi's strict workplace standards. The company is principle driven: A set of corporate "aspirations" guides all key decisions.

Tasks Your Leaders Can Do Right Now

Here are some steps that managers and executives can take right away to put them on the track toward building their personal reputational capital as well as that of the firm.

Practice what you preach.   Does the conduct of the company's leaders square with the values they espouse? Confucius advised leaders never to order others to do what they themselves would not do. There are two kinds of values: espoused values and ones people actually practice day to day. What matters is alignment, leaders demonstrating personal integrity—actually doing what they say they're going to do.

A reputation for hypocrisy comes about when espoused values get out of sync with the values we actually put into practice. Leaders that promote standards to which they themselves don't follow display pretension. Leaders who acquire a reputation for hypocrisy and pretense lose their ability to influence others. The inevitable result is that it becomes necessary to turn to artificial forms of power and authority to attempt to regain control. But we've already seen in this book how that kind of compliance-based, "do this or else" mindset erodes rather than builds reputational capital.

Your clients, associates, investors, and business partners make subtle yet penetrating judgments about whether or not you live up to your firm's espoused values. Here is what they are looking at:

- *Punishing and rewarding.* Do your compensation structures reinforce the values driving your business? Do incentives foster internal cooperation—or do they fuel fighting and office politics? If one of your associates undertakes a reasonable risk, intending to benefit the firm, yet fails, do you praise or punish? How do you react when those reporting to you offer constructive feedback?

- *Allocating money.* Scour the budget for consistency. Do your expenditures match what you value? If you say people are a valued asset of the firm, is that captured in your compensation structures and your policies?

- *Allocating time.* As with money, the way you allocate time reveals where your priorities lay. People spend time doing the things they take to be the most important. Write down a list of the top five values driving your organization. Now take a look at your calendar. See how you are actually using your time. Do you see a fit?

- *Responding to people and events.* How you react to matters—from bickerings to bravos—sends out a strong signal. When your people do something exemplary, do you celebrate their achievements? Jack Welch recounts how he encouraged his people to celebrate successes, to take joy in their accomplishments, to make business fun.

- *Framing Questions.* Do questions you pose to associates reflect your concern for them as people? Do your questions guide people to value clients and maintain long-term relationships with them—or to just meet the numbers for short-term goals? The questions you ask and answer speak legions about what you value.

By living out your values you inspire trust in your people. Why is trust so important for a leader? With high levels of trust, it's easy to talk to your people. You can mess up, stumble a bit, but it doesn't matter—people still catch your drift. But when trust burns low, it's a major energy drain to get things across. Things just don't work well.

Be principle driven. Like a compass, the right principles will always point the way. When you know how to read them, you keep your orientation fixed. You don't get turned around by conflicting values and competing interests. Principles like integrity, justice, honesty, and fair play are not parochial standards that drown in the turbulent sea of relativism. They are honored and practiced by businesspeople of good faith in every corner of the world. They are rooted deep in the human conscience and govern human relationships and organizations in a fundamental, enduring way.

Most leaders too quickly jump on the public relations and marketing bandwagons and divert energy to perfecting the corporation's personality—ignoring its character. Most of the existing books on corporate reputation assume that reputation development is all about creating the right image. But in truth, building reputation means discipline: correcting habits, cultivating virtues, honoring promises, and being compassionate and considerate toward others. Character development manifests the maturity of a leader. The essence of effective business leadership lies in honoring and respecting oneself while, at the same time, sublimating oneself to higher principles of humanity, principles that are greater than oneself, that are beyond our ability to control.[2]

I listened to the CEO of Northrop Grumman explain how he led the company into an *ethics dynamic.* I believe he grasped that he was committing his firm and its people to a process much larger than either himself or his company. It involved signing on, surrendering really, to a process that lays principle over economics, politics, and even law—that has a life and direction of its own.

Principle-driven leaders are people of character and vision who draw principles into the core of their being, into the heart of their relationships, into the center of their negotiations, projections, planning, and promises. These are the principles of integrity and fair play that are the bedrock of reputational capital.

Your firm builds its reputation on the values set out in the vision and mission statement. The question people are always asking is whether the values driving your business and the motivation for burnishing reputation are based on integrity—or just plain greed? Have the values been acquired willy-nilly, as a way of just going through the motions—or have they been instilled with intention and resolve? As a leader, you must carry on the task of value shaper.

Research documents that, paradoxical as it seems, corporate excellence in practice depends on honoring the intrinsic value of values—that is, taking a noninstrumental approach that assigns top priority to moral duties.[3] In other words, it's best if leaders are motivated to improve the firm's reputation not just to improve profits but because they are genuinely motivated to do the right thing. If you doubt the truth of this, just ask yourself this question: Who would you rather do business with, a financial advisor or insurance agent that values integrity and fair dealing for their own sake, or one that cynically tries to show you that he cares as a means to get more money from you?

Be Fair.   A reputation for fairness and even-handedness is essential for sound leadership. You can't bust one associate's chops while looking the other way when somebody else commits the same offense. That decimates respect and saps morale.

It seems easy, yet it takes effort to stick with it day in and day out. There's always a plea to make an exception. "Sure, Ryan was padding his expenses, but Ryan is one of our top producers. He says he's sorry and won't do it anymore. Let's give him a warning. But don't let him go."

In discussions I've had with hundreds of executives in similar circumstances, two sides to the story invariably unfold. A case can always be made for bending rules or carving out exceptions. Looked at individually, an executive can always rationalize granting some special dispensation.

Cumulatively, however, if an executive shows that many exceptions are the rule about how the rules are followed, then leadership will weaken as the trust of associates fades away. Leaders that fail to demand consistent and fair adherence to solid principles and policies will find them dying the death of a thousand exceptions.

Admit mistakes.   Let yourself be human. A company is made up of people. Let your customers and employees see that you're mortal. As Rudy Giuliani put it, your people "need to see someone who is stronger than they are, but human, too."[4] Character comes out in the way we deal with crises, during the hard times.

> Failure is an opportunity.
> If you blame someone else,
> There is no end to the blame.
> Therefore the Master
> Fulfills her own obligations
> And corrects her own mistakes.
>
> —*Tao Te Ching*

Stephen Covey tells a story about the importance of owning up to mistakes. He needed to arrange a big meeting. He chose a novice who failed to execute the assignment. But the employee admitted his mistakes and vowed to go the extra mile to improve if given a second chance. Covey stresses his admiration for those having the guts to admit failure, which influenced his decision to let the employee have another go at it. Covey observes that "my estimation of his character was higher than if he'd done it right the first time."[5]

Find out what people think of your company's reputation.   Recall the famous line "... O wad some Power the giftie gie us To see oursels as ithers see us!" Burns's poem "To a Louse" expresses how lucky we would be if we could know how we are perceived from an external point of view. It takes special effort and some imagination to find ways to gain an illuminating external perspective on your business. Dell Computer Corporation's chairman and CEO, Michael Dell, spent time in Internet chat rooms (under a disguised identity) observing what people were saying about his company, which evidently led to a great payoff.

Be available.   In my presentations to corporate leaders I counsel them this way: "Be there—or beware." I see a lot of executives and managers in firms that are forever running away and hiding. They're avoiding the media's tough questions. Dodging angry customers. Shunning disgruntled employees. Don't do this. As leader, you are the lifeblood of the organization's reputation. Stay passionate about your firm's good name. Hang around to hear what people have to say. The good, the bad, and the ugly. Raw and uncensored. Sometimes just being there makes all the difference.

Be organic: Don't fragment and compartmentalize

I want to urge you to avoid the mistake of dealing with your constituencies in a fragmented way. Some firms spread out responsibility for handling reputation matters across distinct areas, like finance, marketing, human resources, and legal. This poses problems when diffusing like this affords little chance for contact or coordination. These distinct areas may not talk to one another. There must be a consistent reputation strategy backed by senior management.

Conduct reputation audits regularly

A reputational audit is a method for identifying, assessing, and taking full advantage of your firm's reputational capital. It helps in highlighting the deeper cultural features of its reputation so as to distinguish it from its superficial image. Ultimately, you want the firm's image, identity, and reputation all to be aligned.

How does your firm come out? The more yes responses you can circle, the better the prospects for reputation building.

Table 9.1 Reputational Audit

Does the firm have a solid legacy of character, e.g., a founder's vision passed down from generation to generation?	Yes/No
Are reputation concerns brought up and addressed within the company?	Yes/No
Do people in your firm know the difference between good and bad behavior for your industry or profession? (You can find out by giving them a questionnaire.)	Yes/No
Is there day-to-day talk about behavior that impacts the firm's reputation?	Yes/No
Does the firm have a code of conduct?	Yes/No
Is the code of conduct communicated effectively to associates?	Yes/No
Are employees rewarded for decisions that enhance the company's reputation?	Yes/No
Does management recognize the importance of creating a culture that cares about employees?	Yes/No
Do employees treat clients and customers with honesty and fair play?	Yes/No
Is the firm focused on the long run as well as the short term?	Yes/No
Are employees basically satisfied?	Yes/No
Is people's behavior on the job consistent with what they say is right?	Yes/No
Is there an external focus on customers, the environment, and the welfare of society?	Yes/No
Do superiors and subordinates openly talk about their ethical quandaries?	Yes/No
Are employees coached on how to do the right thing?	Yes/No
Is employee turnover low?	Yes/No

BE PROACTIVE, NOT REACTIVE

Time and again I find that companies take note of reputational headaches too late. They scramble for quick remedies when the storm clouds of a scandal are already brewing or after the high winds of a crisis have already brought devastation.

DEVELOP A FRAMEWORK FOR FAIR PLAY AND FORTHRIGHTNESS

Take a hard look at fundamental questions:

- Why does your firm exist?
- Where is the organization headed in pursuit of its mission?
- Who are your firm's key constituencies?
- What are your firm's obligations vis-à-vis these constituents' rights, claims, and legitimate interests?

CREATE A MISSION STATEMENT AND DESIGN A CODE OF CONDUCT

Codes fall into four camps:

1. *Code of conduct.* This is the most prevalent. Sometimes called a statement of business practices, it sets out rules and standards covering a range of circumstances.
2. *Policy manual.* These tend to be lengthy, containing detailed rules covering a multitude of job situations.
3. *Credo/mission statement.* This expresses your firm's core values or vision. A credo affirms your firm's commitments to key stakeholders, like customers, employees, and the community. This is where the soul of the company's reputation finds expression. It embodies the shared values people in the organization aspire to. The mission of Merck and Company is: "to provide society with superior products and services by developing innovations and solutions that improve the quality of life and satisfy customer needs, and to provide employees with meaningful work and advancement opportunities, and investors with a superior rate of return." Hewlett Packard's vision is: "A winning company with a shining soul to lead in an Internet age to invent for the common good." Johnson&Johnson's credo, together with a positive and highly responsive corporate culture, is credited by many commentators with having played a

key role in the preservation of its reputation through the Tylenol tamperings. Its credo is inspirational:

> We believe our first responsibility is to the doctors, nurses and patients,
> to mothers and fathers and all others who use our products and services.
> In meeting their needs everything we do must be of high quality.
> > We must constantly strive to reduce our costs
> > > In order to maintain reasonable prices.
> > Customers orders must be serviced promptly and accurately.
> > > Our suppliers and distributors must have an opportunity
> > > > To make a fair profit.
> > > We are responsible to our employees,
> > the men and women who work with us throughout the world.
> > > Everyone must be considered as an individual.
> > We must respect their dignity and recognize their merit.
> > > They must have a sense of security in their jobs.
> > > > Compensation must be fair and adequate,
> > > and working conditions clean, orderly and safe.
> > We must be mindful of ways to help our employees fulfill
> > > their family responsibilities.
> Employees must feel free to make suggestions and complaints.
> There must be equal opportunity for employment, development,
> > and advancement for those qualified.
> > > We must provide competent management,
> > > and their actions must be just and ethical.
> We are responsible to the communities in which we live and work,
> > and to the world community as well.
> > We must be good citizens—support good works and charities
> > > and bear our fair share of taxes.
> We must encourage civic improvements and better health and education.
> > We must maintain in good order
> > > the property we are privileged to use,
> > protecting the environment and natural resources.
> > > Our final responsibility is to our stockholders.
> > > Business must make a sound profit.
> > > > We must experiment with new ideas.
> Research must be carried on, innovative programs developed
> > and mistakes paid for.
> New equipment must be purchased, new facilities provided
> > and new products launched.
> > Reserves must be created to provide for adverse times.
> > > When we operate according to these principles,
> > > the stockholders should realize a fair return.

4. *Corporate philosophy*. This encapsulates your firm's guiding beliefs. Hewlett Packard's philosophy of diversity is famous: "we believe diversity is a

key driver of success. Putting all our differences to work across the world is a continuous journey fueled by personal leadership from everyone in our company. Our aspiration is that the behaviors and actions that support diversity and inclusion come from the conviction of every HP employee—making diversity and inclusion a conscious part of how we run our business throughout the world." Corporate philosophy statements often crop up in emerging industries that call for new ways of doing business.

Codes are increasingly popular. Seventy-nine percent of employees surveyed in a U.S. study conducted in 2000 stated that their company had one.[6] A study of Fortune 1000 companies done in the mid-nineties found 98 percent of the firms addressed ethical issues in formal guidelines.[7]

A recent study canvassing 124 firms throughout 22 countries documents a trend: Corporate boards of directors are getting increasingly involved in setting standards of conduct. Over three-quarters of corporate boards were active in adopting codes in 1999, up from 41 percent in 1991.[8] One study revealed that over 80 percent of Forbes 500 companies with written guidelines had created or revised them during the nineties.[9]

The best codes blend the general with the specific. Levi-Strauss and Company's "Aspiration Statement" is general. It outlines the sort of company its associates aim for. Their code is midrange. It lists the values and principles for guiding action. Their "Global Sourcing and Operating Guidelines" are specific. It lays out detailed directives for dealing with business partners and selecting countries for operations. The company has long used foreign factories in its production processes. In 1992 a scandal hit Saipan. Subcontractors of Levi-Strauss were operating dangerous, abusive, and illegal facilities. The U.S. Labor Department charged the contractor with making employees work up to 11 hours per day in guarded compounds, compensating them with less than minimum wage. In a sweeping reaction the company adopted rules governing foreign operations. The new terms for engagement excluded suppliers using child labor or forcing employees to work unacceptable hours. By 1993, Levis-Strauss had fired 596 of its 600 suppliers—a dramatic change that carried significant costs. Regarding decisions about whether to make direct investments in countries and in selecting business partners, a senior manager of Levi-Strauss said "[w]e've got to be careful. There are some things we just can't be associated with—and still maintain our reputation."[10]

Just getting engaged in writing a vision and mission statement and code helps your firm define itself. By far, the *process* of bringing the code into being is more valuable than any rules and directives that come about.

The question becomes "what do we stand for?" Involve all levels—as many officers and employees as possible—in writing and updating the code. If there's one feature successful codes share, it's gaining support from people at the top. But codes don't work when they're forced. Making a code work requires everyone owning it.

Of course, we're all familiar with Alpha- and Omega-type firms whose espoused values, printed in mission and values statements, business principles, codes, and credos are dissociated with day-to-day conduct. Enron graphically shows that having a code of ethics doesn't, by itself, mean a whole lot. Enron's code was perfectly fine. The company's dishonored former chairman, Kenneth Lay, wrote these words in the preface to the code: "Enron's reputation finally depends on its people, on you and me. Let's keep that reputation high." In hindsight, Lay's conduct spoke louder than words. After its demise, copies of Enron codes of conduct—billed as "never read"—were hot collectibles up for grabs on eBay.

In my travels between the United States and Europe, I find that Americans are prone to approach business conduct chiefly through rules, while Europeans lay greater stress on informal vehicles for corporate culture control. In the United States, managers are urged to consult checklists, principles, and guidelines to distinguish right from wrong. The prevalence of corporate codes among U.S.-based companies bears witness to this proclivity to associate ethics with rules. Although codes are not as popular throughout much of Europe, companies in Great Britain are increasingly adopting them. I've seen quite a few European executives express surprise at the assumption of U.S. leaders that adopting a code will change employees' conduct. Asian executives are the most perplexed of all by this attitude.

Given that there are ethical companies operating in countries where codes are not common, it seems fair to say that codes are not essential for fostering right decisions and good behavior but rather represent one culture-specific tool for transforming the corporation into a better moral agent.

Codes have their limits. A code that overemphasizes rules can make people stop thinking for themselves, eroding the capacity for sound judgment and common sense. Some firms pass on writing up a code altogether, opting for alternative ways to build culture, like leading by example. India's HDFC, mentioned earlier, has consciously opted not to put out a formal code of ethics. The rationale is to avoid any dampening effect codification might have on their preferred method of communicating standards by actually living them and putting them into daily practice.

The code becomes an expression of your firm's commitment to reputation-raising values like integrity and fair dealing. Since, as we've seen, integrity is not itself a virtue but rather the state of keeping virtues in the right relation and balance, a code can express the virtues that exemplify the character of your firm.

Virtues like courage, compassion, discipline, honesty, loyalty, and responsibility are good candidates. Values like trust, respect, teamwork, and quality typically appear in codes. And codes can lend guidance for associates' handling of specific issues like appropriate use of company resources, acceptable forms of gifts and entertainment, expectations for workplace behavior, protecting confidentiality of information, and avoiding conflicts of interest. Here are some tips for your code:

- Make the code match the audience: your employees.
- Consider what the code is trying to accomplish.
- Prioritize, so that what's most important leads the code.
- Get support and ideas from all levels of the firm.
- Revise periodically.
- Use clear, simple language. Lose the legalese.
- Give underlying reasons for various standards so they don't seem arbitrary and mindless.
- Reinforce in staff meetings, orientations, and seminars.
- Devise a concrete and responsible program for enforcing the code.

Keep in mind that the standards in the code stay on paper until they are triggered by real-life problems and dilemmas. They need to be applied and interpreted. Your associates need the resolve to put them into action. Sometimes, two provisions come to loggerheads. When an associate comes across damaging sensitive information about a colleague, respecting confidentiality could conflict with loyalty to the firm. The code can clarify issues. But it can't resolve dilemmas on its own. That takes insight, common sense, wisdom, and experience. Sometimes asking questions and engaging in thoughtful and reflective dialogue with others on issues is better than looking at a code's preformulated commands. One of my favorite lines from poet Ranier Maria Rilke is "try to love the questions."[11] An inscription at the Unitarian Universalist church on Central Park West I stumbled upon sums it up nicely: "[u]nanswered questions are a lot less dangerous than unquestioned answers."

Set up reward systems that encourage reputation-enhancing conduct

Reward systems are the single most important influence on people's workplace behavior. People will do what gets rewarded. They normally are rewarded for reaching a goal or fulfilling a sales quota, with no regard for how the objective goal is attained. Many people recount their experiences with managers to me. The message they get is: "It doesn't matter how you do it, just do it." In other words, use any means necessary—do *whatever*—make the numbers, seal the deal, satisfy the goal. Since people tend to do those things that are rewarded, your managers need to be sure that performance objectives are realistic. Can people meet your ambitious stretch goals without having to resort to reputation-threatening conduct?

Northrop Grumman works to integrate its performance appraisal systems with its mission. It strives for uniformity in assessing manager's conduct. The company uses a leadership inventory. It's a checklist of behavioral attributes linked to Northrop values, which include customer satisfaction, quality, honesty, and fairness. Employees evaluate managers and the managers receive a summary of the assessment along with recommendations for change.

In almost every company there is a Machiavellian underside. Performance appraisals can be misused for hidden agendas, establishing a ruse for cutting costs by not giving anyone a bonus in an especially lean year. Or, performance appraisals can be used to bring positive change by rewarding reputation-strengthening behavior. Here's the deal: The dark forces that sour your firm's culture—the ones that ply what it *says* it stands for away from what it actually *does*—are inhibiting the growth of the company's reputational wealth. So the potential long-term good of the many is jeopardized by dirty politics.

Give care in designing organizational systems. When they're out of sync with the governing framework, people in the firm get mixed messages. They need support to undertake responsible action. You can build favorable conditions for right conduct into the fabric of the firm by ensuring that members have opportunities, abilities, and incentives to tell the truth and to act responsibly and fairly. Remember the Wicked Witch of the West in *The Wiz?* "Don't nobody give me no bad news!" Suppose she's the boss. Now what was that you keep meaning to tell her about those declining sales figures for your division? The organization's systems should reward, not punish, people for being honest, especially when the news they have to report is not good.

Pay heed to:

- Audit and control
- Budgeting and resource allocation
- Communications and information
- Employee development and education
- Hiring and promotion

- Leadership and supervision
- Performance evaluation and rewards
- Planning and goal setting

Misalignment of reward systems with other aspects of firm culture—code, vision, and mission statement, formal policies—is commonplace. I often hear complaints from managers in organizations where the code of conduct is ignored. Actions speak louder than words.

We've all seen companies where the top producers are winning through unscrupulous behavior. Say that financial services professionals in a company are churning, twisting, and violating suitability rules, not disclosing risks. Suppose that not only do the misdeeds go unchecked, but these are the folks getting huge bonuses, expensive vacations. They're cheered at the annual sales meeting. People see that the company's reward system carries the "real" message. The code becomes meaningless. Top management gets a reputation for hypocrisy.

DO VALUES TRAINING

Conducting training is important. Training sessions should be specially tailored to fit the business issues arising in your firm and its industry. The content should match your firm's unique vision, mission, and culture. Training programs can lead associates to see and appreciate reputational matters they may otherwise miss.

Research shows that ethics programs fare better when employees see them as motivated by values rather than compliance. A 1999 study indicates that when employees view corporate ethics programs as being values oriented instead of compliance oriented, the result is greater commitment to the organization, more integrity, and increased willingness to deliver bad news.[12]

All levels of the organization, not just upper and middle management, should take part in the training seminars. And few things will take the wind out of a seminar as much as this, which I've seen happen more than a few times: The top executives come to the start of the session, stay a short while, and leave. This sends out the message to everyone else: "Oh, this stuff doesn't apply to us; it's not important."

Northrop Grumman put together a video about one of their fiascos involving testing irregularities. This problem had meant closing a facility, suspending a division from government contracting, paying a $17 million fine, along with millions in other costs. The incident rocked the company. Its reputation suffered. The company opted to use the mishap as an opportunity to heighten the reputational perceptions of its associates. Entitled "When Things Went Wrong," the video deploys candid interviews with the chief executive, the defense department, and managers in order to examine the context and causes, both organizational and individual, of the mishap. Used as a tool to raise employee awareness of ethical issues, the video probes ways to avoid a relapse. The video is reported to be a success by the company's employees.[13]

Similarly, Columbia/HCA used a 40-minute video, featuring several ethical scenarios as part of its program to institute a values-based culture in the aftermath of its overbilling scandals.

SET UP RESOURCES

Have a "helpline," "guideline," or "open line" to provide guidance on reputation matters. Let associates pose questions anonymously to the ethics officer or the reputation officer via e-mail. Encourage associates to phone human resources, legal, the auditing department or the ethics office if they need guidance.

TREAT EMPLOYEES RIGHT

Employee loyalty favorably impacts worker longevity—which in turn benefits the firm. The Bureau of Labor Statistics calculates the average tenure of an employee with a company as less than five years. Studies show that worker longevity generates customer loyalty and higher profits. These benefits are especially pronounced in the banking, brokering, and auto service industries. Even in the manufacturing sector, where employees seldom confront customers face to face, long-term employees make better products, enhance consumer value, and improve customer retention.[14]

Employee relationship building matters to employees. After all, they spend the bulk of their waking hours preparing for, travelling to, and working at their jobs. Creating satisfying relationships with employees entails more than just providing a job. It means helping workers pursue their own goals and letting them thrive in a humane, uplifting workplace where the value of their contribution to the business is recognized. A study conducted three separate times over the past 45 years asked one thousand employees to rank work rewards in terms of value.[15] Over the years, the results have scarcely changed. "Full appreciation of work" tops the list. Being aware of the stresses and pressures that employees experience and helping them adapt to forces of change in the world and shifts in the work environment can strengthen employee loyalty. Table 9.2 shows some major trends happening in today's companies.

Table 9.2 Changes in Corporate Structure

Shift From:	*To:*
Stability, predictability	Continuous change
Hierarchical structure	Flat structure
Domestic business	Global organization
Homogeneity	Diversity
Individual contribution	Team contribution
Reward for tenure, loyalty	Reward for performance, skills
Rigid structure	Flexible workforce
Product driven	Client/Customer driven
Company management of career	Co-management of career
Loyalty to organization	Loyalty to self
One-time learning	Lifetime learning
Dependent employees	Self-reliant employees

Efforts your firm can make to accommodate such shifting trends might mean offering flextime, telecommuting, and job sharing. Notice that such endeavors will involve building trust in new ways on both sides.

Employers need to understand what affects employee loyalty and commitment because employee retention is crucial. Studies show that employee commitment grows up around these characteristics:

- Fairness at work
- Care and concern
- Satisfaction with day-to-day activities
- Trust given employees
- Reputation of the organization
- Work and job resources
- Ethical climate and corporate citizenship

According to a recent report on employee loyalty and work practices, companies viewed as highly ethical by their employees were six times more likely to keep their workers. Also, employees who view their company as having a strong community involvement feel more loyal to their employers, are more dependable, and, because they feel better about themselves, are more inspired and productive. Employees that don't feel they've been treated fairly will do the minimum to get by each day, having no commitment to what the organization is trying to accomplish.

Below are several ways to improve relationships with your workforce.

Promoting trust.   Good relationships are grounded in trust. Trust mitigates the fear of betrayal. The people we trust defend us when we're attacked. They safeguard our interests when we're absent. Trust doesn't arise spontaneously in the workplace. Zeta firms make concerted efforts to maintain trustworthiness. The following factors are important in developing trust:

1. Being evenhanded with all associates.
2. Encouraging the free flow of communication.
3. Adopting initiatives, like profit-sharing plans or employee stock ownership plans, that share the rewards of good work and draw employees closer together.
4. Conferring empowerment. Good things happen when people feel empowered and involved in decision making. It makes people feel better about their jobs and companies. Feeling good motivates people to work harder and do better. A positive attitude generates trust and builds teamwork. It fuels creativity and innovation. All of this helps your company act more quickly and outpace competitors. Here's another benefit that involvement brings forth. Since line employees are closest to products, services, and clientele, they are well-positioned to certify the wisdom of key judgment calls. More than 2,500 U.S. companies use quality circles to generate participation and capitalize on employees' ideas for improving operations.[16]

Inspiring pride.   Well-reputed firms—known for extending goodwill and respect—tend to make employees bond with them emotionally. This evokes a sense of pride in their work and the way the firm does business. The more your company takes care of its employees, the more likely they will take care of the company. How do you take care of employees? By keeping a safe work environment, setting competitive salaries, fulfilling contractual obligations, and providing work-family programs and stock ownership plans. Undertaking community service can also elicit employee pride. Home Depot associates participate in disaster relief efforts after hurricanes and tornadoes by rebuilding roofs, repairing water damage, planting trees, and clearing roads. As part of Home Depot's focus on building affordable housing and assisting at-risk youth, associates are encouraged to participate in the company's partnerships with organizations such as Habitat for Humanity.

Showing compassion when laying off employees.   The new paradigm for business calls for compassionate layoff policies—ones that alleviate stress on families, lessen financial hardships, and reduce the likelihood that terminated employees will undergo emotional devastation.

Layoffs are traumatic. Not just for the person fired but also for colleagues left behind. Massive layoffs mean larger work loads for people remaining. People missing the cut experience low morale. Productivity drops. They distrust management. Survivors care about fairness. It helps if they can see that downsizing is prompted by legitimate business reasons. It helps if they see it executed in line with your firm's culture. It helps if people get adequate notice. It helps if people are treated with dignity and respect.

Your company's reputation can be sullied by badly managed layoffs. On the other hand, being decent in the way people are let go can earn your firm a reputation as a nice place for competent people to work at. As compassionate layoffs become more common, firms that fail to practice them run the risk of reputation damage and competitive disadvantage.

If your firm is facing the prospect of downsizing, follow these reputation-preserving principles:

1. explore money-saving strategies that might avoid or minimize layoffs, and explain to employees that this is the purpose;
2. look for options in retraining, job placement, career assessment and redeployments, revamped pay, and benefits packages.

Here are some creative, compassionate alternatives to layoffs:

- Compile a job database. Nine years ago, Canadian-based NOVA Chemicals Corporation experienced a downturn with its ethylene, chemical, and energy products. As part of a downsizing program, its human resources department devised a job database, containing internal and external employment opportunities, available to 6,000 employees. Still in place, the program has been used by over 1,000 employees switching to new jobs. Awards of up to $25,000 are available for employee startup ventures. For associates moving into careers with nonprofits, NOVA offers assistance, including the provision of half-salary and complete medical and pension benefits for a trial period determined by the employee, NOVA, and the nonprofit. Should the employee opt for the nonprofit career, a full severance package is awarded.

- Help employees develop spin-off businesses. When Bell Labs became Lucent Technologies, its marketing area was swollen. Its alternative to layoffs:

a new business unit spin off. The company assisted marketing teams in establishing a new business branching off from the firm's introduction of sophisticated voice messaging systems. The team became so adept in devising internal marketing materials that it began selling them to clients. Building on skill sets and the reputation of the parent company, Lucent managed to lower its payroll while raising its market visibility

- Restructure the workforce. In the mid-nineties, Sweden's Telia Group— now TeliaSonera following its recent merger with a Finnish telecom company—faced the prospect of terminating up to 7,000 associates. Among the ranks of employees of the formerly state-run company, many lacked the requisite skills to keep pace with advancing technologies and stepped-up customer demands. To stay competitive, the company needed to simultaneously lower its workforce while recruiting people with enhanced skills. The solution: doing a makeover of employees' skills so they could be hired back. The plan softened hardships from restructuring while retaining precious firm-specific knowledge of existing employees. The group coordinated efforts with unions to provide training and assistance to its excess workforce. The company helped employees acquire new skills and find alternative jobs. In the end approximately 2,800 of the group of about 5,000 to 7,000 people set to be cut got new assignments within Telia Group. The rest took jobs somewhere else, launched their own businesses, pursued studies, or began early retirement. Less than 1.5 percent got cut. This initiative helped not just employees but Telia, too. The company amassed considerable reputational capital by building favorable relationships with important stakeholders and landed the know-how and expertise it needed to stay flexible and competitive in a rapidly changing business environment.

If layoffs are unavoidable, make sure that goodwill toward the firm stays intact, the remaining workforce feels secure, and departing associates feel empowered. You don't want a reputation for brutality.

- Train managers. When people get fired, ripples of pain spread out wide across the workplace. The core of people's lives, their careers, are imperiled. The company's reputation is at stake. Give managers training in attentive listening and distress-response skills. Check the web to locate organizations and consultants that can provide these services for your firm's managers.

- Devise a care package. Formulate plans to take care of separated employees. A principal means for enhancing your company's reputation is the quality of this package. It should propel people forward personally and professionally. Include in it: Severance pay, financial, and benefits arrangements; professional support for finding a new position; and in-house counseling to help the terminated employees understand what combination of severance pay and support services is appropriate.

- Make the message kind. Delivery matters. Stress each employee's high points. Kind words go far. When people get laid off, a lot hinges on how they get the news. So choose words carefully. When people sense meanness or cruelty, morale is eroded. And the company can take a hit in the form of damaged reputation, not to mention lawsuits seeking vindication.

- Relay good words to prospectives. Find creative ways to pass on good news about people to prospective employers. Empowering people involves helping to propel them ahead with their lives. Putting in a good word for them can have an impact. Prevailing attitudes of catastrophobia commonly frown on providing references. The fear is that they translate into lawsuits. A good reference for a poor employee might lead to a claim of negligence. A poor reference for a good employee might trigger a claim of defamation. As a consequence, some firms refuse outright to provide references beyond verification of dates of employment. As a result, information is pursued via informal channels. This kind of grapevine gossip elevates the likelihood of hearsay and rumors damaging the reputations and careers of your former associates. Studies suggest, however, that providing references doesn't create as much risk as had previously been supposed.[17]

Balance employee privacy against the firm's legitimate interests. You want to cultivate a reputation for honoring the electronic privacy of employees. If people feel their reasonable expectations of privacy are being disregarded their morale drops— along with the firm's reputation. And overreaching carries potential legal liabilities.

On the other hand, insulating your firm from legal—and reputational—liability also demands asserting your firm's right to monitor communications. This is essential because abuses of the Internet at the workplace abound. Salomon Smith Barney fired two high-level analysts for using the firm's e-mail system to swap pornographic material. One study of computer logs at Apple and IBM by Neilsen Media Research tallied the firm's combined employee visits to sexually explicit web sites at 13,000 hits—in just one month! Another study by SurfWatch Software found that 24 percent of the online traffic at companies under review was not work related. Popular sites to check out on work time centered on sex, entertainment, and sports.[18] Some workers go to court when they encounter offensive e-mail messages from colleagues or when coworkers habitually scope out porn sites. A federal court recently held that a class action race discrimination suit seeking $60 million in damages could proceed against brokerage firm Morgan Stanley. The lawsuit alleged repeated propagation of a racist e-mail message through the firm's computer system.

The best approach is to limit monitoring, surveillance, or searches to what has been laid out in a detailed policy distributed beforehand to everyone. It should go over the underlying rationale and purpose for electronic surveillance. All monitoring must be reasonable and confined to business purposes.

Put up a sign-on disclaimer defining just how much leeway you want people to have. You may want to remind people that the e-mail and Internet access systems belong to the company. Alert associates that the company may monitor their e-mail communications and web usage at any time and that by using the system, an employee is presumptively consenting to that. Warn users not to send inappropriate messages. Apprise them that violators face disciplinary consequences— including potential termination.

10

Outside-In Strategies

In a world where intangibles like reputation matter at least as much as tangible assets like plant and equipment, competitiveness demands strong relationships with clients and customers, investors, business partners, the local community, and the media. You build a strong reputation by building these relationships. Relationship strength is about forging lasting, high-quality bonds with your firm's constituents. It's about giving and getting, with openness and honesty. The stable commitment of outside constituencies—customers providing revenue, banks providing financing, firms providing goods, materials, equipment, and services—is essential to your company's survival and success.

The expectations of key constituencies can be satisfied within a range, from unsatisfactory to adequate to superior. In the new paradigm, expectations of key constituencies have risen. What used to be adequate is now, more likely than not, unsatisfactory. A prominent, well-reputed insurance company used to send out letters to clients on an "assumed consent" basis. "Unless we hear back from you, we'll assume you consent to us raising the liability limits on your policy in line with our judgment about what's prudent for you." The agent who dreamed this approach up would have gotten the green light from industry peers. After all, it saves a good deal of time and energy from not having to call every client and persuade them to up their coverage. Today such a practice would trigger a red light from a compliance perspective.

In the chart on p. 136, write in some business practices that your firm currently conducts, that are under consideration, or that are slated to be implemented. Consider where they fall from a reputation standpoint. What consituency does the practice impact? Say there's a business practice you or your company can undertake—it's legal—but doing it could have a negative impact your or your firm's reputation because it falls short of your consitutencies' expectations. Write this in the "Red Light" region. Is there some practice that would be the right thing to do, but you can't seem to find a solid enough financial justification for it? Put this in

Table 10.1 Assessing Conduct from a Reputation Angle

Green Light

Superior: Exceeds constituencies' expectations; long-term payoff from goodwill is clear

1. _____
2. _____

Yellow Light

Adequate: Meets constituencies' expectations

1. _____
2. _____

or

Would exceed constituencies' expectations but can't find solid financial rationale yet

1. _____
2. _____

Red Light

Unsatisfactory: Shortfall relative to constituencies' expectations

1. _____
2. _____

the "Yellow Light" region. Finally, can you identify some practices that will surpass your constituencies' expectations and pay off in the long run? List these in the "Green Light" area.

Try to advance as many practices you can think of into the Green Light region. Practices in the Yellow Light category pose these challenges:

- How can we alter the practice to give more, so that constituencies' expectations of us are not merely satisfied, but exceeded?

- How might we account for the payoff from long-term goodwill that proposed expectation-exceeding practices might generate?

Practices you put in the Red Light area are potential reputation headaches. Possibly they are precursors to legal problems. Either find some way to change them so that they will bring about positive reputation consequences or abandon them going forward.

Cultivating Investor Relationships

Investors obviously look first and foremost at the bottom line for profits and potential for increased stock prices. Investors also hunt for potential cracks, or flaws, in a company. So invest some effort in communicating with investors about your firm's reputation and financial performance. You can use the Internet to host quarterly conference calls for both financial analysts and public investors. This lets your firm proactively shape communication in helping analysts and the public understand complex business models (such as IBM's) and allay post-Enron jitters they may harbor about accounting methods.

Together with your company website, online conference calls give you a chance to set up credible sources of news and information, a forum for addressing relevant issues that lets you broadcast a controlled message to the outside world. Let them know that reputation matters—because it constitutes a major part of their investment—and that your firm cares about its reputation and is actively working to build and protect it.

Here are some factors investors consider important in evaluating your firm for investment potential.[1]

Earnings.   Investors select stocks based on current and historical earnings. They like companies with reputations for better and more stable earnings. Investors typically bid up a company's market value in the wake of announcements of either strong profits or measures likely to improve future profits. This increases reputational capital. This accounts for why managers watch the bottom line so closely. Declining profits signal dampened prospects to investors, lowering the firm's market value along with its reputational capital.

Volatility.   When people assume greater risk due to the uncertainty about the profitability of a company in which they are investing, they anticipate getting rewarded with better-than-average returns. A method of determining the riskiness of a company is to examine the volatility of its earnings for past years. The less steady profits have been, the greater the risk. There needs to be some significant upside to the risk. That means higher potential profits. Over time, the market downgrades firms that fail to deliver on investor expectations. In the process, the firms' reputations take a hit.

Indebtedness diminishes the residual value of a company to investors. Indebtedness is a good predictor of bankruptcy. A company having comparable total assets, yet greater debt relative to another company, is less attractive to investors.

Nobody's interested in investing in a company that's unlikely to pay them back. All told, earnings and risk are key predictors of how investors and analysts rate companies—including their reputations.

Growth outlook. Rating services, like Standard and Poor's and Moody's, help in evaluating the financial strengths of public companies as investments. They rate companies with a letter scale, from AAA, the highest rating, to D. Getting a triple-A grade is understood to be an indicia of sterling credit. It signals a low likelihood of default even under the most troubled conditions. On the other hand, a D rating means a company poses a bad credit risk.

Ratings express reputation judgements about a firm's business and financial prospects. There is no fixed formula by which companies get rated. Ratings are strongly influenced by a company's volatility of earnings, its indebtedness, its business fundamentals, its financial management, and management's credibility.

Investors normally view companies with high price/earnings (p/e) ratios as better prospects than contenders.

Foundations, mutual funds, pension funds, insurance funds, and university endowments have amassed vast pools of money controlled by professional managers responsible for making portfolio investments. In light of their prominence, institutional investors are important to building reputation. Fund managers serve as information brokers to smaller investors. The smaller investors, accordingly, frequently emulate the moves of fund managers.

Analysts make recommendations about stocks based on firms' current and past accounting performance. When companies report their seasonal earnings, investors react quickly. High profits and low risk produce upturns in a company's stock price.

For analysts, a strong earnings report card signals that managers are doing things right. It means a company shows good prospects. Strong earnings incline investors to bid up a company's equity. Strong earnings lend confidence to investors' assessment of a company's ability to service its outstanding debt. All of this raises a company's reputational capital.

Promoting Relationships with Clients and Customers

Building reputations with customers and clients centers around fairness, honesty, and respect. Because the quality of customer service affects customer satisfaction, improvement in the quality of service has a direct impact on your company's image. Customer service quality also bears on the firm's ability to attract new customers. Companies with high-quality products command high customer loyalty: Note the number of people who are loyal to BMW, Saturn, Waterford Crystal, Sony, and Timberland, to name only a few.

By putting customer satisfaction center stage, your business deepens the customer's dependence on the company. As the customer's confidence grows, the firm sees how to better serve the customer so the relationship can endure. Successful businesses solicit customer feedback. This engages customers in cooperative problem solving. Contented customers will return. Disgruntled customers will pass their disdain on to others and discourage friends from dealing with a company they despise.

Service customers are especially sensitive to exploitation or operations that do not respect rights. When information about added service costs is omitted or a guarantee is not honored, the customer reacts negatively to the perceived injustice. The customer's response—complaining or refusing to deal with the business again—may be motivated by the need to punish and the desire to limit a future injustice. Millions of customers are overcharged by retail computer scanners that are not programmed with the correct price. If the customer is overcharged for an item that has a visible sale price displayed, a feeling of injustice arises typically provoking an angry verbal response in earshot of other customers.

Listed below are key components for strengthening bonds with customers.

Gaining customer loyalty. Ethical conduct toward customers builds a strong competitive position that has been shown to positively affect business performance and product innovation.

A study of consumer attitudes found that 70 percent of consumers said that if price and quality were equal among all brands, they would likely switch to a brand tied to a good cause.[2] Results indicated that consumers take it for granted that they can buy high-quality products at low prices. This signals that businesses need to stand out as doing something socially responsible—demonstrating commitment to society. Another way of looking at these results is that perceived unscrupulous behavior triggers disloyalty—switching to a rival's brand. Forthright practices draw customers to you.

Keeping the firm's reputation intact requires maintaining excellent customer service, accomplished by:

- Providing quality products or services at fair prices
- Making sure products or services are safe

- Honestly representing products or services
- Giving reasonably accurate work estimates
- Waiting on customers promptly, returning phone calls
- Establishing eye contact, showing interest, giving respect

In addition, it's important to uphold customer and client confidence by:

- *Protecting client and customer privacy.* The right of privacy is basic. In the financial services industry professionals gain access to sensitive, privileged information. People will provide this kind of information only if they are pledged confidentiality. Respecting privacy involves using sensitive information only for the purpose for which it was provided.

- *Ensuring suitability and appropriateness for customers.* Especially in the financial services area, this issue can seriously affect both corporate and individual reputation. In 1994, Prudential Securities committed malfeasances connected to sales of limited partnerships to individual investors. People lost significant amounts of money as a result of the firm's salespeople overstating the soundness of a number of their financial services products. The portrayal of highly risky investments as sound investments violates a duty to recommend only suitable investments for clients. Not only was the firm excoriated by the press, but it paid more than $700 million in fines and penalties. All in all its reputation took a pounding.

- *Advertising truthfully.* You lose customer trust when products or services get portrayed in a deceptive or inaccurate way. Take the recent Nike ads for Tiger Woods golf balls. The ads enticed golfers to buy the same golf balls the superstar plays with. But Tiger was using custom-designed Nike golf balls not yet publicly available, and customers got angry when they found out. In one of its TV ads, Volvo portrayed its cars as withstanding piggyback rides by monster trucks. What this didn't show were the concrete and steel beams stuck inside the cars before filming. Even if based on an innocent mistake, once your company gets caught handing out dubious data, trust evaporates.

- *Issuing prompt alerts.* Your firm loses trust if it doesn't quickly disclose problems when they're detected. This happened to Chrysler when it dillydallied about replacing safety latches for minivans. And Firestone and Ford were lambasted in the United States for sitting on information about SUV tire defects. The problem had surfaced years earlier in other countries.

Building Goodwill in the Community

IN LAUNCHING CORPORATE CITIZENSHIP PROJECTS, PURSUE JOINT ACTION WITH OTHER ORGANIZATIONS AND BUSINESSES

In December 1977, General Mills teamed up with the Stairstep Initiative, a non-profit community organization, and Glory Foods, a minority-owned food enterprise to start a frozen food company intended to create 150 jobs in Minneapolis's inner city. The Danone Group sponsors employees in Spain to work with a local organization, SOS Children's Villages Network, to support homeless or orphaned youth. Enlisting the assistance of UNICEF, Proctor and Gamble developed Nutri-Delight, a product aimed at alleviating malnutrition in poor countries

TREAT ACTIVISTS AS ADVISORS, NOT ENEMIES

Whether activists are acting in good faith or in bad, they can profoundly impact your business, putting its reputation in jeopardy. Disney's introduction of a theme park outside of Paris was attacked by activists who dubbed it a "cultural Chernobyl."[3] Activist groups have stopped openings of Wal-Mart stores in a number of states. Public outcries prompted Home Depot, the world's largest home-improvement retailer, to stop selling lumber derived from environmentally sensitive regions and to give priority to wood certified as responsibly harvested. Other major retailers followed with similar commitments.

Good-faith activists can help your company anticipate the negative repercussions of your operations. Seek out responsible activists that can help your company merge profit with social and environmental uprightness.

Activists can stimulate efforts to save money from reduced turnover, lawsuits, fines, boycotts, and public relations costs by treating workers better. They can help a company explore linkages between life-cycle product engineering and cost cutting, or assist a firm in finding environmentally responsible suppliers. For instance, Starbucks enlisted the assistance of Conservation International in arranging to buy coffee from farmers that preserve forests. Home Depot developed its eco-friendly lumber supply program with the Rainforest Action Network.[4]

Internet Strategies

With its vast reach, anonymity, and pervasiveness, the Internet is becoming a formidable influence on corporate reputations. Your company's reputation builds, grows, and changes with information transmitted across informal networks of personal contacts. By exponentially increasing indirect interactions between people, electronic networks are a major force in propagating reputation-draining rumors—or spreading reputation-lifting messages of confidence and trust. How can your company use the Internet to burnish its reputation? How it can protect itself from Internet perils?

On the Internet, otherwise disconnected audiences can link up. They share viewpoints, consolidate, plot joint strategies, and pursue agendas that target corporate reputations. In cyberspace, companies are scrutinized as never before. Anyone with a grievance and enough motivation to vent their outrage at your company can do it. Examples abound of disgruntled ex-employees creating sites to lambaste former employers. Activist groups worldwide are sophisticated in their use of the Internet to conduct global protests, targeting specific companies. A Greenpeace campaign took aim at Coca-Cola's use of chlorofluorocarbons. The group appropriated the company's logo, colors, Olympic sponsorship, and advertising.[5] Many sites (for example, www.mcspotlight.org) maintain an ongoing battle against McDonalds. Some sites regularly condemn sundry firms for abusing human rights, the environment, and clientele. Aggressive measures include directing users to deluge a company with messages, which overloads their communications teams and sometimes paralyzes their systems.

Some fresh approaches to promoting and safeguarding corporate reputations on the Internet are in order.

Rebut Internet rumors

The Internet culture breeds information and propagates allegations that target the heart of corporate reputation. Lines between fact and rumor are easily erased. What does this imply for your business? If you mistreat customers, if you're a major polluter, if you violate human rights, then look out—you're in for a bumpy ride. But even if your conduct is impeccable, you still need to beware.

Companies are finding that control over their communications is slipping away in the dot.com world. One study by Cyveillance finds that, on the Internet, 80 percent of major brand names suffer brand abuse, that is, misleading or false claims are made about products or services. This hits Global 500 companies hard: the average firm loses $30 million each year from Internet-based defamatory communications.[6]

To mount an effective rebuttal to cyber rumors: (1) Take them seriously, even if they are preposterous; (2) move swiftly; (3) garner hard evidence to repudiate them; (4) tailor the evidence to a finer level of detail and specificity than the rumors contain; and (5) spread the evidence around to all affected audiences with websites and web-hosted conference calls.

MAINTAIN TRUST IN ONLINE TRANSACTIONS

Because users' identities are easily cloaked, online business transactions are vulnerable to distrust. At the outset of a deal, e-trading partners are complete strangers, clueless about each others' reputations. Some online market sites allow customers to rank firms based on ease of transactions. Others, like eBay and Amazon, are using reputation feedback devices to lower risks associated with anonymous e-business transactions

Just what are those risks? Suppose you're thinking of buying a personal digital assistant on eBay. You face some risk. What if the seller hasn't accurately described the shape it's in? How can you be sure it'll be properly packed and promptly shipped? Is there anything that can be done to give you some ground for trusting the phantom seller?

Ebay uses a reputation management system. Called the Feedback Forum, it lets online business partners pass judgment on each other. A "+ 1" stands for a positive reaction. A "−1" expresses a negative comment. "0" is neutral. The entire set of comments an eBay user gets are captured in a Feedback rating number. This score appears in parenthesis, next to the user's name.

Users with Feedback ratings of −4 or less get suspended. The Feedback rating comprises a portion of the user's Feedback Profile. You can get the full profile, or "ID card," by clicking on the number. It contains the complete text of comments and a table identifying the most recent comments and ratings.

Amazon has a slightly different feedback system. People buying from Amazon marketplace, Auctions, or zShops are asked to rate sellers' performances, leaving a brief comment. Average ratings, from one to five stars, pop up next to sellers' names in each reference.

Generally, such reputation management systems lead to lower levels of fraud. But there are limits. One drawback of reputation management devices is that they can be exploited by unscrupulous sellers that use them to cheat.

Here's the modus operandi. Online con artists first participate in auctions in a forthright manner. This elevates their trust ratings. Then, after their trust scores get high enough for them to participate in high-end deals, they commit a financial hit-and-run. They capitalize on their sterling reputations, initiating auctions for high-buck articles they don't even own. Upon receiving payment for the bogus items, they cash out and vanish into thin air.[7]

Another unscrupulous method involves shill bidders posting positive feedback with another user name, placing themselves or their friends in positive light.

In the wake of such scamming, critics attack e-businesses for not doing more to prevent the misconduct, such as enabling users to obtain more sophisticated data about a seller's feedback. Although eBay has been successful in maintaining a loyal following, if the number and magnitude of such fraudulent practices rises, the resulting disillusionment among scammed users could tarnish the online auction's reputation.

Building mutually beneficial relationships bonded with trust is a must for electronic commerce. Research shows that building and maintaining trust entices customers to keep coming back to websites. Here are key elements for cultivating confident and trusting customers:

- Maintain speed and efficiency, allowing orders to be placed and merchandise dispatched promptly and with little hassle. This gives customers a sense of being in control of the buying process.
- Have state-of-the-art, effective security measures on your site to handle consumers' personal information with sensitivity and iron-clad confidentiality. Advertise this on the site.
- Create linkages between your products or services and established brands to confer legitimacy. For instance, brokers such as TD Waterhouse, Ameritrade, HarrisDirect, and Vanguard are linked with CNBC's website.
- Facilitate customer collaborations with chat groups that let consumers share purchasing experiences.

Also, consider these trust-building methods:

- Maintain feedback mechanisms on your website. This allows your company to maintain communication control.

Dunkin Donuts turned disadvantage to advantage by sponsoring a site where critics could voice their concerns, thus putting them center stage in customer service dealings. Monsanto Corporation and Proctor and Gamble also set up special-purpose sites to respond to matters of customer concern.

- Create online communities. This is a proactive step in cultivating meaningful relationships with key audiences. To help your corporate-sponsored communities succeed, make them:

—— linked to hot topics, especially ones for which your firm has some credibility

—— rich in content

—— associated with a credible sponsor

—— interactive

—— easy to access

—— entertaining and/or informative

As Amazon, AmericaOnline, and GeoCities are showing, virtual communities carry tremendous influence with their members. Using them to endorse your company or brand can enhance its credibility.

11

Harnessing Your Firm's Reputational Strengths

> Use the orthodox to engage.
> Use the extraordinary to attain victory.
>
> —Sun Tzu, *The Art of War*

In the new paradigm, your firm's reputation hinges on its distinctiveness in engaging clients, associates, and investors in ways that fit heightened expectations about balancing conscience and cash flow. Its reputation takes shape by the ways it sets itself apart from competitors.

Admittedly, cross-cultural differences and varying legal standards sometimes make it hard to maintain a consistent identity with geographically diverse audiences. Consider Nike, maker of sports shoes and apparel. Perceptions of fairness about its wages and labor conditions differ radically among workers in its Asian factories, its managers and executives in Seattle, and consumers in the European Union. Not only the images through which the company promotes its products but also the justifications and defenses of its employment practices prove difficult to harmonize across the globe. Nike's advertisments spotlight distinctively American sports images and flash endorsements of celebrities like Michael Jordan and Andre Agassi to project an aggressive, dynamic image. But those images don't mask negative perceptions of the firm's character across national boundaries, especially in light of media revelations about Michael Jordan's compensation (astronomical) relative to that of workers in Southeast Asian sweatshops (abysmal). In other words, a key issue is: How well does your unique reputation travel from region to region?

There are tremendous opportunities for your company to foster a reputation for fair play that will differentiate it from rivals, Especially in countries with corrupt environments and in environments with lax social and environmental regulations.

Let's look at a company that is gaining success from this approach. Incorporated in Mumbai in 1977, Housing Development Finance Corporation (HDFC) is India's largest residential mortgage finance institution. Through the years, HDFC has, due to conservative and strict policies put in place by its promoters, been a consistent performer. It enjoys a reputation for superior management, transparency, strong brands, and outstanding customer service. It has received numerous awards from both domestic and international institutions for corporate governance. The HDFC scrip has received premium valuations because of HDFC's leadership role, a track record of consistent growth, and management's solid reputation.

The company's founder, H. T. Parekh, believed in openness. Assuming that, deep down, borrowers are honest, he wanted to establish mutual trust between his company and its clients. Following Parekh's insight, the company respects delinquent debtors; instead of intimidating them, it works with them to remove whatever barriers might be keeping them from making good on their financial obligations.

This approach surprised me. From discussions I have had with members of the judiciary in India, civil cases in India languish in the courts, sometimes literally for decades, depriving litigants of relief. Typically, lending institutions cannot rely on normal enforcement mechanisms for delinquent borrowers. Consequently, many lenders hire strongarms to coerce repayment, or seize a defaulting borrowers' property on the spot. So, in light of such conditions, HDFC's humane policies seem especially noteworthy.

Skeptics will say that all such respect-based policies do is produce more delinquent borrowers. But the firm's outstanding long-term financial performance seems, on the contrary, to testify to the wisdom of its founder's belief that banking on the inherent goodness of people is good business.[1]

USE GOOD CITIZENSHIP EFFORTS TO REVEAL THE COMPANY'S DISTINCTIVE MORAL CHARACTERISTICS—ITS OWN VIRTUES

It's important for people to be able to distinguish deep reputational attributes (those related to moral character) from superficial image and brand identity attributes (those related to marketing and public relations). Two ways to do this are:

1. Give unconditionally: Don't attach any strings when you donate to charities, schools, or other causes.

    This demonstrates the virtue of courage—your firm is willing to take risks for advancing the good even if the payoff is uncertain and far off. It also displays the virtue of candor—you don't have any undisclosed agenda of expecting something in return.

2. Leave the firm's unique "moral signature" on its good citizenship efforts.
   Coming up with fresh ideas to make positive contributions demonstrates the virtue of imagination. The benefits generated by genuine corporate citizenship—efforts at doing good backed by sincere motivations—cannot be replicated by rivals because they are based on the unique web of positive relationships that a business establishes with its own stakeholders. (Conduct undertaken just to build image or distract attention of wrongdoing somewhere else in the firm, by contrast, tends not to build such positive relationships, but rather generates attitudes of suspicion which dissolve trust and weaken relationships.) The corporate citizenship efforts displayed by Wal-Mart illustrate this dynamic. The retailer makes large donations to communities in which its stores are located. The funds are used to support local schools, local associations, and economic development. Such conduct helps Wal-Mart forge tight bonds with local customers, employees, suppliers, and community leaders. Though they may try to mimic your firm's deeds, competitors will be unable to duplicate the resulting relationships of trust and long-lasting interactions these initiatives foster when backed up by sincere motives of goodwill.

Your company will build reputational capital by pursuing strategies of integrity and fair play that differentiate it from competitors that stick with business-as-usual mindsets. Pursue initiatives that square with the firm's core competency, mission and identity. Find pursuits that unite your people and add value to your firm. Seek something that clicks with your customers and business partners.

Table 11.1 below indicates some of the matches between companies and their distinctive citizenship initiatives:

Table 11.1 Leaving a Unique Social Signature

Company	Competence	Social Initiative
Sony Ericsson	Telecommunications; mobile phones	Developing project on magnetic pollution.
SmithKline Beecham	Pharmaceuticals	Giving away drug to cure lymphatic filarissis.
British Petroleum	Petroleum	Donating solar-powered refrigerators to doctors in Zambia for storing malaria vaccines.
Green Mountain Coffee	Beverage retailing	Buying 25 percent of beans directly from farmers, eliminating middlemen.

Having the right sense of fit between a firm's competencies and its social outreach projects helps to get people on board because the cause feels natural for your business. Another big plus here is that the company's commitment goes much deeper than simply writing a check for a social concern. Even start-up businesses finding themselves strapped for cash can explore ways to contribute to good causes in nonmonetary ways—all of which opens up new possibilities for investing in reputational assets. For instance, a sole practitioner attorney might consider offering free workshops that educate the public on important legal rights, thus conferring a social benefit while simultaneously building credibility for potential clients.

Sometimes naysayers try to move a firm away from undertaking good citizenship, arguing that to do so throws the firm's money away. Here are some illustrations of fairly direct payoffs from investments in good citizenship. Note that the public acclaim these companies receive—what I term the "proximate payback"—often triggers a domino effect leading to more diffuse favorable reputational results touching untold numbers of constituents further down the road.

Hewlett-Packard (HP)

Good deeds: In 2001, HP contributed over $54 million in resources worldwide to educational institutions, community residents, and nonprofits to tackle the most basic difficulties. The donations targeted areas where HP employees live. The company's active volunteer committee, made up of 300 employees, searches for new ways to make HP greener.

Proximate Payback: Along with General Mills, HP was listed among the highest-ranking companies in *Business Ethics* magazine's 2003 annual corporate citizenship awards.[2]

Thanksgiving Coffee Company (TCC)

Good deeds: In 1985, TCC began investing part of its revenues in the Central American villages in which its beans are grown. This community development initiative makes for loyal suppliers. It also enables reasonable prices to be maintained when periods of small harvests occur. The firm has undertaken sustainability initiatives such as:

- Partnering with a nonprofit to plant trees in Ethiopia to offset carbon waste.
- Fueling delivery trucks with biodiesel, an alternative fuel made from vegetable oil.

- Conducting an environmental audit leading to increased recycling and de-creased energy consumption.

Proximate Payback: In 2002, TCC received an award from the state of California for outstanding environmental leadership.

Interface Carpets

Good deeds: In 1994, the company's CEO, Ray Anderson, resolved to turn the firm's 26 factories, spanning four continents, into an environmentally sustainable manufacturing outfit. The goals: Recycle whatever could be recycled, reduce pollution, and dump nothing in landfills. The firm had been using over 500 million pounds of raw material annually. It released about 900 tons of air pollutants, 600 million gallons of wastewater, and 10,000 tons of garbage each year. In two years the company achieved a whopping 23 percent more efficiency from its recycling regimen. Forty million dollars in costs were trimmed.

Proximate Payback: The savings aided Interface in capturing the winning low bid in 1997 to carpet the Gap's new headquarters. The Gap was prompted to solicit Interface's bid in light of the carpet company's environmentally friendly steps.

Best Buy

Good deeds: In 1994, Best Buy began to host the Charity Classic golf tournament, run by employee volunteers. The event teams up the company's vendor partners and golfers from the Ladies' Professional Golf Association to raise funds for the Best Buy Children's Foundation, which supports organizations and programs committed to bettering the lives of school kids. According to the company's website, in 2002 the Charity Classic raised more than $2.2 million.

Proximate Payback: In 2002, Best Buy ranked number six on *Forbes* annual list of America's most philanthropic corporations, with 1.31 percent of its income going to charity.[3]

Degrees of Good and Bad and Their Relevance to Your Firm's Core Character

Just as the law makes distinctions among degrees of offenses in meting out punishments, the court of public opinion and the court of key constitutents assign reputational rewards and penalties to business behavior according to both its gen-

Table 11.2 Evaluating Risks: How Bad? Does It Matter?

	Moral Felony *(severe offense)*	*Moral Misdemeanor* *(minor offense)*
Low relevance to core identity of the business	I. Poses high threat to reputational capital	III. Poses low threat to reputational capital
High relevance to core identity of the business	II. Poses highest threat to reputational capital	IV. Poses moderate threat to reputational capital

Table 11.3 Projecting Impact of Good Behavior

	Gold Deeds	*Silver Deeds*
Low relevance to firm's core identity	I. Moderate payoff	III. Minor payoff
High relevance to firm's core identity	II. Major payoff	IV. Moderate payoff

eral level of significance and its bearing on the particular character of the enterprise in question. The matrix in table 11.2 above relates the *severity* of misconduct— ranging from "moral felonies," which are egregious offenses of moral turpitude, to "moral misdemeanors," which are comparatively trivial missteps—to the *relevance* of the misconduct to the core identity (character) of a firm.

Examples of "moral misdemeanors"—lightweight improprieties that are remote from the core reputational attributes of a business—would include: a real estate agent who inadvertently fails to feed enough coins into the parking meter while conducting a closing; a small car repair shop that unwittingly fails to comply with obscure Occupational Safety and Health Administration regulations requiring that it keep material safety data sheets (which detail possible harmful effects of "possible toxic substances") for Windex and Joy cleaning solutions used for routine cleaning in its employee restroom.

Examples of "moral felonies," on the other hand—misdeeds closely related to the core reputational attributes of a business—would include: a law firm that intentionally misappropriates its clients' trust accounts; a coffee chain that knowingly uses beans treated with pesticides containing known carcinogens.

In devising and implementing strategies for building your company's reputational capital, allocate the most energy toward avoiding any behavior that falls into quadrants and II and I, respectively. Worry less about activities encompassed in quadrant III. Give an intermediate amount of effort toward preventing conduct within quadrant IV.

On the flip side, we can correlate the varying degrees of rightdoing (developed earlier in chapter 8) according to their relevance to core identity of the firm.

Your objective, following table 11.3, is to channel maximum effort into undertaking quadrant II behaviors, since they will lead to maximum payoff as far as reputational benefits go. Effort spent in promoting this type of behavior should be followed (in descending order of importance), by efforts producing conduct falling into quadrants IV, I, and III.

12

Strategies for Building Reputations
across Cultures

How can your firm maintain a consistent, positive reputation across borders? It's easier said than done, since different countries have different laws or government regulations, customary practices, levels of economic development, and cultural understandings.

In the global business environment, integrity and fair play are often less a matter of choosing right over wrong and more a matter of charting a responsible course through a thicket of conflict and ambiguity. Key challenges facing companies operating abroad are:

1. Legitimacy Challenge. Establishing a basic reputation for legitimacy in another country.
2. Character Challenge. Maintaining consistency in the face of cultural diversity.
3. Compliance Conflicts Challenge. Recognizing what is legal and ethical in unfamiliar and unstructured settings—that is, discerning what the rules are.
4. Corruption Challenge. Competing successfully against companies that act unethically and in countries with high levels of corruption.
5. Philanthropy Challenge. Meeting expectations of being a good citizen when operating in host countries.

In the face of these challenges, it's advantageous to start out with a critical mass of reputational capital acquired from a solid track record of conduct in your own country. This will: (1) contribute initial legitimacy that helps to overcome the negative sterotypes attached to multinational companies generally; and (2) provide an immunizing effect when the character of the company is challenged from any of the many frontal attacks afforded by exposure to a multiple cultural, legal, and ethical milieu. In other words, you want to create a presumption of innocence that your firm can carry with it no matter what part of the world it is conducting business in.

Sources of Negative Reputations

The superpower status of many multinational corporations (MNCs) leads to substantial criticism of their conduct. So there is a reputational backdrop—frankly, a rather negative one—against which multinational firms operate. Of course, MNCs bring many positive benefits: providing jobs for people in poor countries, introducing capital, helping people meet their basic needs. But the reputations of MNCs have been darkened over the years by abuses. So, public perceptions of the character of MNCs pose a duck-rabbit problem.[1] How you see them—as legitimate or illegitimate—depends on your frame of reference. Look at this figure:

Depending upon whether you perceive the figure as facing left or right, it appears as either a duck or a rabbit, respectively. Some will see retail giant Wal-Mart as a "duck"—a union-busting, employee-exploiting destroyer of local economies. Consequently, Wal-Mart confronts barriers to entering Germany and other countries skeptical of the social and economic value it provides. Others see it as "rabbit"—a positive-change agent that creates job opportunities in places that otherwise would not have them and spreads a special concern for customers to every corner of the globe. Wal-Mart is making great strides in its entry to China, where it is perceived as bringing positive benefits.

Practices for which MNCs are blamed include the following:

Exploiting people.   Critics accuse MNCs of exploiting the labor markets of less-developed host countries. Some critics, including labor unions, claim that it is unfair for MNCs to move jobs to overseas locations in search of lower wage rates. Others charge that MNCs use labor-saving devices that elevate unemployment in countries where they manufacture. So they are blamed for exacerbating the gap between rich and poor nations. Their size and financial clout enable MNCs to control money supplies, employment, and even the economic existence of less-developed countries.

Some MNCs are taken to task for paying inadequate wages. Recall the attacks on Wal-Mart—and Kathy Lee Gifford—over low wages paid to workers in Honduras. But ethical issues surrounding fair wages are complex. Sometimes MNCs pay higher wages than local employers can afford to match. In that case local businesses complain that the most productive and skilled workers go to work for multinationals.

Depleting natural resources.   Critics ask: Why should MNCs be allowed to pay a low price for the right to remove minerals, timber, oil, and other natural resources from developing countries and then sell products made from those resources for a much higher price? In many instances, only a small fraction of the ultimate sale price of such resources comes back to benefit the country of origin.

Being unfair competitiors.   Due to their diversified nature, MNCs can borrow money, using up local capital resources so that little is left for local firms. MNCs are blamed for not carrying their fair share of social development costs. They often deploy advanced technologies unavailable to local firms: The cost may be prohibitive or there's an absence of qualified people to operate the technology system. The MNCs hence become more productive and can then afford to pay higher wages to workers. Because of their advanced technology, however, they hire fewer people than would be hired by the local firms that produce the same product. And, given their economies of scale, MNCs can negotiate lower tax rates. Through manipulation of transfer payments among affiliates, they may pay little tax anywhere.

Purveying harmful products.   Since unsafe products banned in developed countries are not always banned elsewhere, MNCs sometimes sell such products where they can get away with it, causing direct harm to consumers. In some instances, MNCs cause indirect harm by introducing products that are safe for consumers in developed countries but unsafe for those in underdeveloped regions. Nestle Corporation, a Swiss firm, sustained hits to its reputation for marketing powdered infant formula in African countries. Safe use of the product requires literate consumers who can read instruction labels and use purified water to mix the formula. It is not appropriate to give free promotional samples of the product to indigent mothers who cannot afford to purchase it when the samples run out, particularly if their own natural supply of breastmilk has been let down from formula feeding. Nestle, along with other infant formula makers, promoted infant formula to illiterate mothers who used unsanitary water to mix and dilute the formula. Many babies died as a result. Subsequently, the company agreed to follow a code authored by the World Health Organization for marketing breast milk substitutes.

Importing dangerous technology.   Some MNCs fail to exercise due care with regard to products they bring into less-developed countries. The reputation of Dow Chemical is saddled by reports of illiterate and uneducated workers from developing countries lacking technologically advanced protective gear using their pesticides. People from remote villages have been found using pesticides to help capture fish; others used empty insecticide containers to trap rain for their drinking supply.

Union Carbide's industrial accident in Bhopal, India, involving the leak of deadly methyl isocyanate from a storage facility, killing 2,000 and injuring 200,000, left a black mark on its reputation. The company's executives seriously miscalculated how much hands-on management the Bhopal plant called for in light of the country's poor infrastructure and thin regulation. In the wake of the poisonous gas leak, the firm was faulted for failing to oversee the safe deployment of advanced technology.

Disrupting local economies.   The practices of MNCs sometimes fail to respect the economies of host countries. Many heavy-equipment companies from developed nations promote construction equipment to foreign companies that hope to build major roads, dams, and utility complexes. They say that the equipment will speed up completion of these projects, to the country's benefit. But some critics from less-developed countries counter that such equipment purchases remove hard currency from their economies, increasing unemployment. Some believe it's better in the long run to hire laborers to do construction work than to invest in heavy equipment. This keeps hard currency in the local economy and creates jobs— enhancing the quality of life more than quick projects would.

Supporting rights-violating regimes.   The conduct of some MNCs evince heavy-handed interference with local politics. ITT's involvement with the overthrow of Allende in Chile, Shell Oil's collusion with the military government in Nigeria, and Pepsi's and Unocal's investments in Myanmar create reputations for riding piggyback on brutal regimes that systematically violate the human rights of their populations.

Contaminating cultures.   MNCs are condemned for dominating cultures. Disney's European theme park, Euro Disney, is a classic illustration. Due to critical press, the Walt Disney Company set the park in a European context. French was slated to be the primary language, with multilingual signs, and several park areas were to feature French themes. But even before its doors opened, the park was lambasted for its U.S. cultural imperialism. A theater director from Paris dubbed the park "cultural Chernobyl." Another critic deplored the "horror of cardboard, plastic, atrocious colors, solidified chewing-gum constructions, and idiotic folk stories that come straight out of cartoon books for fat Americans. It is going to wipe out millions of children." Saboteurs destroyed an electricity tower, plunging the park into darkness on the eve of its opening. On opening day, employees of a nearby railway station struck in an effort to discredit the park's reputation.

Working to Establish Legitimacy

MNCs are actively working to counter the unwelcome reputation they have inherited. Some MNCs are trying to help organize labor unions and implement minimum wage laws. Following the tragic incident at Bhopal, Union Carbide has assumed a leadership role, guiding other companies on how to safely implement hazardous techology in developing nations. Cisco Systems donates computer systems to schools, gave $50 million to NetAid for Africa, and pushed for Third World debt relief. In 2001, Hewlett Packard contributed over $54 million in resources across the globe to help teachers, students, nonprofits and community residents.

Coca-Cola, Du Pont, Levi-Strauss, Chevron-Texaco, Wal-Mart, and many other companies endorse business responsibility abroad. These companies support a globally based resource system called Business for Social Responsibility (BSR). BSR tracks emerging issues and trends, provides information on corporate leadership and best practices, conducts educational workshops and training, and assists in developing practical business ethics tools. BSR has also established formal partnerships with other organizations that focus on corporate responsibility in Brazil, Israel, the United Kingdom, Chile, and Panama.

Attracting Criticism Even When Acting Ethically?

Keeping a reputation intact requires not only acting ethically from the vantage point of one's own culture—but also being perceived as forthright from the perspective of other, sometimes radically different, cultures. The following Italian-U.S. tax scenario illustrates how hard balancing divergent cultural viewpoints can be. In most countries, including the United States, it is now considered a violation of the letter and spirit of the law for a company to ignore standard accounting practices. Yet during parts of Italy's history it was accepted practice for companies to understate annual earnings by a third when reporting to the government. Knowing this, the government in turn automatically raised each firm's income statements by one third, imposing taxes on the more accurate estimate, which companies willingly paid. Thus, because of a cultural practice known to both the business community and the government, Italian companies did not actually lie to their government when they understated their income: What looked like a fraudulent scheme to outsiders was, in the cultural context, a clearly understood signal of a company's true income.

Consider also the plight of H. B. Fuller Company. The St. Paul, Minnesota–based adhesives manufacturer has operations in more than 40 countries spanning Asia, Europe, Latin America, and North America. The firm enjoyed a local reputation within the Twin Cities as a socially responsible firm. It endowed a domestic university chair in business ethics and set up a charitable foundation for the environment, the arts, and social programs. The firm's mission statement puts its commitment to customers first, and responsibilities to employees and shareholders second. The statement says H. B. Fuller will do business legally and ethically and be a responsible corporate citizen. But the company's well-constructed reputation for corporate responsibility—grown in the United States—didn't travel well across borders and ended up getting trashed when the company stolidly insisted that it had no responsibility for the misuse of a product manufactured by its Guatemalan subsidiary.

H. B. Fuller's reputation nightmare started in 1985, when media stories emerged that street children in Guatemala, Honduras, Nicaragua, and El Salvador were sniffing Resistol, a shoe glue made by the company.

The debacle took the firm by surprise. Insisting that glue sniffing in Central America was a social ill, not a problem with its product, the company halted marketing of Resistol to retailers in 1993. But it kept selling big containers of glue to industrial customers. The next year the company altered the glue's chemical make-up and raised prices to deter kids' use. Yet activist protests persisted, calling for an end of Resistol sales to industrial customers and to retailers in Central

American countries. Shareholder meetings were picketed, with critics asking how a firm with a conscience could sell a substance that was burning out children's brains. Wrongful-death lawsuits were launched, placing millions of dollars and the reputations of the company's top leaders at risk. Finally, in 1995, the company came to its own defense by dispatching a statement of retrenchment. H. B. Fuller asserted that it didn't actually make or sell Resistol—in fact a subsidiary of a subsidiary of the firm in Latin America manufactured and sold the product.

Why was such a well-reputed firm hammered for its sales of Resistol? The company's rivals were also making and selling glue abused by street children in Central America, yet were not the target of attack. The answer seems to be that not much was expected from the other companies, so critics generally ignored them. Whereas acting good, and advertising it, made H. B. Fuller more vulnerable to being made an example by child advocates, shareholders, plaintiffs, and the news media. By its refusal to assume responsibility for the addiction of street children to the products of its subsidiaries, H. B. Fuller's reputation was left to drift about, unanchored, in parts of the world where it did not see itself as accountable for unintentional, indirect harm.

Such cases stand as reminders that doing business across borders means that frames of reference for values are constantly in flux. Accordingly, you should keep tabs on both the narrow, local reputation of the firm as well as its broader global reputation. An unwelcome reputation can develop in corners of the world that get neglected. Having a great reputation in the eyes of members of the home country alone won't cut it.

How International Contexts Elevate Reputational Risk

Internationally, businesses face heightened reputational risks from the following factors:

Lack of supervision. There is often diluted supervision from the home office. The transgressions leading to the demise of Barings P.L.C., one of the oldest merchant banks, provide a graphic illustration. While stationed in Singapore, employee Nick Leeson wore two hats—he was not only the principal trader but bookkeeper as well, giving him a special opportunity to hide massive losses from his superiors in London.[2]

Lax legal standards. Some foreign governments do not have effective laws to curb unfair or abusive business practices.

Nike has been lambasted for using child labor and underpaying workers in Third World sweatshops to make big-buck sneakers. In October 1996, Nike tried to burnish its image by launching an independent study. Its contention: Laborers in Indonesia and Vietnam owned VCRs and were actually pretty well off. Ernst and Young conducted an audit a few weeks later. Result: Accounts of unsafe workplace conditions in one of the firm's Vietnamese factories hit the *New York Times* front page. News reports disclosed that in 1996 Nike paid Michael Jordan $30 million for his endorsement. That sum surpassed the combined wages of 19,000 non–U.S. factory workers. The reputation-slashing message broadcast around the world: Nike trades off human dignity with marketing.

Intent to help.   Corporate leaders sometimes think that they are helping the people of a country, leading them to believe their behavior is legitimate. This is often a complicated matter. It should be seen from several points of view. If a multinational company does business with a corrupt or rights-violating government, but is actually trying to do all it can to help the citizens of the country, is the company acting with integrity?

U.S. Congress voted in 2000 to establish permanent "normal trading relations" with China. So debate about how multinational companies should deal with human rights violations is becoming prominent. Many companies have a strong presence in China. Among them are Amoco, Boeing, Chevron, Coca-Cola, General Motors, IBM, Kodak, McDonald's, Microsoft, Motorola, Occidental Petroleum, Procter and Gamble, and Texaco. But customers, employees, and investors sometimes press these companies about how they deal with human rights in their China operations.

For instance, in November 2001, at its annual shareholder meeting, executives of Microsoft faced a group of stockholders skeptical of the software company's operations in China. They wanted Microsoft to take measures advancing human rights. The shareholder proposal pointed out that Microsoft is increasingly becoming involved in China, operating a subsidiary at a research and development center in Beijing and an engineering center in Shanghai for which an additional $14 million in investments were slated.

The shareholders behind the proposal, owners of more than 55,000 shares, voiced concern about labor rights problems, human rights problems, and sales of software to police and security services that might assist the Chinese government in suppressing dissent. The proposal alleged that China does not enforce labor laws and has a deplorable human rights record. It criticized China for permitting labor rights abuses such as physical abuse, forced labor, child labor, improper wage deductions, and hazardous work conditions.

The shareholder proposal urged Microsoft to adopt basic standards for companies operating in China. The standards were supported by several nongovernmental organizations and companies including Levi-Strauss, Reebok, and Mattel.

Microsoft's board recommended a vote against the proposal. It was unnecessary, they said. The company's code ensures compliance with the laws of the countries in which it operates, the promotion of a healthy environment, and the prohibition of discrimination and harassment.

Other companies say that multinational firms in China should not promote human rights. By doing so they lose the political neutrality required to be successful in China. Some companies also contend it is wrong for them to impose ideas about human rights on foreign countries and claim, like Microsoft, that they need only comply with the local laws of countries in which they do business.

Delusions of immunity.   Managers perceive that they can easily get away with bad behavior, and it can pay off. This is seen clearly in the case of bribery. Bribery is widespread and seldom prosecuted in many countries. So managers that decide to bribe officials often don't have to worry about getting caught. Also, for the short term at least, bribery can pay, or, at least, a decision not to bribe can be very costly.

On June 2, 1998, an Argentine federal judge issued international arrest warrants for four executives and former executives of IBM on allegations of fraud and bribery. The payments in question were $37 million in kickbacks to directors of the state-owned Banco de la Nacion Argentina in the award of a $250 million information systems contract. There was evidence that top managers of IBM's Argentine unit transferred funds through a shell company to "buy the good will" of the bank's former directors.[3] IBM claimed it did nothing illegal. However, it admitted to errors that were "inconsistent with company policy."[4] As a consequence of the investigation, IBM decided to cease computer engineering deals with the public sector in Latin American governments. Its shift in sales to the private sector, with sales of computer systems to the government only through local distributors, was evidently made to distance itself from the bribery allegations. In Argentina, bribery, kickbacks, and payoffs are accepted as normal. But people's expectations are higher for a world-class corporation such as IBM. They expect IBM to follow nobler norms than those customary in Argentina; the firm is looked to as a leader in helping to eradicate corruption in Argentina.

No adverse consequences.   There is sometimes relatively little pressure on firms to act with integrity and fair play in international settings. For instance, Starbucks was awarded the International Human Rights Award by the Council on Economic Priorities, a consumer organization. This came after Starbucks was under attack for exploiting Guatemalan coffee pickers. A Guatemalan worker was paid an average of $2.50 a day—way below a living daily wage. The reason that Starbucks got the award anyway is that it announced a "framework" for a code of conduct on improving the quality of life in regions where they purchase coffee.[5] Starbuck's senior vice president for corporate social responsibility, David Olsen, said, "We are choosing an approach that is proactive, developmental. Perhaps it's incremental . . . and sometimes too slow for my tastes. . . . But we believe that it is positive."[6] The company promised that a review of plantation conditions was being carried out by the Guatemalan Coffee Growers Association, the very organization accused of perpetuating the low wages. First condemned for labor practices it could not change, Starbucks was then praised for actions it had not yet taken. This shows a trend in which good intentions are becoming the new standards of international corporate ethics. Starbucks hadn't actually done anything to solve the problem with Guatemalan workers, but the fact that it expressed intent seemed to be enough for many in the business community. Companies often practice bribery and unfair labor practices when they can do so without repercussions from governments or the business community. Until they get caught.

Failing to synchronize information across operations in different countries. In August 2000, Bridgestone/Firestone, a U.S. subsidiary of Japan's Bridgestone Corporation, was facing mounting reports of personal injuries due to tread plying from rims, mainly on Ford Explorers. Ford and Bridgestone/Firestone jointly ordered a recall on 6.5 million tires in the United States. Tire-related accidents caused 250 injuries and 88 deaths in the United States and 51 fatalities in countries throughout Latin America, the Middle East, and Southeast Asia.

The reputations of both Ford and Bridgestone/Firestone were at risk. People were wondering how long the companies had known about the risks—and why they hadn't done anything earlier.

Information surfaced showing that both Ford and Bridgestone/Firestone knew about the risk of tread separation well in advance of the recall. Insurance companies were clueing Firestone officials about abnormally high numbers of accidents with their tires as far back as 1997. People at Ford evidently knew about tread separation problems because, in 1999 and 2000 the company replaced Firestone tires on Explorers in 16 countries, including Saudi Arabia, Venezuela, and Thailand.

The reputational liability soon turned into a loss of reputational capital. As the charts below indicate, the stock of both companies took a pounding. Notice the sharp decline in Ford's stock price on the Nasdaq index in the month after the recall announcement:

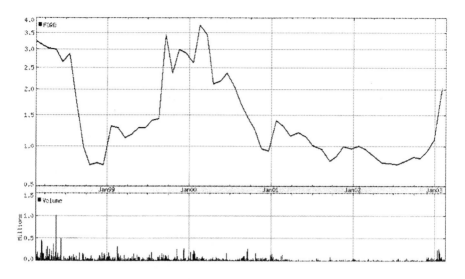

Chart 12.1: Drop in Ford stock price
http://finance.yahoo.com/q?s=FORD&d=c&k=1&a=v&p=s&t=5y&l=on&z=1&q=1.
Copyright © 2002 Yahoo! Inc.

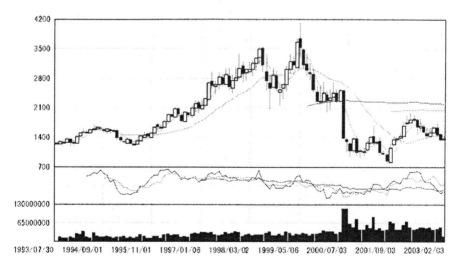

Chart 12.2: Drop in Bridgestone stock price
http://finance.nify.com/cgi-bin/stocks/vchart.cgi?WORD=5108&KUBUN=t1

Likewise, in Japan, as chart 12.2 shows, Bridgestone's stock plummeted on the Tokyo exchange following an investigation launched upon its tire recall.

Initial estimates of the cost of the recall were placed at about $500 million. But toward the end of 2001, that amount was topping $2 billion for Bridgestone/ Firestone. Meanwhile, Ford had earmarked $3 billion to cover the replacement cost for 13 million Bridgestone/Firestone tires on its vehicles because of tread separation risks uncovered by its own tests. The recall and investigation ignited immense negative publicity. Worldwide consumer confidence in the companies fell dramatically; a study emerging shortly after the recall found that consumer trust dropped 39 percent in Asia-Pacific, 47 percent in South America, and 14 percent in Africa.[7] Other polls reveal dramatic declines in consumers' respect for the companies:

- Harris poll: the recall was "extremely or very likely" to influence 25 percent of the respondents in their decision to purchase a Ford product; 22 percent said the recall was "somewhat likely" to influence their decision. Sixty-seven percent said recall was "extremely or very likely" to influence decision to buy a Firestone product.[8]
- E-business.com survey: reported 82 percent judged that Firestone intentionally sat on safety data before recalling the tires.
- *Newsweek* poll: More than 80 percent of U.S. respondents believed Bridgestone/Firestone was culpable for neglecting to warn consumers about the dangers of rollover accidents.[9]

Sales of Firestone tires and Ford Explorers dropped, with distributors and customers switching to alternative suppliers. Bridgestone received downgrades in its credit and investment ratings. Plaintiffs initiated lawsuits, and criminal charges were mounted concerning 1,400 complaints, 525 injuries, and 148 deaths in the United States. Authorities in Venezuela targeted Ford for 46 deaths involving Explorers that occurred in that country.

Given the dramatic impact the tire ply problems had on the companies' reputations, why did the companies parry so long before taking action? The answer seems to be that the right hand didn't know what the left hand was doing—a problem exacerbated in the transnational business context. Even though Bridgestone/Firestone had reams of data detailing tread ply problems, it was dispersed among separate functional silos: engineering, finance, warranty claims, legal compliance, customer relations, marketing, and quality control. Critical data about cases cropping up across many different countries was not compiled and reviewed systematically from a safety point of view—much less from a reputational perspective.

Ford's general counsel and chief safety official, armed with information about cases from a variety of jurisdictions, wasn't on a distribution list for a notorious memo addressed to Ford's CEO, its vice president for international operations, and six vice presidents. In what became an infamous memo of 1999, Ford's group vice president for purchasing showed that he knew about tread ply problems for Explorers driven for long distances at high velocity in Saudi Arabia, Oman, Qatar, and Venezuela. But he was under the misconception that those were the only occurences.

Ford did not compile systematic data on tire performance and was not privy to tire warranty claims. Only after Ford learned of the government's investigation and negotiated access to Firestone's claims and warranty data did the company become equipped to compile and analyze evidence of tread ply problems.

In hindsight, it's clear that the companies should have taken greater care to ensure that their organizational systems were aligned with their espoused values. Upon his installation as CEO of Bridgestone/Firestone shortly after the recall, John Lampe laid plans for breaking down barriers that impeded information flow about the tire defects. In Japan, Bridgestone rolled out new methods for ensuring that claims information would reach Tokyo and designated personnel in order to maintain strict production standards.

Dealing with Conflicting Rules

Conducting business across borders invariably brings up the age-old problem of which folkways to adopt. When in Rome should you do as the Romans do, or just act as you would at home?

BE FLEXIBLE

Many Omega firms operating across borders are caught in a compliance conflict trap. They look at dilemmas with an either-or mindset: Should we follow home or host standards? They turn to mechanical formulas and algorithms that only give an artificial resolution to the tension between "when in Rome" and "foreign imperialist." But this is almost always a dead end. What I tell corporate leaders to do is look for responsible alternative solutions where none seem to be.

You might sponsor a park beautification initiative in a foreign country, earning political support and public trust while thwarting requests for bribes from government officials there. Your company can try to eliminate child labor from the production chain. Or, in cases where unemployed children and their families would be hurt, your company can set up benefits programs that provide medical care and education for child laborers. Levi-Strauss took a creative step by paying children's school tuition, providing uniforms and books, and offering each child a job at age fourteen. Other companies, such as Adidas, are requiring suppliers that hire children to agree not just to keep them in school but also to pay the children normal wages while attending school.

Of course, attention still needs to be given to existing rules. Multinational corporations face an intricate, multilayered array of cultural, ethical, and legal norms. The norms subsist at local, national regional, international, and global levels. The presence of such normative complexity and depth signals the need for ethics programs that assimilate such characteristics. Many companies are taking action to do this. At a meeting in Switzerland of the Caux Round Table—a body of senior business leaders from firms in Europe, Japan, and the United States—the group subscribed to an international code of ethics, providing a global framework for conduct and ethical standards.

GET CLEAR ABOUT WHAT IS ETHICALLY FIXED VERSUS WHAT IS ETHICALLY OPEN

- Some standards (like truth telling and respect for property) are well-defined and established.
- Some norms (such as bans on nepotism) vary from group to group and are context specific.

Here's a checklist to consult to help maintain a positive reputation when doing business across cultures:

- Comply with human rights and fundamental freedoms.[10] Those rights and freedoms applying either directly (because of business practices that violate them) or indirectly (because companies do business with governments that violate them) to multinational firms include:

  Nondiscrimination in employment

  Freedom of movement within one's country

  Due process of law

  Privacy

  Physical security

  Freedom from torture

  Fair wages

Ownership of property

Basic education

Freedom of speech, expression, religion, and assembly

- Respect values and customs of countries in which the firm operates.
- Avoid practices, products, and services that have harmful effects on both immediate and remote stakeholders in host countries or a negative impact on cultural practices.
- Don't interfere in the internal affairs and local politics of host countries.
- Abstain from corrupt practices, refusing to offer, pay, or accept bribes.
- Assist host countries with their long-term economic and social development.
- Negotiate and implement contracts and agreements in good faith.
- Avoid practices that adversely affect the international flow of technology.
- Do not cause injury to health nor jeopardize the safety of consumers.
- Do not create variance in the quality of products in various markets, which might have a detrimental effect on consumers.
- Disclose information to the public about possible hazards from products and services.
- Take measures to protect the environment, and rehabilitate it when it's damaged by the firm's activities.
- Disclose information about products and services that may harm the environment.
- Assist in establishing equitable ethical and legal support systems at the domestic, regional, and international level.
- Foster fair competition; respect tangible and intellectual property rights; avoid collusion; promote open markets; avoid industrial espionage.

Many of those engaged in international business are unaware of the many different ethical issues that arise on multiple levels—that is, at the level of the firm, at the level of host culture and government, at the level of home culture and government, and at the level of international institutions. Some of the reasons for this knowledge gap are:

- Legal and moral standards of a foreign culture may not be known by the associates, or are known only from an "external" point of view.

- The associates have an inadequate understanding of relevant human rights standards and other international guidelines pertaining to their business activities.
- Legal and regulatory institutions may be undeveloped in some host countries and therefore do not serve as a backdrop for normative guidance.
- The corporation may not receive, or may misinterpret, feedback concerning misconduct and harm it is producing in host countries.

So take special care to be sure your company is not deceiving itself with a self-assessment of its reputational posture in the international environment. If its understanding of what it means to "do the right thing" is too parochial, its assessment of reputational risk is in danger of being incomplete, inaccurate, and misleading. It's a good idea to use external consultants with expertise in international ethics, as well as those familiar with the ethical environment of host country operations.

GLOBALIZE YOUR CODE

When business operations expand abroad, a firm's code of conduct should not remain parochial, that is, grounded only in national mores. The code should embody recently evolved standards, many of which have been promulgated especially for international business. "Internationalizing" parts of the code—and communicating what it means as far as day-to-day business is concerned—helps make people in the company more aware of the worldwide ethical context within which the firm is operating. Having an awareness that international ethics standards for business are in place along with national standards tends to make the two sets mutually supportive. Knowing that bribery is forbidden *both* by local law *and* by the global initiatives, the prohibited practice can be seen not simply as the product of domestic political forces but as a norm attracting broad consensus throughout the international community. Conversely, transnational codes enjoy greater credibility the more individual nation-states implement and enforce their norms through their own legislation.

Avoid putting vague, abstract phrases like "avoid corruption and bribery" into the code. There is a danger that the workforce will not understand what this means, much less know how to comply with such a command. It is necessary to communicate what the practical meanings of the standards are as far as the associates' business conduct goes. How is this done?

Consider hooking your firm's ethics hotline (keeping it confidential) and ethics office up to electronic mail. Since e-mail access is now so widespread—and since it's such an excellent medium for international communications especially—it can provide a forum not only for inquiries about what the code means but also for swapping reports of ethical situations that associates are confronting in various legal and cultural settings throughout the world.

American Express uses an "Issues and Answers" column in its newsletter, which is sent out to employees worldwide to address questions concerning the interpretation and application of its code of conduct.[11]

Meeting the Corruption Challenge

Increased global competition adds to the temptation to seek advantages through questionable practices. Companies are more willing than ever before to resort to unconventional methods to make a sale because every sale is cherished. During the next decade the pervasiveness of such corrupt practices means troubled times lie ahead as firms compete for an estimate $1 trillion dollars in overseas infrastructure projects.

Suppose that, while rival firms pass dollars under the table to get regulatory authorities to approve new product introductions, your firm publicly offers a generous gift, say shade trees for the city's parks, that will benefit the people at large.

CHAMPION CORRUPTION COMBAT AS A HUMANITARIAN RESPONSIBILITY

Given their financial resources, firms from developed countries could be said to have a humanitarian obligation to fight corruption and graft. Your rivals that provide bribes and incentives to corrupt public officials and politicians subvert the orderly development of poor nations that are caught in a vicious circle of poverty, hunger, and disease.

JUST SAY "NO"

Consider just walking away from any kind of bribery. In some countries it's said to be impossible to conduct business unless deals are done under the table. But your firm can commit to conducting all transactions above board. If, in a given market, that's not possible, you leave. HDFC of Mumbai, India, firmly opposes bribery. Associates are told to end talks if customers offer bribes. The company wants to send a clear signal: It's not the sort of firm that accepts bribes. This is also the approach that IBM has long been reputed to take, which makes the alleged bribery incidents with its Argentina subsidiary come as a bit of a shock.

Notice that once you gain this kind of reputation it's less likely that your firm and its members will be asked for bribes. The force of the reputation for shunning all bribes makes it easier to say no when bribes are solicited.

CALL CORRUPT PLAYERS ON THE CARPET

Unfair practices, such as bribery and corruption, are most effective in the dark, thriving on people's reluctance to confront them. So publicity accomplishes these tasks:

- Opens up your opponent's unfair fighting to public scrutiny.
- Allows you to mobilize public pressure against the corrupt practices.

One firm pressured to pay bribes began a massive letter-writing campaign to the local government authorities asking why this additional payment was being requested of them.

TEAM UP WITH OTHERS

When competitors contrive to avoid taxes, use bribes or kickbacks to get business, or when they jeopardize worker safety to control costs, honest and forthright companies find themselves at a disadvantage. In regions lacking social and legal structures to support fair business practices, firms are pressured to compromise even basic standards to stay competitive. It may be necessary to work for changes in laws, regulations, or industry practices. Collaboration with government, industry groups, community representatives, or nongovermental organizations may be called for.

GATHER THE COURAGE TO GO AGAINST THE GRAIN

Guaranty Trust Bank (GTB) entered the Nigerian banking industry, one saturated with corruption, with ambitious goals: to attain outstanding financial returns through forthright conduct, provide exemplary customer service, and be a good corporate citizen. Because of nationwide trends toward deregulation and liberalization, Nigeria had experienced a rise in its number of banks and finance companies. Aspiring Nigerians were clamoring to seize the opportunities that were opening up due to the departure of a lot of big international banks. GTB aimed to conduct business professionally, with a commitment to integrity in all its operations. It wished to achieve superior results on the basis of talent and effort— not through graft. The founders saw a chance to build a venerable and enduring enterprise.

Yet soon after opening its doors, the bank's vision met a serious challenge. At years' end the bank had yet to start earning money. Should it report a first-six-month loss, or pass it on to next year? Some board members made a bid for nondisclosure. But founders Fola Adeola and Tayo Aderinokun believed the loss should be published. After all, this would be a candid move that would announce GTB's credibility to the market. Garnering the board's endorsement, they published the loss. Miraculously, no adverse consequences flowed from the bold, unorthodox transparency.

A second challenge came up in connection with a tax audit showing shortages in prior tax payments from the bank's employees. GTB instituted a policy mandating proper withholding and requiring employees to pay the bank back for deficiencies it had advanced on their behalf. But that stance drew ire from employees, some of whom resigned, lowering overall morale. In turn, the bank scrutinized its culture, engaging everyone in the process. This became a way of turning a problem into an opportunity for leading recruits down a new path consistent with the bank's vision and culture.

In 1996, GTB, along with a Citibank subsidiary, earned a top risk rating. Getting listed on the Nigerian stock exchange led to a president's merit award for advancing corporate governance and fostering healthy competition among quoted enterprises. The bank won the award again in 1999. Recently, Nigeria's leading rating firm, Agusto and Company, conferred a A+ rating, confirming the bank's solid financial performance for 2002.

CONDUCT ANTICORRUPTION TRAINING

To establish itself as a Zeta company your organization needs a company-wide training program that will serve to reinforce its commitments overseas. Effective methods of training are interactive workshops, small group exercises, and case studies that assist in training employees to recognize ethical dilemmas in foreign contexts and then demonstrate how to work through them. Your corporation should ensure that its code of conduct clearly and concisely spells out in practical terms its stand on corrupt actions by its associates. Employees should be made to understand that they should not compromise personal integrity in the face of a job situation. They should be helped to see that once you compromise yourself or your company, you will always be expected by others to operate in a similar corrupt manner. In most cases there is no turning back.

In the training program, companies should emphasize that an aggressive approach works best when doing business in the international arena. This means that the company representative should make it clear to any foreign customer that his or her corporation doesn't make payoffs or questionable "consultant fees" and so on.

An integral part of the training program should be to gain a complete understanding of international business practices. This training program should have phases that begin before the prospective company representative leaves the host country and continue once she relocates. Often the company representative will not relocate, but will travel back and forth among the host country and several international locations. In this case, the program should be comprehensive enough at the firm's headquarters as to fully prepare the employee for numerous dilemma situations. The program should explore subjects such as: cultural awareness, local laws, local customs, speaking with local (foreign) lawyers, speaking with expatriate managers experienced in working in various overseas markets, speaking with members of the local chamber of commerce, and if possible, speaking with the in-country state department representative, possibly the commercial attaché at the local embassy or consulate for the home country.

A supplement to the training program can come from information compiled by a local business journalist contracted by your firm. This person theoretically should have a better read on local business conditions than a journalist from your home country would have. The information supplied should include how seriously corruption and bribery are viewed in the host country. In addition, you would want to know which companies recently have been involved in a corruption scandal and how the local government authorities and courts dealt with the matter.

Finally, upon relocating to the host country, the expatriate manager should follow a procedure of completing a cursory background investigation of everyone who will work for the company as a consultant, representative, distributor, wholesaler, agent, licensee, and joint venture partner. The focus of the investigation should be the reputation that person has in the local business community—with an obvious emphasis on discovering any hints of past dishonest business practices. Upon approval, all employees must be made to fully understand the corporation's policy, translated into all local dialects, with regard to corruption and bribery. It might seem unusual to many foreign workers, but each should be made to sign a statement that they have read, understand, and will abide by the company's rules with regard to corrupt business practices.

Global Corporate Philanthropy

A significant number of multinational companies are practicing global corporate philanthropy. As multinationals derive large portions of their profits from foreign endeavors, the firms are finding that local communities, nongovernmental organizations (NGOs), and governments expect multinationals to play a positive role in local affairs. Transnational involvement is often viewed as a strategic investment as well as goodwill by fostering stable business environments, training programs, and overall economic growth.

There are a wide variety of methods your firm can adopt to give charitably. Large corporations with deep pockets often choose to create their own programs, not trusting their funds to the charitable distributions of foreign governments or to NGOs that use a large percentage of donations for administrative costs. This method also allows them to expand their world vision as a branding tool.

Many large corporations, such as Mobil Exxon, J. P. Morgan, Ford, IBM, and International Paper, have corporate citizenship programs. Such programs help companies manage their reputational risk, increase their reputational capital, and enhance their performance. In the context of globalization, transnational companies feel a need to acknowledge the powerful impact that they have upon the local society and consequently become more actively engaged with social or environmental issues.

Nike created a loan program to help women in communities where the company has suppliers. Originating in Vietnam in 1998, the program later was set up in Indonesia and Thailand as well. The initiative helps women grow small businesses. After making sure that borrowers have developed a business plan and undergone business training, the company has extended loans for raising livestock and manufacturing products such as clothing and incense.[12]

Another popular method of philanthropy is the foundation. The Soros Foundation has several of its own international initiatives, all removed from its core business. They include the Burma Project, Central Eurasia Project, Forced Migration Projects, and the Landmines Project made famous by Princess Diana's involvement in countries such as Angola. There are also several joint projects with the United Nations and affiliated NGOs. The projects have extensive strategies that dig down into the roots of the problems they are attempting to change. Joint effort with the United Nations and NGOs provides a third-party entity to organizations that assures donors and preserves the integrity of the project from the self-interest of organizations.

But interpreting the apparent goodwill of philanthropic decision making in the global context can be problematic. Even when the best of intentions are behind international philanthropy and goodwill giving of multinational corporations, the results can potentially cause more harm than good. In worst-case scenarios they can be disastrous. Moreover, different cultures have different opinions on what is ethical or not, and in extending goodwill gestures, corporations must be attuned to these differences.

Although no international laws, guidelines, or governing bodies exist to police gestures of corporate goodwill, several regional organizations provide guidelines for multinational corporations to follow.

Many agencies set voluntary codes of conduct for doing business around the world. They call for businesses to engage in practices that encourage good corporate citizenship and make a positive contribution to the communities in which the company operates. They hope to create environments where ethical conduct is recognized, valued, and exemplified by employers.

Here are some ways your firm can balance its reputational, or self-promotional, needs with philanthropic activities:

Create global community mission statements.   Write global community involvement mission statements to express your company's goals and objectives in helping local communities. You should allow local operating units a certain amount of autonomy in implementing projects within host countries.

Make global community involvement strategic.   Incorporate community involvement into your company's business plan for given regions. Think strategically about such initiatives, harnessing corporate assets with the aim of fulfilling key business goals, such as supporting local infrastructure development (including health care, education, and agriculture), enhancing job skills of local residents, providing investment and income flows through various community economic development initiatives, supporting local business development, introducing technology, and sharing standards and business practices with local companies.

Examine the project's impact.   Take a big-picture perspective of projects. In other words, ensure that addressing community needs does not unintentionally cause environmental, human rights, or workplace problems.

Seek local advice.   Solicit local advice on how to best be of service to the local community and on what types of resources could best serve its needs. In some instances, it may be appropriate to provide personnel, supplies, or facilities. In other situations, needs may best be served through financial grants that help local communities address their own challenges. Whenever possible, collaborate with and seek feedback from the most diverse group possible, one that includes representatives of both government and citizen groups. Operate with transparency, keeping publicly accessible records of meetings and projects.

Take a supply-chain perspective. Seek opportunities within your supply chain and examine the key issues of suppliers and the communities where they operate. Also consider making grants or offering assistance based on raw material sourcing. Doing so can engender goodwill among key trading business partners and can also help ensure a sustainable supply of materials by helping to stabilize suppliers' local economies and communities.

Budget and monitor fund use carefully. Beware of misappropriation of resources by taking care not to inadvertently perpetuate traditional hierarchies and economic inequalities by dealing exclusively with local leaders who may have only their own self-interests at heart. Ensure that funds exist not only to create programs or facilities but also to keep them in operation.

Communicate the company's commitment. Use both internal and external communication mechanisms to demonstrate your company's commitment to the communities in which you operate. Whenever possible, partner with local government agencies and local nonprofit organizations to issue communiqués about specific projects and initiatives.

Assess and measure. Take stock of the impact your company is having. Use this information to review and revise initiatives on an ongoing basis. Whenever possible, describe the impact of company community activities in quantifiable terms, as in a cost-benefit analysis. Some companies measure the direct and indirect cost savings and benefits realized by both the company and the community.

Link rewards to community involvement. Include global community involvement in managers' performance reviews and compensation. This underscores your company's commitment to these projects and also helps to link them with the company's business goals in the minds of those at all levels of the company.

Possible Objections

Let's consider a few criticisms of global corporate philanthropy. First, some may object that it is contrary to conventional roles of business to expect profit-driven corporations to give up revenues or resources for "charitable" purposes. Such critics ought to bear in mind that today's business paradigm imposes a corporate duty of aid. The reputations of companies doing business internationally are measured against background norms intimately bound up with and presupposed by familiar direct legal duties of the corporation that are themselves widely accepted in the international business community. This helps to explain why critics justifiably blame multinational companies for evading their fair share of taxes imposed by governments of developing host countries. The host governments have *pro tanto* less revenue available to assist their own indigent citizens in need of aid as a consequence of this maneuver.

It may be argued that if corporations assume general responsibility for philanthropic duties, the price tag becomes astronomical. Restoring physical security, property, and civil liberties, or providing food and shelter to the homeless, are awesome tasks that could even outstrip the coffers of some nation states. Yet, as business academics have argued in recent years, there is a social contract between corporations and communities. Corporations need society to exist, and society in turn needs the corporations' products. As an extension of this ideal, many multinational corporations set out to improve communities related to their operations in host countries with varying degrees of self-interest. The critics' argument also fails to recognize the solid reputational benefits that international philanthropy can generate for multinational corporations.

Another objection might point to potential dangers such as aid abandonment. Say a multinational corporation establishes itself in a host environment and sets out to raise local standards of living such as health and education. The multinational pulls out after a few years and discontinues its aid. With no available funding for such programs, the community falls into a worse situation than it was in before: The conditions may be the same, but the expectations for a better life have been raised.

Mobil Exxon has established itself in Equatorial Guyana. It is already developing its community consciousness in the widely destitute area. Mobil has several different programs in the various countries in which it operates to elevate local benchmarks in health, education, and environmental issues. As it enters a new host environment, part of Mobil Exxon's entry strategy is to leverage these programs to gain acceptance by local government and populations. But if the region turns out to be barren of oil deposits in a few years, what would become of these initiatives as the company moves elsewhere?

Similarly, a shortsighted aid program can be problematic. Pharmaceuticals may "donate" large quantities of a certain medication to a region in great need of it. The medication may in turn save many lives and create dramatic changes for those who would have otherwise been victims of disease and epidemic. But once the promotional handout is completed and the supply of free drugs finished, how can the poor survive if their survival depends on the drug? Financial contributions by multinationals made directly to foreign governments are sometimes questionable, especially when such donations are not directed toward a government charity of social or ecological initiative.

Finally, there are some pitfalls connected with cause-related marketing. The mutual benefits of cause-related marketing to both nonprofit organizations and the corporation are evident. The company sells more products, and the nonprofit receives money to further its mission. If prices and quality are the same, consumers often opt for the brand associated with the charity. The danger to the nonprofit organization is that if it does not exercise caution in entering a cause-related marketing partnership, it may lend its name and logo to potential scandal. Another danger is exemplified by the American Medical Association (AMA) which was the target of a breach of contract suit filed by Sunbeam after the AMA had second thoughts about their cause-related marketing partnership with the company.

All of these philanthropic dangers coincide with the degree of promotion of the corporate image. It is granted that every corporate action of charity has some basis in self-interest, just as does any kind gesture from one human being to another. The saying "what goes around comes around" is applicable. The lesser the amount of immediate self-interest gratification, the greater the return, or rather, the benefits are less tangibly connected to the action. The differentiation between appropriate and inappropriate is related to the level of self-interest inherent in the charitable act. Generally, the resulting good of the act is more beneficial to both the recipient and the corporation if it is made with long-term and far-reaching goals. This is the most efficient way for a corporation to develop a long-term trustworthy image. If a company is attempting to promote a new product by donating it to a needy population, it seems obvious that it is more interested in launching its product than in the population it is helping. On the other end of the spectrum, a company like the Soros Foundation, which organizes projects that fund land mine removal in places like Angola, seems to truly care about bettering the global human condition, particularly because a direct relation cannot clearly be drawn. The result is a long-lasting and striking image of a company that cares, a wise investment in a priceless asset.

Granted, due to the many unexpected risks that can result from poorly managed programs, multinational corporations' philanthropic decision making remains complex and ambiguous. Finding the harmonious balance between self-interest and the resulting benefits of philanthropic action is the key to evolving healthy philanthropic strategies.

13

Reputation Rescue

Lose money for the firm, I will be very understanding; lose a shred of reputation for the firm I will be ruthless.

—Warren Buffett

Success is not in never falling, but in rising every time we fall.

—Confucius

Losing Reputational Capital

All organizations sustain reputational loss sometime. Reputational damage occurs in innumerable ways. Sometimes it is foreseeable. Other times it flies in out of the blue.

At this juncture, accumulated decisions and relationships—what a firm and its people say and do, who it is associated with, how it treats others—all stand out in the stark light of judgment from the court of key constituencies and the court of public opinion. The intensity of scrutiny a firm's soul undergoes in a moral crisis shows how superficial the battle cry of the Alpha firm—"the business of business is business"—really is. It also highlights a fault with Omega firm approaches that treat the symptoms rather than the underlying causes of reputational liability and loss. Responses to a reputational crisis must address the problems that cause it.

Reputation damage can stem from:

Social irresponsibility. Notable examples include Nike's questionable labor practices in Southeast Asia; Wal-Mart's use of sweatshop suppliers in Honduras and anti-union tactics in the United States; Pepsi's maintenance of contracts in Myanmar while otherwise seeming to disengage from that rights-violating country; tobacco companies' cover-up of evidence of the addictive properties of nicotine from consumers and the public; AT&T's beefing up of executive compensation packages after announcing massive worker layoffs; and Burger King's use of cattle pastures cut from rain forests.

One-shot event. Consider the grounding of Exxon's oil tanker in Prince William Sound, NBC's *Nightline* episode that used a staged ignition of GM trucks, Perrier's bottled water that was tainted with benzenyne at one of its plants, or Martha Stewart's insider trading debacle.

Misdeeds of leaders. Dennis Koslowski of Tyco listed a mega birthday party hosted on the island of Sardinia for his wife as a corporate "entertainment expense." Along with Koslowski, Tyco's former chief financial officer, Mark Swartz, and former corporate counsel, Mark Belnick, used bonuses and loans to finance lavish lifestyles, using the company as their own source of funds. Another example is Texaco's executives uttering racial epithets in corporate meetings.

The SEC, its reputation hobbled in the aftermath of U.S. accounting scandals, needed to rebuild its reputation. The opportunity arose when Harvey Pitt named William Webster head of the agency's accounting oversight board. The move backfired though, when it turned out that Pitt neglected to disclose to the other four commissioners Webster's connection to U.S. Technologies, Inc., an Internet company being investigated for fraud.

Marketing gaffes. Examples include Beech-Nut's infant apple drink that was falsely billed as "100 percent pure juice," Volvo's TV ads that used cars secretly rigged with concrete and steel beams in their interiors to seem invulnerable to attack from monster trucks trampling over them, and Listerine's audacious claim that its mouthwash could cure common colds.

Reputations can sustain dents from new product flubs like New Coke or The Body Shop's rollout of hemp-based products in Asia, where governments abhor anything even remotely tied to drug culture. In other instances, a company's own myopic marketing tactics are the culprit, as witnessed in connection with the Nestle infant formula nightmare.

Not-for-profits' greed. The United Way, once regarded as a "blue chip" charity, is a case in point. In 1992, the United Way's reputation as a revered philanthropic organization was undermined by exposure of its leader's excesses. President William Aramony resigned amid charges of nepotism and misuse of agency funds to support his posh lifestyle. For the United Way, reputation translates into monetary contributions. In the aftermath of the scandal, the organization strained to recover its lost reputational capital. The United Way network raised $66 million less in

1992 than in the preceding year. Trying to recoup public trust, the United Way named a new president and imposed cost controls and accountability standards. It set up an ethics program. For the United Way, doing business differently is a matter of survival. However, recent reports suggest that the organization is still suffering shock waves from the scandal. Twenty percent of its former donors have stopped giving to the charity, while many of those remaining are cutting back their contributions. Recent news says that some United Way organizations are using creative methods to make donors' contributions look bigger and expenses smaller. Different branches in Chicago and Washington counted the same contributions. This double-counting inflated both their own numbers and those of the overall system.

These crises present a challenge: How do you resuscitate a reputation when it's gasping for air? There is room for optimism. You can see a reputation tragedy as an opportunity for bringing positive, fundamental change. Many people transcend personal hardship by adopting such an attitude. Some use a crisis like alcoholism as a vehicle for moving to a deeper understanding of themselves—confronting an old character in a raw, uncensored form and forging a new one with dedication and discipline. Similarly, a company can use a crisis of confidence to deepen its character and ultimately sharpen its competitive edge.

Key points to keep in mind:

- Taking the right steps now reduces the need for the court of law, court of key constituencies, and court of public opinion to continue to punish your firm.

- There is a "life cycle" every reputation crisis moves through. The crisis need not permanently deflate your company's reputation. Speeding up this life cycle is to your firm's benefit.

- Measures to rebuild reputation must be as deep and as complex as the crisis itself. All that image creation gets you is an image. But a reputation crisis is a crisis of character. And the currents of character run deep with the organization and its people.

How to Rebuild Reputation: General Steps to Take

Accept responsibility.   Leaders need to promptly accept responsibility for a scandal. Those responsible must be reprimanded and punished. This signals to regulators and investors that the company owns up to its misdeeds and is committed to doing what's needed to prevent a relapse.

Taking responsibility is not necessarily the same as admitting guilt. But if your company is indeed wrong, it's best to confess. Frank admissions of wrongdoing help to neutralize a crisis. But admissions alone are rarely enough.

Promptly express concern to all stakeholders affected. Following Union Carbide's Bhopal disaster, its president, Warren Anderson, flew immediately to Bhopal. Consequently, the company got at least somewhat favorable acclaim for the way it handled the crisis. On the other hand, Exxon's CEO Lawrence Rawls delayed a visit to Alaska for three weeks in the aftermath of the *Valdez* oil spill, causing resentment toward the company's conduct to fester in the meantime.

Set up face-to-face meetings. Build constructive working relationships with current and potential critics. This helps you establish and understand expectations. Don't fill up the dialogue with complicated technicalities. That just increases paranoia, suspicion, and mistrust.

Reveal information openly. Take measures to reassure all stakeholders. They want to know how changes will impact them. How will their interests be protected? Run open letters to shareholders in the press. Step up the staff meetings. Be constantly in touch with customers. Never say "no comment." This gets taken as your admission of culpability. It does nothing to establish confidence.

Clean House. Follow this checklist:

- Extend complete, good-faith cooperation to all regulatory officials.
- Get rid of the inept managers.
- Replace any agents and suppliers linked to the inept managers.
- Enlist independent accountants, attorneys, auditors, investigators, and PR people.
- Redesign systems to maintain more control (align formal and informal systems).
- Implement strict procedures governing compensation and incentives.
- Track down the underlying cause(s) of the malfeasance.
- Keep close tabs on compliance efforts.
- Proactively negotiate with regulatory agencies.

"Before we dump him, have something nice said about him to the press."

Drawing by Bernard Schoenbaum © 2002, Barrons

Salomon Brothers Case

Salomon's embranglement illustrates how a firm can pull itself back from the rim of the abyss—how reserves of reputational capital lost from a scandal can be replenished. In stark contrast to Drexel Burnham Lambert, E. F. Hutton, and Kidder-Peabody—Wall Street firms toppled by misdeeds—Salomon resurrected itself from the depths of a crisis that imperiled the firms' franchise in trading government bonds.

How It Lost Reputation

The venerable brokerage firm was almost ruined in 1991 when traders in its government securities division tried to rig a series of auctions of treasury notes.

A number of trading desk officials submitted false bids, using the names of Salomon clients. This enabled them to circumvent rules that limit the size of bids and awards to a single firm in an auction. In some cases they were able to acquire control of securities beyond the established maximum. Several times, starting in 1990, traders used the names of established firms, such as S. G. Warburg and Mercury Asset Management, without the clients' knowledge or consent.

How It Rebuilt

By introducing new leadership at Salomon Brothers, the board of directors managed to reclaim the bank's reputation with clients, employees, and regulators while simultaneously recapturing economic value. Salomon's managers undertook measures to invigorate discipline. They retooled compliance and control systems and established a board-level compliance committee. A firm-level business practices committee scrutinized ethical issues tied to the firm's businesses. Salomon fired associates responsible for the fraudulent bids. CEO John Gutfreund and President Thomas Strauss tendered their resignations, pressured by government authorities and the firm's senior managers. Gutfreund, along with other top executives, had withheld news about improprieties for four months before bringing it to the Treasury Department. Two hundred ninety million dollars in fines and damages were imposed. The firm's saving grace: no criminal charges were leveled against it.

All told, the scandal cost upward of $1 billion dollars. This encompassed lost business, legal expenses, and the $290 million in penalties.

Salomon's reputation rescue strategy was spearheaded by Warren Buffett, Deryck Maughan, and Robert Denham. Buffett shelled out $600,000 for a letter to shareholders set in two-page advertisements that ran in the *Financial Times,* the *New York Times,* the *Wall Street Journal,* and the *Washington Post.* In the letter, Buffett hailed Salomon's new compliance procedures. The firm's associates, he said, will "be guided by a test that goes beyond rules: contemplating any business act, an employee should ask himself whether he would be willing to see it immediately described by an informed and critical reporter on the front page of his local paper, there to be read by his spouse, children and friends. At Salomon we simply want no part of any activities that pass legal tests but that we, as citizens, would find offensive."[1] Buffett insisted that Salomon could earn superior returns without having to push the envelope, since profitmaking is consistent with good conduct. But the effects of the scandal lingered. Two years after the crisis, the company had still not fully recovered its lost underwriting business. When the merger with Travelers Group was announced in 1997, observers linked favorable terms extended to Travelers to the scandal.

Shell Oil Case

How It Lost Reputation

In 1995 Shell was set to sink a huge oil buoy storage rig the *Brent Spar* six thousand feet into the North Atlantic. But activists protested that the rig would emit substances harmful to the environment. In view of television crews, members of

Greenpeace dramatically intervened in small boats to stop Shell's ships from sinking the rig. Millions of consumers began a boycott, and violent protests against Shell erupted in Europe. The *Financial Times* cited Shell's ethical troubles as the chief reason its ranking dipped in the 1997 annual survey of the most respected European companies.[2] Shell's CEO alluded to "a ghost in the system . . . some sort of slight blurring that causes us to make subtle, but in the end far-reaching, mistakes in assessing developments."[3]

This wasn't Shell's only problem. The company began oil drilling in Nigeria in the mid-1950s. The shareholders in the joint venture consisted mainly of Shell and the National Nigerian Petroleum Corporation.

But government corruption negatively impacted Shell's oil venture. Unrest sparked by various ethnic groups had led to repeated military overthrows of the government and a civil war. Following elections in 1990, the president was deposed by a coup d'état, which installed General Sani Abacha. Fraud was so elevated under Abacha that *The Economist* concluded "these days the main activity of the state is embezzlement."[4] Corruption and theft left indigents poorer and crooks wealthier.

With escalating profits came oil spills. Between 1982 and 1992 Shell was responsible for about 1.6 million gallons of spilled oil in Nigeria, close to 40 percent of the company's worldwide spills.

The Ogoni people, residing near the Niger River Delta, were but one ethnic group out of about 300 in Nigeria. Numbering only 500,000 a decade ago, they constituted a tiny part of the population. With oil exploration depleting once fertile land, pleas for aid went unheard by the government.

As oil spills and pollution spread, Shell failed to make substantial efforts to assess damage. Initially peaceful Ogoni demonstrations turned into protests as the people became more aggravated by the indifferent response they received from the company as well as the Nigerian government.

The Ogoni complained that they were not compensated for Shell's use of their land as promised at the beginning of the venture. The Ogonis felt they deserved a share of profits for not only surrendering parts of their land but also for the damage to their sacred grounds.

Ken Saro-Wiwa, a successful writer, businessman, and political journalist, formed the Movement for the Survival of the Ogoni People to take a stand against the increasing problems with the oil company and the government. The opposition team sparked such upheaval that Saro-Wiwa was arrested in 1992 without charges. He was later released as protests escalated.

As clashes between the people and the government intensified, Shell kept quiet. The company later admitted supplying arms to the military to keep order around its plants and protect company assets. However, critics charged that the company endorsed brutal forces that the military regime used on its own people. Close to 2,000 people were killed from such clashes. Another 80,000 were displaced from their homes into the bush, many suffering rape and torture.

While the corporation was sweeping in annual revenues of $109.8 billion, local people saw the barest fraction of that, whether in monetary payments or infrastructure development.

The most atrocious incident was the 1995 execution of Saro-Wiwa. Upon a second arrest, Saro-Wiwa, along with nine others, was tried for the murder of four Nigerian officials, a fabricated accusation. Saro-Wiwa was not tried by a traditional court but instead by a special tribunal that refused to admit evidence showing innocence. As the defendants were found guilty and sentenced to death, Shell stated that political issues in the host country were not their concern. Granted, Shell sent a letter to the government at the eleventh hour, yet the firm expended no further efforts. The tribunal proceeded with the executions.

Voices around the world expressed outrage. Foreign sanctions cut off Nigerian trade. A World Bank loan of $100 million was denied. Noteworthy magazines and newspapers called for punishment of Nigeria and Shell. Celebrities urged a U.S. oil embargo and the Sierra Club launched a massive boycott campaign.

How It Rebuilt

The *Spar* and Nigerian entanglements posed a formidable reputation crisis for the company. For several years, the world's largest company faced relentless media inquiries and powerful political pressures akin to those encountered by Union Carbide, after its Bhopal chemical gas leak, and Exxon, in the wake of the *Valdez* oil spill incident.

Shell took a holistic approach—a Zeta orientation—to turning itself around. The company addressed both "hard" and "soft" aspects of its performance. Virtually every corner of the company was touched in its efforts to change.

A member of the firm's committee of managing directors, Mark Moody-Stuart, asked if the strong emphasis on rationality and technical competence in the company culture—normally seen as a plus—could be a liability instead. He mused that management misread the reactions of environmentalists and human rights activists triggered by the Spar and Nigeria imbroglios.

Shell's first step harkens to Michael Jackson's famous lines: "I'm starting with the man in the mirror. I'm asking him to change his ways. . . . If you want to make the world a better place, take a look at yourself and then make a change." Senior management took a hard look at Shell's organizational ethos. Their soul-searching revealed a propensity for insularity and an attitude of arrogance with investors, customers, nongovernmental organizations, and the public. Analysis and hard facts took precedence over dialogue and empathy. People inside and outside the company were found to be inhibited, unable to talk freely about problems and concerns.

At a meeting of top leaders, a fine-grained analysis of Shell's financial performance was brought up to nail down the business case for a deep, broad-based transformation. Data that benchmarked Shell's financial performance against rivals were presented, exposing a relatively weak growth rate. All in all, it was a wake-up call. Even though the company was immensely profitable, it was not attaining superior performance. The sobering statistics supporting that reality helped chip away at the arrogance and insularity that was beginning to be deemed so undesirable by the company's leaders.

The second stage in Shell's reputation revolution ushered in a new corporate vision. Senior management composed a list of culture changes deemed necessary for superior performance. These changes included:

- Adopting a new mindset to unleash creativity and talent of employees
- Stopping insularity, arrogance, and secrecy
- Managing from the outside-in
- Communicating openly inside and outside the firm
- Maintaining transparency of information and operations
- Establishing single-point accountability to replace diffuse accountability

Shell rolled out fact-finding initiatives along three fronts:

1. *Staff Survey.* The company created a survey that asked associates about working conditions and their aspirations for themselves and the company. The survey attested to employees' slumping motivations resulting from red tape, poor financial incentives, and dead-end career tracks. It showed that employees wanted more freedom, a voice in decisions, and a stake in financial performance. Employees thought the company should promote the environment and human rights.
2. *Customer Survey.* The survey suggested that customers had brand loyalty but disapproved of the *Spar* and Nigeria situations. It also revealed that they saw Shell as old fashioned.
3. *Changing Social Expectations Study.* Shell commissioned interviews with more than 100 leaders from business, government, and NGOs, across 50 nations, concerning the social role of global companies.

Overall, Shell's studies of changing expectations about social and environmental performance showed that most folks don't put credence in what businesses say. They look at what they do. People rank showing over telling. So transparency is all important. Shell put together a social accountability team to show whether the company was being true to its business principles.

Shell had its operating company chief executives attest that laws and guidelines were followed. They hired external auditors to corroborate statistics. Senior executives ignoring the business principles were fired.

A second report offered an assessment of Shell's economic, social, and environmental performance. The document merged information from Shell's annual financial report and health, safety, and environmental audit with newly collected social data to give a panoramic view of the company.

In Response to the Brent Spar

Shell set up a website giving visitors background information and updates about the *Spar*. Visitors could voice their viewpoints. They could link to websites of corporate watchdogs like Greenpeace, or even to rival firms. The company set up roundtable discussions in 14 countries that brought together many constituencies including executives, activists, journalists, and academics. Shell announced its commitment to protecting health, safety, and the environment.

Representatives from churches, environmental groups, engineering firms, universities, and trade unions, congregated in London to review developments in a dialogue facilitated by the Environmental Council. Shell and Greenpeace joined together in a seminar about media coverage of the imbroglio, and technical experts of the two organizations met periodically to look over proposals on how to dispose of the *Spar*.

Shell solicited proposals for the on-shore disposal of the *Spar*. Independent evaluators looked over a short list of proposals, pared down from two hundred, and dialogued with interested parties. Ultimately, Shell decided to recycle the rig as a ferry quay on the Norwegian shore. News coverage of this decision was consistently favorable.

In Response to Nigeria

Shell put out a review of its environmental record in Nigeria. It hosted an in-house workshop to brief executives and equip them with a communication package. Throughout 1996, it hosted more than 20 European journalists in Nigeria and gave them full access to Shell facilities and people. Articles about the situation, many pro-Shell in tone, subsequently appeared in the world press.

Furthermore, as it had done with the *Spar,* Shell created a website to tell its story about Nigeria and to solicit feedback. Over the course of 1997 it met with various NGOs, among them the World Council of churches, a strong voice for justice in Africa.

Regarding Shareholders

A shareholder resolution requested that Shell implement and report on the company's environmental and corporate responsibility policies. The resolution failed to pass, although it attracted 10.5 percent of shares voted. One op-ed piece pointed out the tremendous hit the company took from the resolution. The activity prompted Shell to start including nonfinancial information in investor communications.

Shell hosted events in 1998 and 1999 that brought more than five hundred managers and professionals together to critique the business and interface with analysts, industry watchers, and outside experts. The company started an outside-in strategy: dialoguing with investors, surveying customers, and benchmarking themselves against the cream of the crop. Tabulations of corporate reputation rankings produced upbeat results. A *Financial Times* poll taken in early 1997 landed Shell eleventh among Europe's "most respected companies."[5] Later that year, *Fortune* listed Shell among the world's "most admired companies."[6]

Ongoing Efforts to Sustain Reputation

In each of the 135 countries in which Shell operates the company has a senior leader responsible for managing reputation by assuring that behavior in the country conforms to the country's general principles, including its commitment to human rights, diversity and inclusiveness, security, health and safety, and concern for climate change, biodiversity, and sustainable development. Shell's annual reports detail its so-called social investments. In Nigeria, the company slated $36 million for vocational training to 1,700 Ogoni youth and for funding college scholarships, immunizing 100,000 children, and supporting local agriculture. Shell partnered with a U.K. NGO, Living Earth, to profile other community needs and respond to them. This involved interviewing 700 men and women in the Niger Delta and evaluating existing programs.

The Jury Is Still Out

A glance at the scores of anti-Shell websites across the Internet reveals that critics of Shell's social and environmental practices remain unplacated. Only time will tell whether Shell's transformation will definitively resurrect its character and reputation. The Shell case shows some of the challenges of reorienting a company's reputation when it's gone astray. Like turning an ocean liner around, it takes time and effort. One thing is clear: Shell's social and environmental reporting, endorsement of the United Nation's Global Compact, participation in multisector forums, and interest in ecocommerce have set it squarely on a course to building reputational capital.

Sears Auto Service Centers Case

How It Lost Reputation

In the early nineties Sears was flooded with complaints from attorneys general and consumers across the United States about its auto service centers. People accused Sears of misleading customers and selling unnecessary parts and services, from shock absorbers to break jobs. The company was accused of passing off used batteries as new. Why? Faced with shrinking revenues, a declining market share, and an increasingly competitive market for car repairs, Sears's leaders had tried to stimulate performance at its auto centers by setting ambitious employee goals. The company upped minimum work quotas and introduced productivity incentives for mechanics. Service personnel were issued product-specific quotas—sell this number of alignments per shift—and paid commissions based on sales. Missing quotas meant reduced work hours or job transfers. Employees recounted being pushed to pump up sales. With mounting corporate pressures and incentives, and few options for making sales goals on the up-and-up, employees' judgments blurred. Management's failure to clarify the boundary between unnecessary service and legitimate preventive maintenance, coupled with consumer vulnerability, left employees to navigate their own path through ambiguous terrain. Without hands-on support for fair practices, and no way to signal and check questionable sales behavior and shoddy work, it's no surprise that employees resorted to unfair tactics like exaggeration and misrepresentation.

The lawsuits were settled. But Sears suffered $60 million losses. The fraud allegations led to national negative press, loss of auto center customers, and a dramatic reduction in income. Its reputation was severely tarnished.

How It Rebuilt

Soon after the charges came to light, Sears's CEO Edward Brennan confessed to the firm's hand in setting up the compensation and goal-setting systems that pushed it into perilous waters. However, he denied the charges of fraud and systemic problems in the auto centers. He insisted that the auto centers were promoting reasonable preventive maintenance. The company conducted internal checks and hired an independent firm to run random shopping audits to deter overcharging incidents. Sears took out full-page advertisements in newspapers around the country to reassure customers that with changed operations at the auto centers they could now trust Sears. The company's customer reassurance program gave out $46.6 million in customer coupons. People charged over $50 for unnecessary work received refunds.

A reward system based on customer satisfaction was installed to replace the compensation and goal-setting system for service advisers. Sears also set up a values program. Brennan's successor, CEO Arthur Martinez, started to rechart the company's course. Steering a path toward good business ethics, Martinez vowed to "revisit and intensify the theme of our customer being the center of our universe."[7]

Not long after the auto center scandal, I witnessed Sears's CEO giving a talk about his firm's reputation for trust to a gathering of business ethics specialists. The general message seemed to be that the company didn't need to worry about monitoring ethics since everybody working at Sears was already honest and forthright. In a low-key, understated delivery, he relayed a folksy anecdote in which a cashier at a fast food restaurant reassured a Sears employee who was paying for his order with a bunch of nickels and dimes: "that's OK, sir, I don't need to count it ... you're from Sears." This is an example of using myths or stories to convey messages about values embedded in a firm's culture. The trick with making such examples work, I find, is to make sure they don't come off as smug, cartoonish and two-dimensional. I confess that hearing the Sears story in the wake of its systemic auto center foibles I would have been more persuaded by some hard evidence of improvements to the company's tarnished reputation resulting from changes in its corporate governance.

Columbia/HCA Healthcare Corporation Case

How It Lost Reputation

Columbia/HCA became the world's largest for-profit hospital chain with Alphafirm methods. Profits came before health care. Relentless cost-cutting, a focus on bottom-line performance and the pursuit of business acquisitions were paramount. Training periods were slashed shorter than those of competitors. A former administrator noted that training that should have lasted six months was done in two weeks.[8] The company stood accused of patient dumping—discharging or relocating emergency-room patients before they could reach stable condition.

INFACT, a public interest coalition, put Columbia/HCA in their Hall of Shame, excoriating the company's irresponsible behavior in elevating its own financial interests above public health.

Columbia/HCA's management had put in place high financial incentives for doctors and administrators to stimulate earnings and growth. Physicians got earnings bonuses by performing more surgeries than monthly benchmarks. They made extra pay if they upped hospital admissions. Some owned shares in facilities they worked at. As the hospitals' earnings rose, the value of the shares increased. Administrators won sizeable bonuses—some up to 80 percent of their salaries—if they reached aggressive growth and profitability goals.

The strategy worked to turn what was a two-hospital operation in 1988 into one of the largest health care service companies in the United States by 1997. The company ran 343 hospitals, 136 outpatient surgery centers, and 550 home health locations. Its outpatient and ancillary facilities ranged across 37 states, Switzerland, and the United Kingdom. Annual revenues hit $20 billion.

But in 1997 the U.S. Justice Department got wind of Columbia/HCA's questionable business practices, mounting the largest criminal probe ever taken against a health-care provider. The government investigation produced indictments of three mid-level Columbia/HCA executives, who were charged with filing fraudulent cost reports, miscoding patient illnesses to get larger reimbursements, and rewarding doctors for admitting patients into hospitals.

The government alleged that Columbia/HCA fraudulently overstated expenditures for home health care lab tests and knowingly miscategorized other expenses to increase reimbursements. The investigation led consumers, physicians, and the public to mistrust Columbia/HCA.

In December 2000, the company forked over $840 million in criminal fines, civil penalties, and damages in partial settlement of charges that it had overbilled government health insurance programs. In the end, it was the biggest government fraud settlement on record. Its stock price fell over 50 percent from its all-time highpoint.

How It Rebuilt

Following the public disclosure of misconduct, Columbia/HCA adopted strong measures to reform its bad practices. A press release expressed its resolve to put an internal ethics, compliance, and responsibility initiative in place. In July 1997, Dr. Thomas Frist, Jr., vice chairman of Columbia's board and its largest noninstitutional shareholder, was named chairman and chief executive. Frist outlined changes to reshape the company. A senior executive position would cover compliance and quality concerns. A mission statement would underscore the importance of honesty and a commitment to delivering quality medical services. All physician investments and performance-based bonuses would be nixed.

The company designated more than five hundred employees as facility ethics and compliance officers (ECOs). The ECOs were intended to help maintain a responsible culture. Employee training sessions covering the company's code and compliance program were implemented locally by each ECO.[9]

Columbia/HCA's guidelines covered topics like acceptable ranges for nurses' tips and the nature of Medicare fraud. The company also set up certification exams for employees charged with determining billing codes. In August 2000, HCA attained a stunning reputational victory. It earned the distinction of being the first corporation taken off of INFACT's Hall of Shame roster.

Arthur Andersen Case

There were two preludes to Arthur Andersen's reputation implosion due to collateral damage from the Enron catastrophe: (1) the legal fallout from a savings and loan crisis; (2) its confusion of identity crisis.

In 1992 Arthur Andersen agreed to pay $65 million to settle federal charges that its audits of failed savings and loan banks were negligent or misleading. Although consenting to pay fines, the firm declined to admit guilt. They calculated that paying a fine was preferable to deflating the firm's economic value in a court battle. Settling sidesteps protracted litigation and attracts publicity that tarnishes a firm's name and lowers the underlying value of its most treasured intangible asset—its reputation.

Arthur Andersen enjoyed a reputation as one of the world's most prestigious accounting firms for decades. Having an admirable collection of blue-chip clients helped it attract yet more big-name clients worldwide. Brushing aside government warnings of potential conflicts of interest, the firm created Andersen Consulting as an independent business unit in 1989 to serve as an advisor to companies the firm audited. Arthur Andersen offered assurances that total integrity could be maintained by separate groups of professionals wearing accounting and consulting hats. It insisted that such an arrangement would not compromise the firm's role as auditor of its clients.

Andersen's consulting business turned out to be a big hit. In fact, it was so successful that its consultants were quick to point out that they were bringing in more revenue than the accountants, yet without corresponding pay increases. The resulting imbalance of earnings to compensation ratios fueled resentments. Following a time of high-visibility bitterness, arbitration proceedings completed in 2000 enabled the consulting business unit to become an independent company. The next year, it was renamed Accenture, an international management and technology services organization that today is a public company with 75,000 consultants in 47 countries.

Consequently, the massive worldwide firm that used to be Arthur Andersen, conducting an array of different operations and doing business under multiple variations on the Andersen name, morphed into an accounting firm sans consulting practice. Interestingly, the Andersen accounting-consulting debacle didn't lead to significant reputation loss.

How It Lost Reputation—Fatally

Though Andersen survived its breaking away from Accenture, it perished altogether from a massive reputational heart attack brought on by its association with both Enron and WorldCom and the revelation of other accounting improprieties. In June 2002, Andersen was convicted of obstructing justice by destroying Enron Corporation documents while on notice of a pending federal investigation. Following the conviction, the firm handed over its license to practice public accountancy.

The Andersen case demonstrates that image, public relations, and marketing alone don't cut it. While Andersen managed to rebuild their image in the wake of the breakup with Accenture, in the end, the character damage from accounting fiascos did them in. Big name clients dropped Andersen like a rock. In 2002, the firm lost over 650 of its 2,300 public audit clients.

Can companies experiencing reputional crises of the magnitude of Shell, Salomon, Sears, and Columbia/HCA ever fully regain their reputations? It depends. In truth, there are many shareholders, customers, and others who will never be won back, for whom trust, confidence, and respect will not return, no matter how hard a firm might work to transform itself.

Years ago, an article by Peter French, "The Hester Prynne Sanction," suggested that a court might sanction a miscreant company by forcing it to fund an independent ad agency that would launch a negative campaign publicizing their wrongdoing so as to taint their reputation—where it hurts the most.[10] His rationale was that ordinary legal sanctions are too easily passed along as a necessary "cost of doing business" and serve as no effective deterrent for corporate wrongdoing. French believed such an approach would force firms to redouble efforts to remove the cloud of impropriety that a court-imposed reputational sanction would impose. As it turns out, the times have caught up with French's suggestion. The reputational penalties for corporate wrongdoing are increasingly being imposed by the court of key constituencies and the court of public opinion and are often far more severe than anything a court of law could concoct.

Rebuilding reputation is no substitute for keeping a sterling one from the start. Avoid building up reputational debts. Remember Humpty Dumpty. After a big fall it may be too late to put everything back together again.

Conclusion

> To leave the world a bit better, whether by a healthy child, a garden patch, or a redeemed social condition. . . . To know that one life has breathed easier because you have lived; this is to have succeeded.
>
> —Ralph Waldo Emerson

> Leave a good name in case you return.
>
> —Kenyan proverb

I hope that this book has stimulated you to consider just how important building reputational capital is to the success of your business. You may be asking what the shift in emphasis toward creating reputational wealth through forthright conduct means for the company you now manage or advise, or for a business you are planning to start up or invest in. Use the website www.reputationalcapital.com as a further resource to get up-to-date ideas for building reputational capital in light of ever-shifting business trends and changes in laws and regulations.

The reputation-enhancing strategies provided in this book should not be viewed as limited to the specific kinds of companies or industries offered up as examples. Rather, the strategies are intended to have a wide range of applicability. The strategies can lend guidance to small and large firms alike, across the entire range of different industries in all countries. Needless to say, however, specific details and methods of execution for the strategies vary from firm to firm, meaning that everything cannot be transmitted in advance of your company's own special circumstances. There is no one-size-fits-all strategy when it comes to building reputational capital.

Nevertheless, there are some constants. Since reputation-inspired corporate governance embraces what we called the business integrity thesis—that a business is a moral agent that possesses and demonstrates character—it is clear that successful firms need to carefully consider the short- and long-term consequences of their conduct, their moral as well as legal responsibilities, and their impact on the wider community. In other words, attaining an excellent reputation means taking the high road. Doing so will earn self-respect for the members of the organization. That self-respect is a necessary condition for gaining the respect of others, and it also forms a big part of the firm's will to excel.

Looking forward, business leaders need to evolve new standards for dealing with the powerful status accorded to reputation. Clearly, morality cannot be effectively legislated, no matter how stringent corporate governance rules continue to become.[1] If reputation is the precious intangible asset we've found it to be from the arguments and evidence presented in this book, a hard challenge arises: Just how far should one go in making and safeguarding a good name? To what lengths, legal[2] and otherwise, is it appropriate to go in keeping the reputational assets of your firm—once successfully acquired—secure? How should we separate rational from irrational responses to reputational threats? What distinguishes prudent from fanatical when maintaining the firm's moral probity?[3] I would urge business leaders to be guided by common sense and good judgment.

Whether you suppress or pay close heed to reputation issues, they tend to turn into something unpredictable and larger than life. In reputation matters, there is a sensitive dependence on initial conditions: A chain of events can be magnified, either raising your firm to a glistening apex of triumph—or, on the other hand, plummeting it into a deep dark pit of shame, humiliation, and financial ruin. Certainly, many companies, from tobacco firms with their hidden nicotine agendas to advisors with creative financial vehicles, have learned this firsthand. Ignoring reputation problems just creates a downward spiral in which dimly perceptible ethical issues fester into moderately severe reputation issues. Then, if ignored further, full-blown legal problems erupt, eventually morphing into enormous, often catastrophic reputational nightmares than can lead to hard asset meltdown.

Paying close attention to even small, seemingly insignificant good deeds can—like the butterfly effect of chaos theory—engender surprising colossal consequences that better the bottom line. When handing out scads of leaflets on a crowded street corner, or doing a mass mailing, you can't always be sure just what final impact such acts will have. It all happens behind the scenes. If it's done right, reputational capital grows and grows even as you sleep.

Considering matters from a wider perspective, could it be that the recognition of a deep connection between moral value and economic value that underpins the conception of reputational capital developed in this book is a part of a larger evolution in worldview—an enlarged understanding of all phenomena, whether social institutions or nature, by grasping interpenetrating layers of interconnection and interdependence? To say, as this book has, that a firm's hard physical assets are fundamentally linked to how it deploys its intangible (reputational) assets is not unlike the assertion of contemporary physicists that the physical objects of our everyday world are created by energy fluctuations occurring on the subatomic level. And the paradoxical relation between acting morally for the intrinsic value of doing so and being rewarded financially recalls the contradictory behavior of the probability waves of quantum theory,[4] which act as both a wave and a particle.

It is my personal wish that one day a collective awareness will emerge from an expanded perspective of economics: that business enterprises ought to serve humanity and not the other way around. To that end, I hope that the concept of reputational capital developed herein may serve as a connecting bridge between the material and moral impulses of humankind.

A final bit of wisdom: In business as in life, karma counts. In due course, what goes around comes around. Concerning reputation, that principle holds true, amplified by laws of exponential growth. Tiny acts of compassion, goodwill, and generosity often fetch great financial returns, exceeding one's expectations. As for their nonfinancial returns, virtue is its own reward. What we do echoes in eternity.[5]

I can't think of a more worthy investment than that.

Notes

Introduction

1. The concept of first mover advantage comes from the theory of games, which is applicable to many fields, including economics. A game is formed by a set of rules dictating a situation in which competitors select strategies aimed at maximizing their winnings. The first mover advantage arises when the player moving first chooses a strategically optimal self-reinforcing equilibrium (a Nash equilibrium). See J. F. Nash, Jr., *Essays on Game Theory* (Northampton, MA: Edward Elgar Publishing, Ltd., 1997). The concept is applied to business strategy in M. Porter, *Competitive Advantage: Creating and Sustaining Superior Performance* (New York: The Free Press, 1985).
2. Various benefits of a good reputation are laid out in G. Dowling, *Creating Corporate Reputations* (Oxford: Oxford University Press, 2001), pp. 12–16.
3. See the studies on the linkage between corporate social responsibility and corporate financial performance listed in Chapter 3, "A Fresh Economic Concept with Strategic Significance."

Chapter 1

1. The study is the *2002 Corporate Reputation Watch*. Quoted in A. Ray, "Customers Hold the Key to Reputation," *PR Week* (13 September 2002): 9.
2. The eighteenth-century jurist Lord Chancellor Thurlow said that the corporation has "no body to kick and no soul to damn, and by God, it ought to have both." C. D. Stone, *Where the Law Ends: The Social Control of Corporate Behavior* (New York: Harper and Row, 1975), p. 3.
3. S. Anderson and J. Cavanagh, *Top 200: The Rise of Corporate Global Power* (Washington, D.C.: Institute for Policy Studies, 2000), pp. 3, 10.
4. In *Misguided Virtue: False Notions of Corporate Social Responsibility* (London: Institute of Economic Affairs, 2001), British economist David Henderson contends that the present movement toward corporate social responsibility is harmful to the global economy and places developing countries at a disadvantage.
5. *A. P. Smith Manufacturing Company v. Barlow*, 98 A.2d 581 (NJ, 1953).
6. P. E. Murphy, "Corporate Ethics Statements: Current Status and Future Prospects," *Journal of Business Ethics* 14 (1995): 727–740
7. T. Donaldson, "Adding Corporate Ethics to the Bottom Line," *Financial Times* (13 November 2000): 6.
8. The use of a corporate ethics office can be traced at least as far back as 1985, when General Dynamics established one in an effort to devise and enforce an internal code of conduct that had been decreed by the U.S. Secretary of the Navy. L. K. Trevino and K. A. Nelson, *Managing Business Ethics*, 3d ed. (New York: John Wiley & Sons, 2004), p. 276.
9. F. D. Baldwin, *Conflicting Interests: Corporate-Governance Controversies* (Lexington, MA: D. C. Heath and Company, 1984), pp. 75–84.

10. W. H. Shaw and V. Barry, *Moral Issues in Business* (9th ed., Belmont, CA: Wadsworth, 2004), p. 395.

11. S. Lipset and W. Schneider, " 'How's Business?' What the Public Thinks," *Public Opinion* (July/August 1978): 41–47.

12. L. Talner, *The Origins of Shareholder Activism* (Washington, D.C.: Investor Responsibility Research Center, 1983), pp. 8–9, 22–23.

13. P. Johansson, "Social Investing Turns 30," *Business Ethics* (January/February 2001): 12–16.

14. The U.S. Federal Sentencing Guidelines, appearing in 1991, direct judges to consider a company's culpability when fashioning sentences for criminal misconduct. Companies with compliance programs aimed at preventing and detecting wrongdoing may receive a reduced assesment of culpability, getting a lowered fine. Firms assuming responsibility for their misconduct gain moral credit, cashed out in reduced fines. United States Sentencing Commission, *Guidelines Manual* (Washington, D.C.: United States Sentencing Commission, 2001), pp. 431–432.

15. The American Law Institute promulgated principles of corporate governance in 1994. The standards specify that corporations can take ethical considerations into account in decisions and can allocate reasonable levels of resources for public and humanitarian causes. American Law Institute, *Principles of Corporate Governance: Analysis and Recommendations,* vol. 1 (St. Paul, MN.: American Law Institute Publishers, 1994), p. 55.

16. In 1989, a U.S. court held that preserving a corporate culture was a legitimate concern in corporate decision making. The Delaware Court of Chancery upheld a board of directors' authority to rebuff a hostile takeover bid favored by a shareholder majority. The board argued that a previously arranged alliance would better maintain the company's culture and ability to serve the public. *Paramount Communications v. Time, Inc.* (Delaware Chancery Court, 1989), affirmed, *Paramount Communications v. Time, Inc.,* 571 A.2d 1140 (1990).

17. A majority of U.S. states have laws allowing corporate directors to consider the interests of nonshareholder constituents in making decisions on behalf of the firm, especially in takeovers. G. Subramanian, "The Influence of Antitakeover Statutes on Incorporation Choice: Evidence on the 'Race' Debate and Antitakeover Overreaching," Harvard NOM Research Paper No. 01-10 (December 2001), available online at http://papers.ssrn.com/abstract=292679 (visited June 20, 2003).

18. R. H. Koppes, "Corporate Governance," *National Law Journal* (December 29, 1997): B5.

19. In 2001, the SEC began considering the effectiveness of a company's compliance program in deciding whether to bring charges of violating federal securities laws. D. H. Freyer and R. S. Walker, "How the SEC Will Credit Compliance Programs in Enforcement Decisions," 15(4) *Ethikos* (January–February 2002): 1. The Environmental Protection Agency's "Incentives for Self Policing: Discovery, Disclosure, Correction, and Prevention of Violations," 65 Fed. Reg. 19618, lowers civil penalties and erases criminal sanctions for firms that set up programs for compliance, self-policing, and risk disclosure.

20. The London Stock Exchange's listing requirements mandate that companies disclose how they manage not only financial and technological risks but also risks bearing on legal, health, safety, environmental, reputation, and business probity issues. "Internal Control, Guidance for Directors on the Combined Code," (London: The Institute of Chartered Accountants in England and Wales, September 1999), p. 13.

21. The act impacts all corporate functionaries from senior executives to board members to auditors to legal counsel to front-line employees. It requires the CEOs and CFOs of all public companies, as well as foreign issuers with U.S.-listed securities, to certify quarterly and annual reports. It shrinks periodic-deadline filing deadlines from 45 to 35 days for 10Qs and from 90 to 60 days for 10Ks. Plus, companies have to report any deficiencies in internal controls to their independent auditors and audit committees. The new rules saddle companies with more costs, more challenges, and more potential liabilities. Corporate executives are, understandably, edgy about personally certifying the veracity of their company's financial statements. Some contend that although they maintain a high-level macroperspective of their company, they lack a microperspective into its day-to-day operations and therefore lack the knowledge necessary to certify disclosures. Investors are divided about the impact of reforms. Forty percent of portfolio managers and investors responding to a FD Morgen-Walke survey said the Sarbanes-Oxley Act reforms are insufficient to enhance accountability. Fifty-six percent say they are unconvinced that a public accountability board will be more effective than the current system. More than 53 percent believe Enron-like corporate scandals are not just the work of a few bad apples, as the SEC and the Bush administration indicated. On the other hand, investors see the new legislation as a step in the right direction. More than half of the survey respondents said that stiffer penalties for securities fraud and document shredding will serve as deterrents. Two out of three said CEO/CFO certifications enforced with stiff penalties will improve the accuracy of financial reporting. Quoted on PR Newswire August 12, 2002.

22. T. Herman, "Survey Says Many Think Selfishness, Greed Are Widespread on Wall Street," *Wall Street Journal* (18 October 1996): B3. In the survey, 52 percent of the respondents disagreed with the statement, "In general, people on Wall Street are as honest and moral as other people."

23. As reflected in articles in the business press such as: A. Fisher, "How Can We Be Sure We're Not Hiring a Bunch of Shady Liars?" *Fortune* (26 May, 2003): 180.

24. *Fortune* (18 March, 2002): 62–76.

25. Since the Enron scandal broke, a cornucopia of corporate scandals has dominated U.S. business headlines. Exposés of executive greed, management excess, corruption, and fraud encompass firms stretching from the banking, accounting, and legal professions to the mutual fund, energy and telecommunications industries. Previous high fliers like Enron, WorldCom, Tyco, and Global Crossing were led into Chapter 11 bankruptcy. Some of their highest-ranking executives now face criminal charges carrying possible prison terms. In the wake of the scandals, lawmakers, regulators, and industry professionals are stepping up to defend their own positions, pointing the finger of blame elsewhere. Meanwhile, thousands of employees have lost jobs. Many, like the private investors who put faith in the profit-and-loss and balance-sheet figures these companies fabricated, have seen their life savings eviscerated. Small wonder that there is a widespread public concern about the credibility of the business community.

26. With respect to assets in socially screened portfolios, from 1995 to 1999, the sector grew at a compound annualized rate of 74 percent, in contrast to a rate of 25 percent for all mutual fund assets in this period (*1999 Report on Socially Responsible Investing Trends in the United States*). Report by the Social Investment Forum, 4 November 1999. Socially screened portfolios amounted to $162 billion (for 1995), $529 billion (for 1997), and $1,497 billion (for 1999).

27. Investment companies have developed socially responsible portfolios using several different methods. Historically, the popular method has been exclusion. Portfolio managers exclude specific stocks or sectors of stocks that they deem unethical. The sectors often excluded are tobacco, alcohol, and defense company stocks, or any corporation seen as contributing to unworthy causes or those detrimental to the greater good of society. This is a subjective approach that focuses on the negative aspects of a corporation's business. It raises questions about the effectiveness of such selection criteria. Some claim that an exclusion approach impedes a fund's chances for success by eliminating certain sectors of the market. This hinders diversification, which historically has been known to reduce the volatility of a portfolio and eliminate risk.

    An option that is becoming more widely accepted takes basically the opposite approach. It involves a more positive selection criteria method, where fund managers pick and choose industries or companies that they think are contributing a greater amount of good. These companies may have distinct employee relation policies, environmentally sound waste removal systems in place, or any other practices that may lead a fund manager to think they are consciously doing right. Using this method, a manager may not necessarily exclude an entire sector based on its definition. It may use a best-of-sector option, where it might include the stock of a tobacco or alcohol company if it is considered the best in the industry based on its contribution to affecting change in the socially conscious environment.

28. K. Burgess, "Why Ethical Indices Still Have Their Critics: Socially-Responsible Investment," *Financial Times* (10 December 2002): 4.

29. R. K. Dhanda, *Guiding Icarus: Merging Bioethics with Corporate Interests* (New York: John Wiley and Sons, Inc., 2002).

30. O. W. Holmes, Jr., "The Path of the Law," 10 *Harvard Law Review* (1897): 457–468.

Chapter 2

1. See, F. Capra, *The Tao of Physics* (Boston: Shambhala, 2000), pp. 106–108.

2. In other words, a company cannot give away what it doesn't yet have. A company just starting out on a shoestring budget cannot match the largess of a global pharmaceutical giant. However, it should be noted that many good deeds that magnify reputational assets can be undertaken by low-budget start-up companies at little or no financial cost.

Chapter 3

1. J. F. Tomer, *Organizational Capital: The Path to Higher Productivity and Well-Being* (New York: Praeger, 1987).

2. J. F. Tomer, *Organizational Capital* (New York: Praeger, 1987), p. 37.

3. R. De George, *Competing with Integrity in International Business* (New York: Oxford University Press, 1993).

4. The survey, Hill & Knowlton's Corporate Reputation Watch, found that 65 percent of Belgian, 56 percent of Italian, and 50 percent of British CEOs cited a link between a better reputation and sales. A. Ray, "Customers Hold the Key to Reputation," *PR Week*, (13 September 2002): 9.

5. J. D. Margolis and J. P. Walsh, *People and Profits? The Search for a Link between a*

Company's Social and Financial Performance (Mahwah, NJ: Lawrence Erlbaum Associates, 2001). The areas included community investment, product safety, human resource practices, and environmental performance. Eighty of these studies investigated whether better social performance was a predictor of improved financial performance. Nineteen looked in the opposite direction: Could stronger financial performance predict higher social performance? Some of the studies documented the relationship in both directions. Only 4 out of the entire 95 studies detected a negative relationship between social and financial performance. Fifty-five studies discovered a positive correlation between better financial performance and better social performance. Twenty-two uncovered no relationship between the two. Eighteen found a mixed relationship.

6. R. M. Roman, S. Hayibor, and B. R. Agle, "The Relationship Between Financial and Social Performance: Repainting a Portrait," 38(1) *Business and Society* (1999): 109–125.

7. Sustainable Asset Management Group. Quoted in *Fortune* (26 May 2003): 152.

8. The study was conducted by marketing research firm Nima Hunter, Inc. in collaboration with *Ethical Corporation* magazine. "Managing Corporate Social Responsibility: What Business Leaders Are Saying and Doing 2002–2007," p. 4. Quoted in *Id.*, at p. 154.

9. C. C. Vershoor, "A Study of the Link Between a Corporation's Financial Performance and Its Commitment to Ethics," *Journal of Business Ethics*, (October 1998): 1509.

10. This study used a composite measure of financial performance for 1997 and the previous two years. It should be noted, however, that language in annual reports (used by the study to determine commitment to ethics) is not, as such, a very credible indicator. C. C. Verschoor, "Principles Build Profits," *Management Accounting* (October 1997): 42–46.

11. Ronald Coase, followed by a lineage of other economists, gave us the contract picture of the firm. R. M. Coase, "The Nature of the Firm" 4 *Economica* (1937): 386–405; S. N. S. Cheung, "The Contractual Theory of the Firm," 26 *Journal of Law and Economics* (1983): 1–22; H. N. Butler, "The Contractual Theory of the Firm," 11 *George Mason Law Review* (1989): 99–123.

12. Paul Romer separates private returns to capital from social returns. Investment produces not only new machines but new ways of doing things well—sometimes because of deliberate investment in reasearch, yet sometimes due to serendipitous spinoffs. P. Romer, "Increasing Returns and Long-Run Growth," *Journal of Political Economy* 94(5) (October 1986): 1002–1037.

Chapter 5

1. J. R. Rest and S. J. Thoma, "Educational Programs and Interventions," in J. R. Rest, ed., *Moral Development: Advances in Research and Theory* (New York: Praeger, 1986), pp. 59–88.

2. T. R. Piper, M. C. Gentile, and S. D. Parks, *Can Ethics Be Taught?* (Boston: Harvard Business School Press, 1993).

3. Ethics Resource Center, *Ethics in American Business: Policies, Programs, and Perceptions* (Washington, D.C., 1994), pp. 31–32.

4. S. Milgram, *Obedience to Authority* (New York: Harper and Row, 1974). In the experiments research subjects willingly doled out painful electric shocks to others when directed by an experimenter. The subjects later accounted for their action with the rationale that they were just following orders.

5. L. S. Paine, *Cases in Leadership, Ethics, and Organizational Integrity: A Strategic Perspective* (Chicago: Irwin, 1997), p. 14.

6. J. Rawls, *A Theory of Justice* (Cambridge, MA: Harvard University Press, 1971), p. 3.

7. L. K. Trevino, K. D. Butterfield, and D. McCabe, "The Ethical Context in Organizations: Influences on Employee Attitudes and Behaviors." 8(3) *Business Ethics Quarterly* (1998): 447–476.

8. J. Galvin, "The New Business Ethics," *Smart Business Mag.com* (June 2000), p. 94.

9. J. Joseph, *2000 National Business Ethics Survey Volume I: How Employees Perceive Ethics at Work* (Washington, D.C.: Ethics Resource Center, 2000), p. 67.

10. Ibid., p. 5.

Chapter 6

1. See C. A. Kotchian, "The Payoff: Lockheed's 70-Day Mission to Tokyo," *Saturday Review* (9 July 1977): 7–12. In 1977, Lockheed Corporation was implicated in paying $12.5 million in bribes to Kakuei Tanaka, then prime minister of Japan, to facilitate its sale of aircraft to All Nippon Airways.

2. See, R. T. De George, *Business Ethics*, (5th ed. Upper Saddle River, NJ: Simon & Schuster, 1999), pp. 73–76.

3. The neglect of reputational impact is even more pronounced in deontological or rights-based approaches.

Chapter 7

1. Quoted in L. K. Trevino and K. A. Nelson, *Managing Business Ethics: Straight Talk About How To Do It Right* (2nd ed, New York: John Wiley and Sons, Inc., 1999), p. 30.

2. Ibid., pp. 30–31.

3. J. A. Byrne, *Chainsaw: The Notorious Career of Al Dunlap in the Era of Profit-at-Any-Price* (New York: HarperBusiness, 1999), p. 68.

4. W. Zellner, S. Anderson, and L. Cohn, "A Hero—and a Smoking-Gun Letter," *Business Week* (28 January 2002): 34.

5. B. McLean and P. Elkind, "Partners in Crime: The Untold Story of How Citi, J. P. Morgan Chase, and Merrill Lynch Helped Enron Pull Off One of the Greatest Scams Ever," *Fortune* (27 October 2003): 78–100.

6. Ibid., p. 35.

7. J. Cummings, T. Hamburger, and K. Kranhold, "Law Firm Reassured Enron on Accounting," *Wall Street Journal* (16 January 2002): A18.

8. J. Entine, "Shattered Image: Is The Body Shop Too Good to Be True?" *Business Ethics* (September/October 1994).

9. D. Koehn, "Where and Why Did Business Ethicists Go Wrong? The Case of Dow Corning Corporation," in L. P. Hartman, *Pespectives in Business Ethics* (2nd ed., New York: McGraw Hill/Irwin, 2002), p. 208.

10. T. Smart, "This Man Sounded the Silicone Alarm—In 1976" *Business Week* (27 January 1992): 34.

11. J. C. Stauber and S. Rampton, "Confidence Game: Burson-Marsteller's PR Plan for Silicone Breast Implants" 3(1) *PR Watch* (1996).

12. J. A. Byrne, "Informed Consent," *Business Week* (2 October 1995): 104–116; J. Foreman, "Women and Silicone: A History of Risk," *The Boston Globe* (19 January 1992): 1.
13. D. Koehn, op. cit. at p. 212.
14. D. Bollier, *Merck and Company* (Stanford: The Business Enterprise Trust, 1991).

Chapter 8

1. This is not to say that Arthur Andersen did not engage in its own dishonest practices.
2. D. Koehn, "Where and Why Did Business Ethicists Go Wrong? The Case of Dow Corning Corporation," reprinted in L. P. Hartman, *Perspectives in Business Ethics*, 2d. ed. (New York: McGraw-Hill, 2002), pp. 205–214; J. A. Byrne, *Informed Consent: A Story of Personal Tragedy and Corporate Betrayal* (New York: McGraw-Hill, 1995).
3. J. Harr, *A Civil Action* (New York: Random House, 1996).

Chapter 9

1. J. Welch and J. A. Byrne, *Jack: Straight From the Gut* (New York: Warner Business Books, 2001).
2. I excerpt the following passages from the Tao Te Ching because I believe they are as relevant and inspirational now as when they were set down by Lao Tze, an ancient sage from China, thousands of years ago. He wrote them during a time of great competition, political intrigue, suspicion, and mistrust amongst the warring states. Not unlike the brutal battlefields of business you walk across today.

> If you want to be a great leader,
> You must learn to follow the tao.
> Stop trying to control.
> Let go of fixed plans and concepts,
> And the world will govern itself.
>
> —*Tao Te Ching*

3. D. P. Quinn and T. M. Jones, "An Agent Morality View of Business Policy," 20(1) *Academy of Management Review* (1995): 22–42.
4. R. W. Giuliani, *Leadership* (New York: Hyperion, 2002), p. xiii.
5. S. Covey, "Why Character Counts," in *Reader's Digest* (January 1999): 132–135.
6. J. Joseph, *2000 National Business Ethic Surveys, Volume I: How Employee Perceive Ethics At Work* (Washington, D.C.: Ethics Resource Center, 2000), p. 6.
7. G. R. Weaver, L. K. Trevino, and P. L. Cochran, "Corporate Ethics Practices in the Mid-1990s: An Empirical Study of the *Fortune* 1000" 18(3) *Journal of Business Ethics* (1999): 283, 294.
8. R. E. Berenbeim, *Global Corporate Ethics Practices: A Developing Consensus* (New York: The Conference Board, Research Report 1243-99-RR, 1999).
9. P. E. Murphy, "Corporate Ethics Statements: Current Status and Future Prospects," 14 *Journal of Business Ethics* (1995): 727–740.
10. Levi Strauss and Company: Global Sourcing (A) Harvard Business School case 395-127, p. 1.

11. R. M. Rilke, *Letters To a Young Poet*. S. Mitchell trans. (New York: Random House, 1984), p. 34.

12. G. R. Weaver and L. K. Trevino, "Compliance and Values-Oriented Ethics Programs: Influence on Employees' Attitudes and Behavior," *Business Ethics Quarterly* 9(2) (April 1999): 315–335.

13. L. Trevino and K. Nelson, *Managing Business Ethics*, 3d. ed. (New York: John Wiley and Sons, 2004), pp. 301–302.

14. F. F. Reichheld and T. Teal, *The Loyalty Effect: The Hidden Force Behind Growth, Profits, and Lasting Value* (Boston: Harvard Business School Press, 1996), p. 101.

15. K. A. Kovach, "Employee Motivation: Addressing a Crucial Factor in Your Organization's Performance." *Employment Relations Today* (Summer 1995), pp. 93–107.

16. A quality circle is a small group of workers performing the same or similar tasks who meet regularly to talk over problems in an effort to continually improve the quality of products or services.

17. The studies are cited in J. L. Seglin "Too Much Ado About Giving References," *New York Times* (21 February 1999): D4.

18. K. A. Kovach, S. J. Conner, T. Livneh, K. M. Scallan, and R. L. Schwartz, "Electronic Communication in the Workplace—Something's Got to Give," *Business Horizons* (July/August 2000): 59–64.

Chapter 10

1. Traits that impress investors are described in C. J. Fombrun, *Reputation: Realizing Value from the Corporate Image* (Boston: Harvard Business School Press, 1996), pp. 117–123.

2. 1997 Cone/Roper survey, reported in *Business Ethics* (March-April 1997): 14–16.

3. A. Gentleman, "Tourist Drought Hits Disneyland Paris," *The Guardian* (London) (9 August 2003): 16.

4. "Confronting Anti-Globalism," *Business Week* (6 August 2001): 92.

5. A. Laurence and M. Blakstad, "Managing Reputation in the Internet Age," in A. Jolly, ed., *Managing Corporate Reputations* (London: Kogan Page, Ltd., 2001), p. 14.

6. The study is cited in Laurence and Blakstad, "Managing Reputation," p. 12.

7. M. Warner, "eBay's Worst Nightmare," *Fortune* (26 May 2003): 89–94.

Chapter 11

1. The company was incorporated in 1977 with a share capital of Rs. 10 crores. It has had a series of share issues that raised its capital to Rs. 121 crores. The net worth of the corporation (book value) as of March 31, 2002, was Rs. 2,703 crores. As of March 31, 2003, the net worth climbed to 3,043.86 crores.

2. Other companies included in the 2003 awards were: Cummins Engine (for funding the construction of a school and health clinic near its factory in Brazil), Intel (for maintaining a worker injury rate at 4 percent of the industry average), Procter & Gamble (for diversity in employment), IBM (for implementing child- and elder-care programs), Avon (for funding cancer research, prevention, and treatment), and Green Mountain Coffee (for purchasing 25 percent of its beans directly from farmers).

3. A. Weinberg, "America's Most Philanthropic Corporations," available online at www.forbes.com (visited 21 November 2002).

Chapter 12

1. L. Wittgenstein, *Philosophical Investigations* (Oxford: Basil Blackwell, 1952); L. Wittgenstein, *Remarks on the Philosophy of Psychology*, Volume I (University of Chicago Press, 1980), p. 16.
2. Leeson's conduct is connected with the $1.35 billion in trading losses that collapsed the firm. Leeson's main job was to arbitrage minute differences in prices between future contracts for the Nikkei 225 stock average on the Osaka and Singapore exchanges. While appearing to trade for clients as well as for Barings, Leeson hedged the positions he took to avoid losses if the Nikkei suddenly turned in one direction or another. In 1993, Leeson began accumulating unhedged positions in Nikkei futures. At first this strategy was successful. But as the market headed south, Leeson faced increasing margin calls on his losing positions. To pay the margin calls, he sold Nikkei options contracts called "short straddles." This let him raise money from the premiums on the call and put options, but it also meant he was betting on the market to go nowhere. Leeson began trading furiously: 5,000 futures contracts a day on the Singapore International Monetary Exchange—a quarter of all its trades. By February 1995 he had amassed 20,000 contracts in Singapore, worth $1.89 billion, and 15,000 contracts in Osaka, worth $2.83 billion. The bet did not pay off. On January 17 an earthquake destroyed most of Kobe, Japan, sending the index to 17,785.49 on January 23. Leeson's contracts hinged on the index staying above 18,500. The financial losses incurred by Barings were too large for even the Bank of England to risk trying to save. Barings was eventually purchased by Dutch ING Financial Services Group. See, K. T. Jackson, "Globalizing Corporate Ethics Program: Perils and Prospects, 16 *Journal of Business Ethics* (1997): 1227–1235.
3. "Argentine Judge Requests Extraditions," *Wall Street Journal* (25 September 1998): A12.
4. C. Sims, "Argentine Cloud Over IBM Grows Darker," *New York Times* (29 June 1996): 33.
5. P. Lim, "Starbucks' 'Code' for Suppliers Is Criticized," *The Seattle Times* (24 October 1995): E1.
6. C. Solomon, "Coffee Giant Slow To Keep Guatemala Promise," *The Seattle Times* (6 March 1997): D1.
7. M. McKegney, "Ford, Firestone Woes Extend Beyond the U.S.; Scrutiny Most Intense in S. America; PR Effort Questioned," *Ad Age Global* (1 September 2000): 4.
8. R. L. Simison, "For Ford CEO Nasser, Damage Control Is the New 'Job One,' *Wall Street Journal* (11 September 2000): A1, A8.
9. http://pollingreport.com
10. I give philosophical justifications for applying human rights to international companies in *Charting Global Responsibilities: Legal Philosophy and Human Rights* (Lanham, MD: University Press of America, 1994; rpt. New Delhi: East-West Press, 1997).
11. Here's an example of one such inquiry, quoted in K. T. Jackson, note 2 above, p. 1230.

Q: What if I work in a country where lavish gift-giving is expected and would help the company get business or services?

A: You need to consider a business gift in light of the prevailing practices. This can vary by country, just like it can by industry. Nevertheless, American Express doesn't want a reputation for extravagance. Gifts should never exceed what is reasonable and customary and, of course, must be accurately reported on your expense account. You must be careful, however, not to offer gifts to foreign government officials, political candidates or political parties. Even if such gifts seem to be customary in that country, offering such gifts to get business would violate the U.S. Foreign Corrupt Practices Act. It may also violate local law. In some countries, expediting or "grease" payments are customarily demanded by low-level government clerical workers. That kind of payment is not always illegal, but the company strongly discourages them. If necessary, such payments can be made if you follow the procedures in effect in your business unit. For example, in Travel Related Services, any such payment over $100 needs the prior approval of the President of TRS International, the TRS Controller, and the General Counsel's Office, and all such payments must be reported on a quarterly Management Representation Certificate.

12. Nike, Inc., "Corporate Responsibility Report, 2001;" see also, R. Wokutch, "Nike and Its Critics: Beginning a Dialogue," 14(2) *Organization and Environment* (June 2001): 207–237.

Chapter 13

1. Quoted in L. S. Paine, "Forging the New Salomon," in *Cases in Leadership, Ethics, and Organizational Integrity: A Strategic Perspective* (Chicago: Irwin, 1997), p. 131.
2. "Europe's Most Respected Companies: BP Steals the Limelight From Shell," *Financial Times* (London) (24 September 1997): I–II.
3. "Shellman Says Sorry," *The Economist* 343 (1997): 65.
4. "Nigeria Foaming," *The Economist* (18 November 1995): 15.
5. PriceWaterhouse/*Financial Times* survey, April 1997.
6. A. Fisher, "The World's Most Admired Companies," *Fortune* 136(8) (27 October 1997): 220.
7. J. Steinhauer, "Time To Call a Sears Repairman; A Turnaround Is Sidetracked By Its Own Oversell," *New York Times* (15 January 1998) D1.
8. L. Lagnado, "Ex-Manager Describes the Profit-Driven Life Inside Columbia/HCA," *Wall Street Journal* (30 May 1997): A1.
9. K. Eichenwald, "Reshaping the Culture at Columbia/HCA," *New York Times* (4 November 1997): C2.
10. P. A. French, "The Hester Prynne Sanction," 4(2) *Business and Professional Ethics Journal* (1984): 19–32.

Conclusion

1. A 2003 survey commissioned from Opinion Research Corporation International found that only 19 percent of chief executives believe that stepped-up corporate-governance rules in the wake of recent U.S. business scandals will lead to more ethical business conduct. A. Parker, "Few Put Faith in Corporate Reforms," *Financial Times*, 13 October 2003, p. 1.
2. Defamation law is of course one avenue to take after reputation is affected by untruths or reckless disregard for truth. In addition, a firm may seek damages for actual harm to its reputation sustained from interference with its contractual relations. Restatement

(2d) of Torts, section 774A. See *Texaco, Inc. v. Penzoil, Co.,* 729 W.W. 2d 768 (1987). But the law provides a clumsy and imperfect method of protecting a name. After all, by the time those legal protections are triggered, the damage has already been done. *Ex post* the effort is merely compensatory and remedial, seldom making matters whole.

3. Consider, for instance, that Aaron Burr challenged Alexander Hamilton to a duel to the death to defend Burr's name after Hamilton publicly insulted him.

4. A somewhat similar reflection is offered by Deepak Chopra in *The Seven Spiritual Laws of Success* (San Rafael: Amber-Allen, 1994), pp. 21, 69.

5. This is paraphrased from a line in the movie *Gladiator,* 2000.

Bibliography

Books

Abbott, E. A. 1952. *Flatland*. New York: Dover.

American Law Institute. 1994. *Principles of Corporate Governance: Analysis and Recommendations*, Volume 1. St. Paul, MN: American Law Institute Publishers.

Anderson, S. and Cavanaugh, J. 2000. *Top 200: The Rise of Corporate Global Power*. Washington, D.C.: Institute for Policy Studies.

Baldwin, F. D. 1984. *Conflicting Interests: Corporate-Governance Controversies*. Lexington, MA: D. C. Heath and Company.

Benninga, S. Z. and Sarig, O. H. 1997. *Corporate Finance: A Valuation Approach*. New York: McGraw-Hill.

Berenbeim, R. E. 1999. *Global Corporate Ethics Practices: A Developing Consensus*. New York: The Conference Board, Research Report.

Berry, L. L. 1999. *Discovering the Soul of Service*. New York: The Free Press.

Boatright, J. R. 1999. *Ethics in Finance*. Oxford: Blackwell.

Bollier, D. 1991. *Merck and Company*. Stanford: The Business Enterprise Trust.

Byrne, J. A. 1999. *Chainsaw: The Notorious Career of Al Dunlap in the Era of Profit-at-Any-Price*. New York: HarperBusiness.

Capra, F. 2000. *The Tao of Physics*. Boston: Shambhala.

Carter, S. L. 1996. *Integrity*. New York: BasicBooks.

Chopra, D. 1994. *The Seven Spiritual Laws of Success*. San Rafael, CA: Amber-Allen.

Covey, S. R. 1990. *The Seven Habits of Highly Effective People: Restoring the Character Ethic*. New York: Fireside.

De George, R. T. 1999. *Business Ethics*. Upper Saddle River: Prentice-Hall.

De George, R. T. 1993. *Competing with Integrity in International Business*. New York: Oxford University Press.

Dhanda, R. K. 2002. *Guiding Icarus: Merging Bioethics with Corporate Interests*. New York: John Wiley and Sons.

Dowling, G. 2001. *Creating Corporate Reputations*. Oxford: Oxford University Press.

Dunlap, A. J. 1996. *Mean Business: How I Save Bad Companies and Make Good Companies Great*. New York: Random House.

Ethics Resource Center. 1994. *Ethics in American Business: Policies, Programs, and Perceptions*. Washington, D.C.: Ethics Resource Center.

Ferrell, O. C., Fraedrich, J., and Ferrell, L. 2002. *Business Ethics: Ethical Decision Making and Cases*. Boston: Houghton Mifflin.

Fombrun, C. J. 1996. *Reputation: Realizing Value from the Corporate Image*. Boston: Harvard Business School Press.

Gerstner, L. V., Jr. 2002. *Who Says Elephants Can't Dance?: Inside IBM's Historic Turnaround*. New York: HarperBusiness.

Gianaris, N. V. 1996. *Modern Capitalism: Privatization, Employee Ownership, and Industrial Democracy*. Westport: Praeger.

Giuliani, R. W. and Kurson, K. 2002. *Leadership.* New York: Hyperion.

Gleick, J. 1987. *Chaos: Making a New Science.* New York: Penguin.

Griffin, G. 2002. *Reputation Management.* Oxford: Capstone.

Harrison, L. E. 1992. *Who Prospers? How Cultural Values Shape Economic and Political Success.* New York: Basic Books.

Hartman, L. P. 2002. *Perspectives in Business Ethics.* New York: McGraw-Hill/Irwin.

Henderson, D. 2001. *Misguided Virtue: False Notions of Corporate Social Responsibility.* London: Institute of Economic Affairs.

Hodess, R., Banfield, J., and Wolfe, T. 2001. *Global Corruption Report: Transparency International.* Berlin: Medialis.

Kafka, F. 1964. *The Trial.* New York: Alfred A. Knopf.

Jackson, K. T. 1994. *Charting Global Responsibilities: Legal Philosophy and Human Rights.* Lanham, MD: University Press of America; reprinted New Delhi: East-West Press, 1997.

Jennings, M. M. 2002. *Business: Its Legal, Ethical and Global Environment.* Cincinnati: West Legal Studies in Business.

Joseph, J. 2000. *National Business Ethics Survey Volume I: How Employees Perceive Ethics at Work.* Washington, D.C.: Ethics Resource Center.

Marconi, J. 2002. *Reputation Marketing.* New York: McGraw-Hill.

Margolis, J. D. and Walsh, J. P. 2001. *People and Profits? The Search for a Link between a Company's Social and Financial Performance.* Mahwah, NJ: Lawrence Erlbaum Associates.

McKinnon, C. 1999. *Character, Virtue Theories, and the Vices.* Ontario: Broadview Press.

Milgram, S. 1974. *Obedience to Authority.* New York: Harper and Row.

Mitchell, S. 1988. *Tao Te Ching.* (English translation.) New York: HarperCollins.

Nash, J. F. 1997. *Essays on Game Theory.* Northampton, MA: Edward Elgar.

Newburry, W. E. and Gladwin, T. N. 1997. *Shell and Nigerian Oil.* New York: New York University.

Paine, L. S. 1997. *Cases in Leadership, Ethics, and Organizational Integrity: A Strategic Perspective.* Chicago: Irwin.

Paine, L. S. 2003. *Value Shift: Why Companies Must Merge Social and Financial Imperatives to Achieve Superior Performance.* New York: McGraw-Hill.

Piper, T. R., Gentile, M. C., and Parks, S. D. 1993. *Can Ethics Be Taught?* Boston: Harvard Business School Press.

Porter, M. 1985. *Competitive Advantage: Creating and Sustaining Superior Performance.* New York: The Free Press.

Rawls, J. 1971. *A Theory of Justice.* Cambridge: Harvard University Press.

Reichheld, F. F. and Teal, T. 1996. *The Loyalty Effect: The Hidden Force Behind Growth, Profits, and Lasting Value.* Boston: Harvard Business School Press.

Rest, J. R. 1986. *Moral Development: Advances in Research and Theory.* New York: Praeger.

Rilke, R. M. 1984. *Letters to a Young Poet* (S. Mitchell, trans.) New York: Random House.

Shaw, W. H. and Barry, V. 2004. *Moral Issues in Business.* (Belmont: Wadsworth).

Solomon, R. C. 1999. *A Better Way to Think about Business.* New York: Oxford University Press.

Solomon, R. C. 1984. *Ethics: A Brief Introduction.* New York: McGraw-Hill.

Stone, C. D. 1975. *Where the Law Ends: The Social Control of Corporate Behavior.* New York: Harper & Row.

Stowe, J. D., Robinson, T. R., Pinto, J. E., and McLeavey, D. W. 2002. *Analysis of Equity Investments: Valuation.* Baltimore: United Book Press.

Talner, L. 1983. *The Origins of Shareholder Activism.* Washington, D.C.: Investor Responsibility Research Center.

Tomer, J. F. 1987. *Organizational Capital: The Path To Higher Productivity and Well-Being.* New York: Praeger.

Trevino, L. K. and Nelson, K. A. 1999. *Managing Business Ethics: Straight Talk About How to Do It Right.* New York: John Wiley & Sons.

Tzu, S. 2002. *The Art of War: The Denma Translation.* Boston: Shambhala.

United States Sentencing Commission. 2001. *Guidelines Manual.* Washington, D.C.: United States Sentencing Commission.

Velasquez, M. G. 2002. *Business Ethics: Concepts and Cases.* Upper Saddle River: Prentice Hall.

Weiss, J. W. 1998. *Business Ethics: A Stakeholder and Issues Management Approach.* Orlando: Harcourt Brace & Company.

Welch, J. F., Jr., and Byrne, J. A. 2001. *Straight From the Gut.* New York: Warner Business.

Wittgenstein, L. 1952. *Philosophical Investigations.* Oxford: Basil Blackwell.

Wittgenstein, L. 1980. *Remarks on the Philosophy of Psychology.* Volume I. Chicago: University of Chicago Press.

Articles

Armour, S. 2003. "Wal-Mart Takes Hits on Worker Treatment." *USA Today,* 10 February: B1.

Baucus, M. S. and Baucus, D. A. 1997. "Paying the Piper: An Empirical Examination of Longer-Term Financial Consequences of Illegal Corporate Behavior." *Academy of Management Journal* 40: 129–151.

Bayer, R. 2000. "Termination With Dignity." *Business Horizons* (September/October): 4–10.

Bickerton, I., Voyle, S., and Buckley, N. 2003. "Europe Faces Accounting Scandal." *Financial Times* (25 February): 1.

Boutchkova, M. K. and Megginson, W. L. 2000. "Privatization and the Rise of Global Capital Markets." *Financial Management* (Winter): 31–76.

Bradsher, K. 2000. "Documents Portray Tire Debacle as a Story of Lost Opportunities." *New York Times* (11 September): 1.

Bradsher, K. 2000. "Firestone Struggles in Center of an Ever-Widening Storm." *New York Times* (1 September): A1.

Bradsher, K. 2000. "Ford Is Conceding S.U.V. Drawbacks." *New York Times* (12 May): A1.

Burgess, K. 2002. "Why Ethical Indices Still Have Their Critics: Socially-Responsible Investment." *Financial Times* (10 December): 4.

Butler, H. N. 1989. "The Contractual Theory of the Firm." *George Mason Law Review* 11: 99–123.

Byrne, J. A. 1995. "Informed Consent." *Business Week* (2 October): 104–116.

Byrne, J. A., France, M., and Zellner, W. 2002. "The Environment Was Ripe for Abuse." *Business Week* (25 February): 118–120.

Carroll, A. B. 2000. "Ethical Challenges for Business in the New Millennium: Corporate Social Responsibility and Models of Management Morality." *Business Ethics Quarterly* (January): 33–42.

Chaffin, J. 2003. "Enron Fuels Calls for Tax Reform." *Financial Times* (14 February): 1.

Cheung, S. N. S. 1983. "The Contractual Theory of the Firm." *Journal of Law and Economics* 26: 1–22.

Cohen, R. 1993. "The French, Disneyed and Jurassick, Fear Erosion." *New York Times* (21 November): E2.

Coase, R. M. 1937. "The Nature of the Firm." *Economica* 4: 386–405.

Covey, S. 1999. "Why Character Counts." *Reader's Digest* (January): 132–135.

Cummings, J., Hamburger, T. and Kranhold, K. 2002. "Law Firm Reassured Enron on Accounting." *Wall Street Journal* (16 January): A18.

Davids, M. 1999. "Global Standards, Local Problems." *Journal of Business Strategy* (January/February): 38–43.

Daviss, B. 1999. "Profits From Principle." *The Futurist* (March): 28–32.

Donaldson, T. 1996. "Values in Tension: Ethics Away From Home." *Harvard Business Review* (September/October): 48–62.

Donaldson, T. 2000. "Adding Corporate Ethics to the Bottom Line." *Financial Times* (13 November): 6.

Duffy, M. 2002. "What Did They Know and When Did They Know It?" *Time* (January 28): 16–22.

Eichenwald, K. 1997. "Reshaping the Culture at Columbia/HCA." *New York Times* (4 November): C2.

Entine, J. 1994. "Shattered Image: Is The Body Shop Too Good to Be True?" *Business Ethics* (September/October).

Fisher, A. 2003. "How Can We Be Sure We're Not Hiring a Bunch of Shady Liars?" *Fortune* (26 May): 180.

Foreman, J. 1992. "Women and Silicone: A History of Risk." *The Boston Globe* (19 January): 1.

Freyer, D. H. and Walker, R. S. 2002. "How the SEC Will Credit Compliance Programs in Enforcement Decisions." *Ethikos* 15(4) (January/February): 1.

Freiberg, K. 1998. "Leaders as Value Shapers." *Executive Excellence* (November): 7–8

French, P. A. 1984. "The Hester Prynne Sanction." *Business and Professional Ethics Journal* 4(2): 19–32.

Friedman, M. 1970. "The Social Responsibility of Business Is to Increase Its Profits." *New York Times Magazine* (13 September): 33.

Gentleman, A. 2003. "Tourist Drought Hits Disneyland Paris." *The Guardian* (London). (9 August): 16.

Greider, W. 2002. "Crime in the Suites." *The Nation* (4 February): 11–14.

Herman, T. 1996. "Survey Says Many Think Selfishness, Greed Are Widespread on Wall Street." *Wall Street Journal* (18 October): B3.

Hill, A. 2003. "Kozlowski Speaks Out on Tyco Loan Deal." *Financial Times* (10 February): 19.

Holmes, O. W. 1897. "The Path of the Law." *Harvard Law Review* 10: 457–468.

Hunt, S. D. 1997. "Resource-Advantage Theory and the Wealth of Nations: Developing the Socio-Economic Research Tradition." *Journal of Socio-Economics* 26: 351–353.

Jackson, K. T. 1997. Globalizing Corporate Ethics Programs: Perils and Prospects." *Journal of Business Ethics* 16: 1227–1235.

Johansson, P. 2001a. "Social Investing Turns 30." *Business Ethics* (January/February): 12–16.

Johansson, P. 2001b. "The 100 Best Corporate Citizens." *Business Ethics* (March/April): 12–15.

Karpoff, J. M. and Lott, J. R. Jr. 1993. "The Reputational Penalty Firms Bear from Committing Criminal Fraud." *Journal of Law and Economics* 36 (October): 757–802.

Koehn, D. 2002. "Where and Why Did Business Ethicists Go Wrong? The Case of Dow Corning Corporation" in Hartman, L. P., ed., *Perspectives in Business Ethics*. New York: McGraw-Hill/Irwin, 205–214.

Koppes, R. H. 1997. "Corporate Governance." *National Law Journal* (29 December): B5.

Kotchian, C. A. 1977. "The Payoff: Lockheed's 70-Day Mission to Tokyo." *Saturday Review* (9 July): 7–12.

Kovach, K. A. 1995. "Employee Motivation: Addressing a Crucial Factor in Your Organization's Performance." *Employment Relations Today* (Summer): 93–107.

Kovach, K. A., Conner, S. J., et al. 2000. "Electronic Comunication in the Workplace—Something's Got to Give." *Business Horizons* (July/August): 59–64.

Krauss, C. 1998. "Argentina to Seek Extradition of Two Executives from U.S.." *New York Times* (5 May): A8.

Kuczynski, A. 2002. "Companies Dig Deeper into Executives' Pasts." *New York Times* (19 August): A1.

Lagnado, L. 1997. "Ex-Manager Describes the Profit-Driven Life Inside Columbia/HCA." *Wall Street Journal* (30 May): A1.

Lagnado, L. 1999. "Columbia/HCA Whistleblowers to Fight for Gold." *Wall Street Journal* (24 November): B1-B4.

Lantos, G. P. 1999. "Motivating Moral Corporate Behavior." *Journal of Consumer Marketing* 16: 222–233.

Lim, P. 1995. "Starbucks' 'Code' for Suppliers is Criticized." *The Seattle Times* (24 October): E1.

Lipset, S. and Schneider, W. 1978. "'How's Business?' What the Public Thinks," *Public Opinion* (July/August): 41–47.

McLean, B and Elkind, P. 2003. "Partners in Crime: The Untold Story of How Citi, J. P. Morgan Chase, and Merrill Lynch Helped Enron Pull Off One of the Greatest Scams Ever." *Fortune* (27 October): 78–100.

McKegney, M. 2000. "Ford, Firestone Woes Extend Beyond the U.S; Scrutiny Most Intense in S. America; PR Efforts Questioned." *Ad Age Global* (1 September): 4.

Meyer, H. 2000. "The Greening of Corporate America." *Journal of Business Strategy* (January/February): 38–43.

Mirvis, P. 2000. "Transformation at Shell: Commerce and Citizenship." *Business and Society Review* 105: 63–84.

Murphy, P. E. 1995. "Corporate Ethics Statements: Current Status and Future Prospects." *Journal of Business Ethics* 14: 727–740.

Parker, A. 2003. "Few Put Faith in Corporate Reforms." *Financial Times* (13 October): 1.

Piturro, M. 1999. "Alternatives to Downsizing." *Management Review* (October): 37–41.

Quinn, D. P. and Jones, T. M. 1995. "An Agent Morality View of Business Policy." *Academy of Management Review* 20(1): 22–42.

Ray, A. 2002. "Customers Hold the Key to Reputation." *PR Week* (13 September): 9.

Roman, R. M., Hayibor, S. and Agle, B. R. 1999. "The Relationship Between Financial and Social Performance: Repainting a Portrait." *Business and Society* 38(1): 109–125.

Romer, P. 1986. "Increasing Returns and Long-Run Growth." *Journal of Political Economy* 94(5) (October): 1002–1037.

Shirouzu, N. 2000. "Ford Earnings Decline on Firestone Tire Recall." *Wall Street Journal* (19 October): A3.

Seglin, J. L. 1999. "Much Ado About Giving References." *New York Times* (21 February): D4.

Simison, R. L. 2000. "For Ford CEO Nasser, Damage Control Is the New 'Job One.' " *Wall Street Journal* (11 September): A1, A8.

Sims, C. 1996. "Argentine Cloud Over I.B.M. Grows Darker." *New York Times* (29 June): 33.

Singer, A. W. 2000. "The Perils of Doing the Right Thing." *Across the Board* (October): 14–19.

Smart, T. 1992. "This Man Sounded the Silicone Alarm—in 1976." *Business Week* (27 January): 34.

Solomon, C. 1997. "Coffee Giant Slow to Keep Guatemala Promise." *The Seattle Times* (6 March): D1.

Stauber, J. C. and Rampton, S. 1996. "Confidence Game: Burson-Marsteller's PR Plan for Silicone Breast Implants." *PR Watch* 3(1). www.prwatch.org/prwissues/1996Q1/silicone10.html (last accessed 4 January 2004).

Stein, N. 2000. "The World's Most Admired Companies." *Fortune* (2 October): 183–186.

Steinhauer, J. 1998. "Time to Call a Sears Repairman: A Turnaround is Sidetracked By its Own Oversell." *New York Times* (15 January): D1.

Sugawara, S. 2000. "IBM Settles to End Bribery Case." *Washington Post* (22 December): E3.

Taylor, P. 2003. "Ethics in Business: Can Virtue Be Taught?" *Fordham Business Magazine* (Winter): 15–17.

Trevino, L. K., Butterfield, K. O., and McCabe, D. 1998. "The Ethical Context in Organizations: Influences on Employee Attitudes and Behaviors." *Business Ethics Quarterly* 8(3): 447–476.

Verschoor, C. C. 1997. "Principles Build Profits." *Management Accounting.* (October): 42–46.

Verschoor, C. C. 1998. "A Study of the Link Between a Corporation's Financial Performance and Its Commitment to Ethics." 17(13) *Journal of Business Ethics* (October): 1509–1516.

Waddock, S. and Graves, S. 1997. "The Corporate Social Performance-Financial Perforance Link." *Strategic Management Journal* 18: 303–319.

Warner, M. 2003. "eBay's Worst Nightmare." *Fortune* (26 May): 89–94.

Wartick, S. L. 1992. "The Relationship Between Intense Media Exposure and Change in Corporate Reputation." 31(1) *Business and Society* (Spring): 33–50.

Weaver, G. R., Trevino, L. K., and Cochran, P. L. 1999. "Corporate Ethics Practices in the Mid-1990s: An Empirical Study of the *Fortune* 1000." *Journal of Business Ethics* 18(3): 283–294.

Weaver, G. R. and Trevino, L. K. 1999. "Compliance and Values Oriented Ethics Programs: Influence on Employees' Attitudes and Behavior." *Business Ethics Quarterly* 9(2): 315–335.

Weber, J. 2000. "3M's Big Cleanup." *Business Week* (5 June): 96–98.

Welch, D. and Protos, J. 2000. "John Lampe: A Mr. Fixit for Firestone?" *Business Week* (23 October): 56.

Wiggins, J., Boland, V., and Pretzlik, C. 2003. "SEC Urged to Get Tougher on Credit Rating Agencies" *Financial Times* (25 January): 9.

Wokutch, R. 2001. "Nike and its Critics: Beginning a Dialogue." *Organization and Environment* 14(2): 207–237.

Zaun, T. 2000. "A Blowout Blindsides Bridgestone." *Wall Street Journal* (7 August): A8.

Zellner, W., Anderson, S. and Cohn, L. 2002. "A Hero—and a Smoking Gun Letter." *Business Week* (28 January): 34.

Case Studies

1993. "Sears Auto Centers (A), (B), (C)." HBS Case Nos. 9-394-009, 9-394-010, 9-394-011. Boston: Harvard Business School Publishing.

1994. "Forging the New Salomon." HBS Case No. 9-395-046. Boston: Harvard Business School Publishing.

1997. "Levi Strauss & Co.: Global Sourcing (A)." HBS Case No. 9-395-127. Boston: Harvard Business School Publishing.

1999. "Guaranty Trust Bank PLC Nigeria (A), (B), (C), (D)." HBS Case Nos. 9-399-110, 9-399-111, 9-399-112, 9-399-116. Boston: Harvard Business School Publishing.

1999. "Royal Dutch/Shell in Transition (A), (B)." HBS Case Nos. 9-300-039, 9-30-040. Boston: Harvard Business School Publishing.

2000. "Housing Development Finance Corporation (A)." HBS Case No. 9-301-093. Boston: Harvard Business School Publishing.

2001. "Recall 2000: Bridgestone Corp. (A), (B)." HBS Case Nos. 9-302-013, 9-302-014. Boston: Harvard Business School Publishing.

Index

LaVergne, TN USA
25 July 2010
190822LV00001B/1/A